Teach Yourself Windows® 2000 Professional

VISUALLY™

IDG's **3-D Visual**™ Series

IDG BOOKS *From* **maranGraphics**™

IDG Books Worldwide, Inc.
An International Data Group Company
Foster City, CA • Indianapolis • Chicago • New York

Teach Yourself Windows® 2000 Professional VISUALLY™

Published by
IDG Books Worldwide, Inc.
An International Data Group Company
919 E. Hillsdale Blvd., Suite 400
Foster City, CA 94404

Copyright©   1999 by maranGraphics Inc.
5755 Coopers Avenue
Mississauga, Ontario, Canada
L4Z 1R9

Library of Congress Catalog Card No.: 99-068240

ISBN: 0-7645-6040-9

Printed in the United States of America
10 9 8 7 6 5 4 3 2 1

Distributed in the United States by IDG Books Worldwide, Inc.

Distributed by CDG Books Canada Inc. for Canada; by Transworld Publishers Limited in the United Kingdom; by IDG Norge Books for Norway; by IDG Sweden Books for Sweden; by IDG Books Australia Publishing Corporation Pty. Ltd. for Australia and New Zealand; by TransQuest Publishers Pte Ltd. for Singapore, Malaysia, Thailand, Indonesia, and Hong Kong; by Gotop Information Inc. for Taiwan; by ICG Muse, Inc. for Japan; by Intersoft for South Africa; by Eyrolles for France; by International Thomson Publishing for Germany, Austria and Switzerland; by Distribuidora Cuspide for Argentina; by LR International for Brazil; by Galileo Libros for Chile; by Ediciones ZETA S.C.R. Ltda. for Peru; by WS Computer Publishing Corporation, Inc. for the Philippines; by Contemporanea de Ediciones for Venezuela; by Express Computer Distributors for the Caribbean and West Indies; by Micronesia Media Distributor, Inc. for Micronesia; by Chips Computadoras S.A. de C.V. for Mexico; by Editorial Norma de Panama S.A. for Panama; by American Bookshops for Finland.
For corporate orders, please call maranGraphics at 800-469-6616.
For general information on IDG Books Worldwide's books in the U.S., please call our Consumer Customer Service department at 800-762-2974.
For reseller information, including discounts and premium sales, please call our Reseller Customer Service department at 800-434-3422.
For information on where to purchase IDG Books Worldwide's books outside the U.S., please contact our International Sales department at 317-596-5530 or fax 317-596-5692.
For consumer information on foreign language translations, please contact our Customer Service department at 1-800-434-3422, fax 317-596-5692, or e-mail rights@idgbooks.com.
For information on licensing foreign or domestic rights, please phone 1-650-655-3109.
For sales inquiries and special prices for bulk quantities, please contact our Sales department at 650-655-3200.
For information on using IDG Books Worldwide's books in the classroom or for ordering examination copies, please contact our Educational Sales department at 800-434-2086 or fax 317-596-5499.
For press review copies, author interviews, or other publicity information, please contact our Public Relations department at 650-655-3000 or fax 650-655-3299.
For authorization to photocopy items for corporate, personal, or educational use, please contact maranGraphics at 800-469-6616.
Screen shots displayed in this book are based on pre-release software and are subject to change.

Trademark Acknowledgments

maranGraphics Inc. has attempted to include trademark information for products, services and companies referred to in this guide. Although maranGraphics Inc. has made reasonable efforts in gathering this information, it cannot guarantee its accuracy.

All brand names and product names used in this book are trade names, service marks, trademarks, or registered trademarks of their respective owners. IDG Books Worldwide and maranGraphics Inc. are not associated with any product or vendor mentioned in this book.

FOR PURPOSES OF ILLUSTRATING THE CONCEPTS AND TECHNIQUES DESCRIBED IN THIS BOOK, THE AUTHOR HAS CREATED VARIOUS NAMES, COMPANY NAMES, MAILING ADDRESSES, E-MAIL ADDRESSES AND PHONE NUMBERS, ALL OF WHICH ARE FICTITIOUS. ANY RESEMBLANCE OF THESE FICTITIOUS NAMES, COMPANY NAMES, MAILING ADDRESSES, E-MAIL ADDRESSES AND PHONE NUMBERS TO ANY ACTUAL PERSON, COMPANY AND/OR ORGANIZATION IS UNINTENTIONAL AND PURELY COINCIDENTAL.

maranGraphics has used their best efforts in preparing this book. As Web sites are constantly changing, some of the Web site addresses in this book may have moved or no longer exist.
maranGraphics does not accept responsibility nor liability for losses or damages resulting from the information contained in this book. maranGraphics also does not support the views expressed in the Web sites contained in this book.

Permissions

Adobe
Adobe and Acrobat are trademarks of Adobe Systems Incorporated.

Internet Shopping Network
Internet Shopping Network, ISN, First Auction and First Jewelry and their related logos are registered United States trademarks of Internet Shopping Network, LLC.

Microsoft
© 1999 Microsoft Corporation. All rights reserved.

Smithsonian
Copyright © 1996 by Smithsonian Institution.

Spiegel
© Spiegel, Inc. Used with permission.

Wal-Mart
Copyright © 1998 Wal-Mart Stores, Inc.

Yahoo!
Text and artwork copyright © 1996 by Yahoo!, Inc. All rights reserved. Yahoo! and the Yahoo! logo are trademarks of Yahoo!, Inc.

Permissions Granted

CNN	Nasdaq-Amex
Discovery Channel Online	Ragu
Flower Stop	Sunkist
Minolta	

© 1999 maranGraphics, Inc.

The 3-D illustrations are the copyright of maranGraphics, Inc.

U.S. Corporate Sales	**U.S. Trade Sales**
Contact maranGraphics at (800) 469-6616 or Fax (905) 890-9434.	Contact IDG Books at (800) 434-3422 or (650) 655-3000.

ABOUT IDG BOOKS WORLDWIDE

Welcome to the world of IDG Books Worldwide.

IDG Books Worldwide, Inc., is a subsidiary of International Data Group, the world's largest publisher of computer-related information and the leading global provider of information services on information technology. IDG was founded more than 30 years ago by Patrick J. McGovern and now employs more than 9,000 people worldwide. IDG publishes more than 290 computer publications in over 75 countries. More than 90 million people read one or more IDG publications each month.

Launched in 1990, IDG Books Worldwide is today the #1 publisher of best-selling computer books in the United States. We are proud to have received eight awards from the Computer Press Association in recognition of editorial excellence and three from Computer Currents' First Annual Readers' Choice Awards. Our best-selling *...For Dummies*® series has more than 50 million copies in print with translations in 31 languages. IDG Books Worldwide, through a joint venture with IDG's Hi-Tech Beijing, became the first U.S. publisher to publish a computer book in the People's Republic of China. In record time, IDG Books Worldwide has become the first choice for millions of readers around the world who want to learn how to better manage their businesses.

Our mission is simple: Every one of our books is designed to bring extra value and skill-building instructions to the reader. Our books are written by experts who understand and care about our readers. The knowledge base of our editorial staff comes from years of experience in publishing, education, and journalism — experience we use to produce books to carry us into the new millennium. In short, we care about books, so we attract the best people. We devote special attention to details such as audience, interior design, use of icons, and illustrations. And because we use an efficient process of authoring, editing, and desktop publishing our books electronically, we can spend more time ensuring superior content and less time on the technicalities of making books.

You can count on our commitment to deliver high-quality books at competitive prices on topics you want to read about. At IDG Books Worldwide, we continue in the IDG tradition of delivering quality for more than 30 years. You'll find no better book on a subject than one from IDG Books Worldwide.

John Kilcullen
Chairman and CEO
IDG Books Worldwide, Inc.

Steven Berkowitz
President and Publisher
IDG Books Worldwide, Inc.

WINNER

Eighth Annual Computer Press Awards≥1992

WINNER

Ninth Annual Computer Press Awards≥1993

WINNER

Tenth Annual Computer Press Awards≥1994

WINNER

Eleventh Annual Computer Press Awards≥1995

IDG is the world's leading IT media, research and exposition company. Founded in 1964, IDG had 1997 revenues of $2.05 billion and has more than 9,000 employees worldwide. IDG offers the widest range of media options that reach IT buyers in 75 countries representing 95% of worldwide IT spending. IDG's diverse product and services portfolio spans six key areas including print publishing, online publishing, expositions and conferences, market research, education and training, and global marketing services. More than 90 million people read one or more of IDG's 290 magazines and newspapers, including IDG's leading global brands — Computerworld, PC World, Network World, Macworld and the Channel World family of publications. IDG Books Worldwide is one of the fastest-growing computer book publishers in the world, with more than 700 titles in 36 languages. The "...For Dummies®" series alone has more than 50 million copies in print. IDG offers online users the largest network of technology-specific Web sites around the world through IDG.net (http://www.idg.net), which comprises more than 225 targeted Web sites in 55 countries worldwide. International Data Corporation (IDC) is the world's largest provider of information technology data, analysis and consulting, with research centers in over 41 countries and more than 400 research analysts worldwide. IDG World Expo is a leading producer of more than 168 globally branded conferences and expositions in 35 countries including E3 (Electronic Entertainment Expo), Macworld Expo, ComNet, Windows World Expo, ICE (Internet Commerce Expo), Agenda, DEMO, and Spotlight. IDG's training subsidiary, ExecuTrain, is the world's largest computer training company, with more than 230 locations worldwide and 785 training courses. IDG Marketing Services helps industry-leading IT companies build international brand recognition by developing global integrated marketing programs via IDG's print, online and exposition products worldwide. Further information about the company can be found at www.idg.com. 1/24/99

maranGraphics is a family-run business
located near Toronto, Canada.

At **maranGraphics**, we believe
in producing great computer
books–one book at a time.

Each maranGraphics book
uses the award-winning
communication process that
we have been developing over
the last 25 years. Using this
process, we organize screen
shots, text and illustrations in
a way that makes it easy for
you to learn new concepts
and tasks.

We spend hours deciding
the best way to perform each
task, so you don't have to!
Our clear, easy-to-follow
screen shots and instructions
walk you through each task
from beginning to end.

Our detailed illustrations go
hand-in-hand with the text to
help reinforce the information.
Each illustration is a labor of
love–some take up to a week
to draw!

We want to thank you for
purchasing what we feel
are the best computer
books money can buy.
We hope you enjoy using
this book as much as we
enjoyed creating it!

Sincerely,

The Maran Family

Please visit us on the Web at:
www.maran.com

CREDITS

Authors:
Kelleigh Wing
Ruth Maran

Technical Consultants:
Paul Whitehead
Eric Kramer

Project Manager:
Judy Maran

Editors:
Raquel Scott
Janice Boyer
Stacey Morrison

Screen Captures:
James Menzies

Layout Designer:
Treena Lees

Illustrators:
Russ Marini
Jamie Bell
Peter Grecco
Sean Johannesen
Steven Schaerer

Screen Artist & Illustrator:
Jimmy Tam

Indexer:
Raquel Scott

Permissions Coordinator:
Jenn Reid

Post Production:
Robert Maran

**Senior Vice President,
Technology Publishing
IDG Books Worldwide:**
Richard Swadley

**Editorial Support
IDG Books Worldwide:**
Barry Pruett
Martine Edwards

ACKNOWLEDGMENTS

Thanks to the dedicated staff of maranGraphics, including
Jamie Bell, Cathy Benn, Janice Boyer, Peter Grecco,
Sean Johannesen, Eric Kramer, Wanda Lawrie,
Frances Lea, Treena Lees, Jill Maran, Judy Maran,
Robert Maran, Sherry Maran, Russ Marini, James Menzies,
Stacey Morrison, Jenn Reid, Steven Schaerer, Raquel Scott,
Jimmy Tam, Roxanne Van Damme and Paul Whitehead.

Finally, to Richard Maran who originated the easy-to-use
graphic format of this guide. Thank you for your
inspiration and guidance.

TABLE OF CONTENTS

Chapter 1

Chapter 2

CREATE DOCUMENTS

Chapter 3

CREATE PICTURES

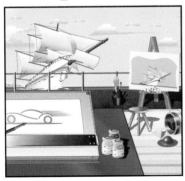

TABLE OF CONTENTS

Chapter 4

VIEW FILES

Chapter 5

WORK WITH FILES

Chapter 6

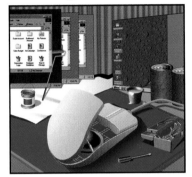

Chapter 7

TABLE OF CONTENTS

Chapter 8

OPTIMIZE YOUR COMPUTER

Chapter 9

WORK WITH FAXES

Chapter 10

WORK ON A NETWORK

Chapter 11

Chapter 12

INTRODUCTION TO WINDOWS 2000

**Microsoft®
Windows® 2000
is a program
that controls the
overall activity of
your computer.**

Windows ensures
that all parts of your
computer work
together smoothly
and efficiently.

WORK WITH FILES

Windows provides ways to
organize and manage the files
stored on your computer. You
can open, sort, rename, move,
print, find and delete files.

Windows includes a word
processing program, called
WordPad, and a drawing
program, called Paint, to help
you quickly start creating files.

CUSTOMIZE WINDOWS

You can customize Windows
in many ways. You can add a
colorful design to your screen,
change the way your mouse
works and change the amount
of information that fits on the
screen.

OPTIMIZE YOUR COMPUTER

Windows provides tools to help
you optimize your computer.
You can check your hard disk
for errors, remove unnecessary
files and defragment your hard
disk to improve its performance.

HAVE FUN WITH WINDOWS

You can use Windows to play games, listen to music CDs and assign sounds to program events.

BROWSE THE WEB

Windows lets you browse through the vast amount of information on the World Wide Web. You can move between Web pages you have viewed, create a list of favorite Web pages and search for Web pages of interest.

WORK ON A NETWORK

Windows allows you to share equipment and information on a network. You can specify exactly who you want to have access to your printer and each folder on your computer by assigning permissions.

EXCHANGE E-MAIL AND FAXES

Windows allows you to exchange electronic mail with people around the world. You can reply to, forward and print e-mail messages. Windows also includes a program that allows you to send and receive faxes using your computer's modem.

PARTS OF THE WINDOWS 2000 SCREEN

The Windows screen displays various items. The items that appear depend on how your computer is set up.

My Documents

Provides a convenient place to store your documents.

My Computer

Lets you view all the folders and files stored on your computer.

My Network Places

Lets you view all the folders and files available on your network.

Recycle Bin

Stores deleted files and allows you to recover them later.

Start Button

Gives you quick access to programs, files and Windows Help.

Quick Launch Toolbar

Gives you quick access to commonly used features, including the desktop, Internet Explorer and Outlook Express.

Title Bar

Displays the name of an open window.

Window

A rectangle on your screen that displays information.

Desktop

The background area of your screen.

Taskbar

Displays a button for each open window on your screen. You can use these buttons to switch between open windows.

A mouse is a handheld device that lets you select and move items on your screen.

When you move the mouse on your desk, the mouse pointer on your screen moves in the same direction. The mouse pointer assumes different shapes, such as ⬉ or I, depending on its location on your screen and the task you are performing.

Resting your hand on the mouse, use your thumb and two rightmost fingers to move the mouse on your desk. Use your two remaining fingers to press the mouse buttons.

MOUSE ACTIONS

Click

Press and release the left mouse button.

Double-click

Quickly press and release the left mouse button twice.

Right-click

Press and release the right mouse button.

Drag

Position the mouse pointer over an object on your screen and then press and hold down the left mouse button. Still holding down the button, move the mouse to where you want to place the object and then release the button.

START WINDOWS

Windows starts when
you turn on your
computer. You need
to enter your user
name and password
to log on to Windows.

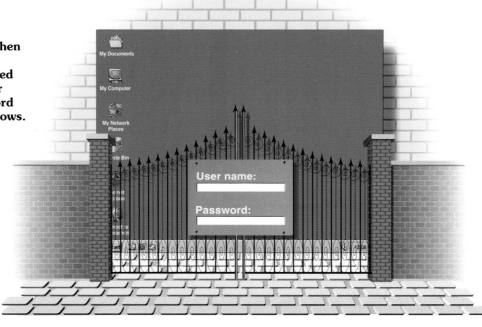

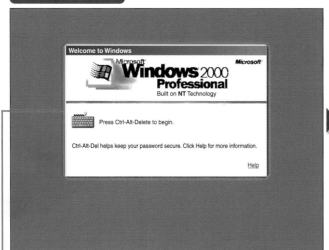

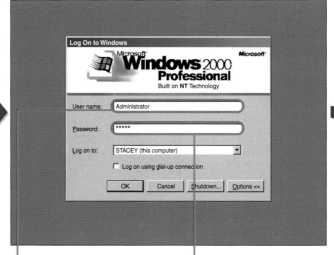

1 Turn on your
computer and monitor.

■ The Welcome to
Windows dialog box
appears.

2 To log on to Windows,
press and hold down the
`Ctrl` and `Alt` keys as you
press the `Delete` key.

■ The Log On to Windows
dialog box appears.

■ This area displays
your user name.

*Note: To enter a different user
name, drag the mouse I over
the current name until the text
is highlighted. Then type a
new name.*

3 Click this area and then
type your password. An
asterisk (*) appears for
each character you type
to prevent others from
seeing your password.

What is a domain?

A domain is a group of computers on a network that are administered together. When logging on to Windows, you can log on to a domain on the network or your own computer. If you are not connected to a network, you will not be able to log on to a domain.

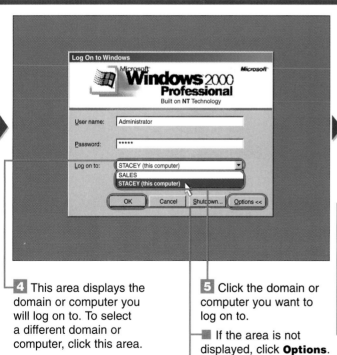

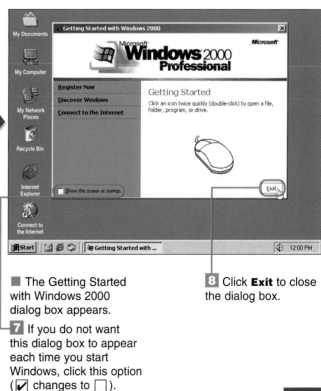

4 This area displays the domain or computer you will log on to. To select a different domain or computer, click this area.

5 Click the domain or computer you want to log on to.

■ If the area is not displayed, click **Options**.

6 Click **OK**.

■ The Getting Started with Windows 2000 dialog box appears.

7 If you do not want this dialog box to appear each time you start Windows, click this option (☑ changes to ☐).

8 Click **Exit** to close the dialog box.

START A PROGRAM

You can use the
Start button to start
your programs.

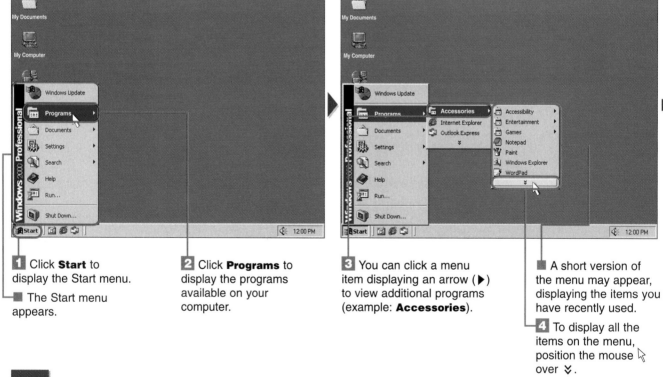

1 Click **Start** to
display the Start menu.

■ The Start menu
appears.

2 Click **Programs** to
display the programs
available on your
computer.

3 You can click a menu
item displaying an arrow (▶)
to view additional programs
(example: **Accessories**).

■ A short version of
the menu may appear,
displaying the items you
have recently used.

4 To display all the
items on the menu,
position the mouse
over ✕.

? Which programs does Windows provide?

Windows comes with many useful programs.

WordPad is a word processing program that lets you create letters, reports and memos.

Paint is a drawing program that lets you draw pictures and maps.

CD Player is a program that lets you play music CDs while you work.

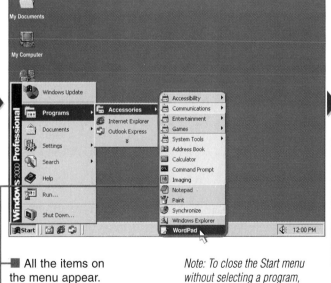

■ All the items on the menu appear.

5 Click the program you want to start (example: **WordPad**).

Note: To close the Start menu without selecting a program, click outside the menu area or press the **Alt** *key.*

■ In this example, the WordPad window appears.

■ A button for the open window appears on the taskbar.

MAXIMIZE A WINDOW

You can enlarge a
window to fill your
screen. This lets
you view more of
the window's
contents.

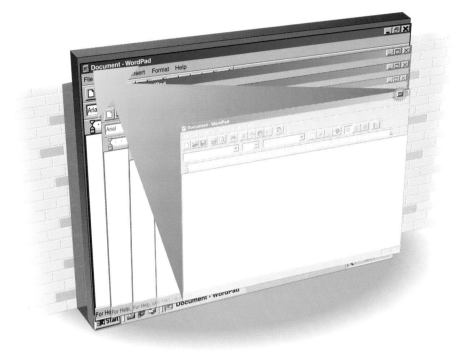

MAXIMIZE A WINDOW

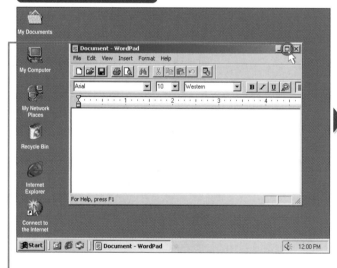

1 Click ▢ in the window
you want to maximize.

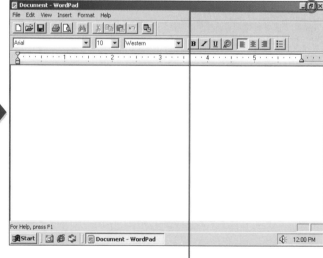

■ The window fills
your screen.

■ To return the window to
its previous size, click ▢.

10

MINIMIZE A WINDOW

If you are not using a window, you can minimize the window to remove it from your screen. You can redisplay the window at any time.

MINIMIZE A WINDOW

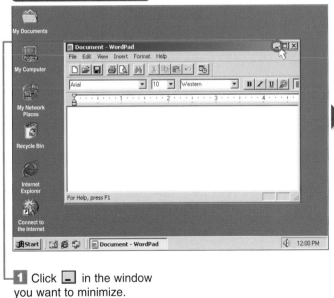

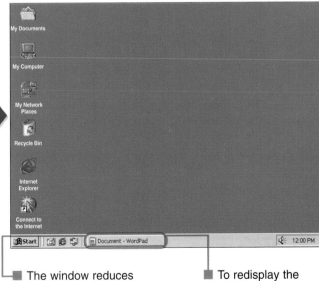

■1 Click ▬ in the window you want to minimize.

■ The window reduces to a button on the taskbar.

■ To redisplay the window, click its button on the taskbar.

MOVE A WINDOW

If a window covers
items on your screen,
you can move the
window to a different
location.

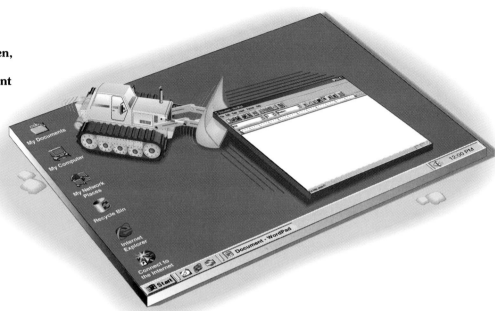

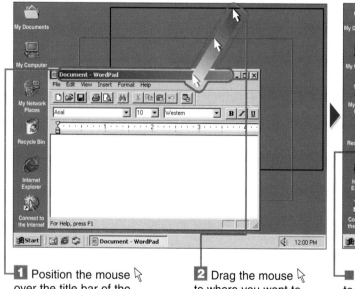

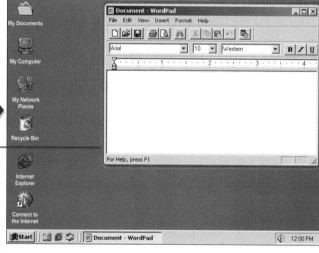

1 Position the mouse ⟨ᛣ over the title bar of the window you want to move.

2 Drag the mouse ⟨ᛣ to where you want to place the window.

■ The window moves to the new location.

You can easily change the size of a window displayed on your screen.

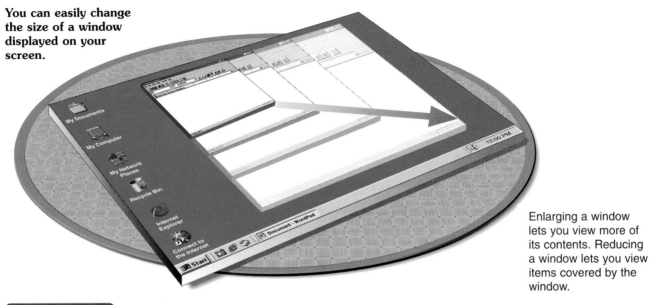

Enlarging a window lets you view more of its contents. Reducing a window lets you view items covered by the window.

SIZE A WINDOW

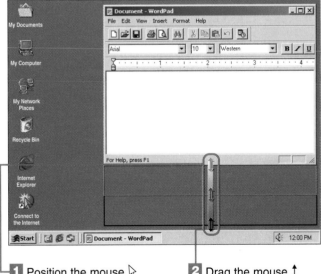

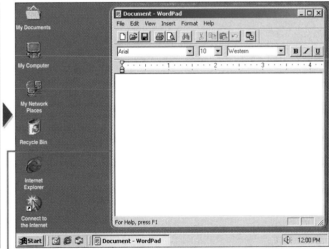

1 Position the mouse ⌖ over an edge of the window you want to size (⌖ changes to ↕, ↔ or ↘).

2 Drag the mouse ↕ until the window displays the size you want.

■ The window displays the new size.

SCROLL THROUGH A WINDOW

You can use a scroll bar to browse through the information in a window. This is useful when a window is not large enough to display all the information it contains.

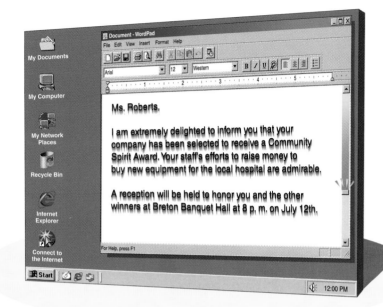

SCROLL DOWN

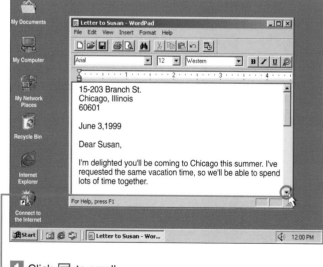

1 Click ▼ to scroll down through the information in a window.

SCROLL UP

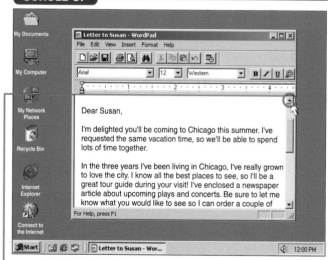

1 Click ▲ to scroll up through the information in a window.

Is there another way to use a mouse to scroll through a window?

You can purchase a mouse with a wheel between the left and right mouse buttons. Moving this wheel lets you scroll through a window.

SCROLL TO ANY POSITION

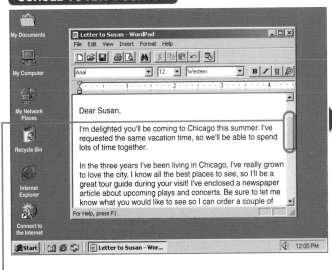

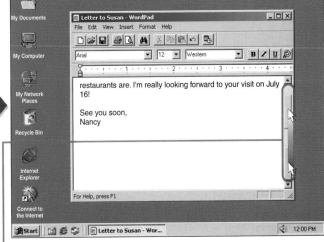

■ The location of the scroll box indicates which part of the window you are viewing. For example, when the scroll box is halfway down the scroll bar, you are viewing information from the middle of the window.

Note: The size of the scroll box varies, depending on the amount of information the window contains and the size of the window.

1 Drag the scroll box along the scroll bar until the information you want to view appears.

SWITCH BETWEEN WINDOWS

You can have more than one window open at a time. You can easily switch between all the windows you have open.

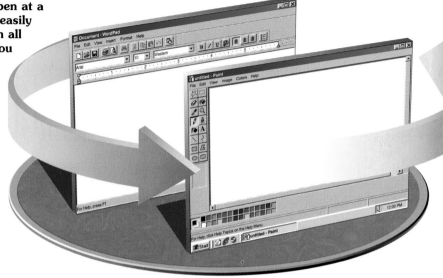

Each window is like a separate piece of paper. Switching between windows lets you place a different piece of paper at the top of the pile.

SWITCH BETWEEN WINDOWS

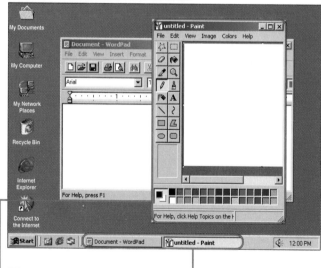

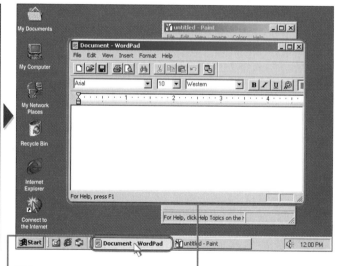

■ You can work in only one window at a time. The active window (example: Paint) appears in front of all other windows and displays a blue title bar.

■ The taskbar displays a button for each open window.

1 To display the window you want to work with in front of all other windows, click its button on the taskbar.

■ The window appears in front of all other windows. This lets you clearly view the contents of the window.

CLOSE A WINDOW

When you finish
working with a
window, you can
close the window
to remove it from
your screen.

CLOSE A WINDOW

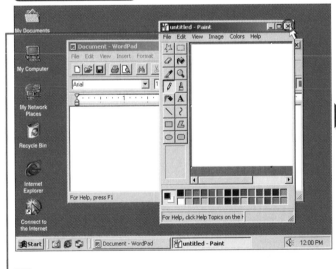

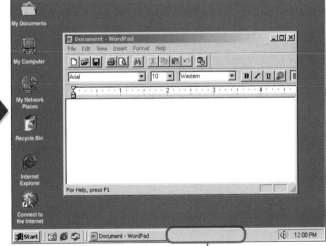

■1 Click ☒ in the window
you want to close.

■ The window disappears
from your screen.

■ The button for the
window disappears
from the taskbar.

SHOW THE DESKTOP

You can instantly minimize all your open windows to remove them from your screen. This allows you to clearly view the desktop.

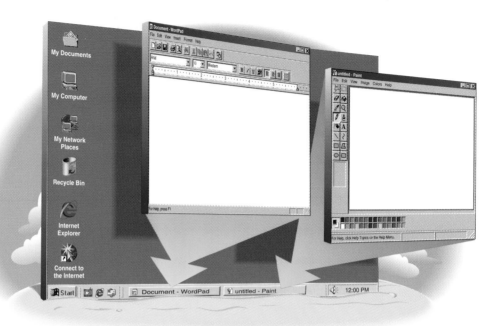

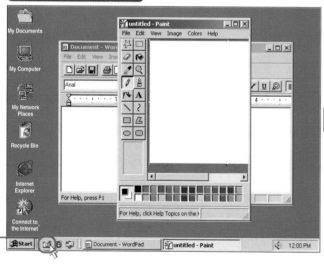

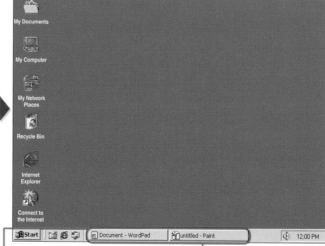

1 Click 📇 to minimize all the open windows on your screen.

■ Each window minimizes to a button on the taskbar. You can now clearly view the desktop.

■ To redisplay a window, click its button on the taskbar.

18

SHUT DOWN WINDOWS

When you finish using your computer, shut down Windows before turning off the computer.

■ Do not turn off your computer until this message appears on your screen.

Make sure you close all open programs before shutting down Windows.

SHUT DOWN WINDOWS

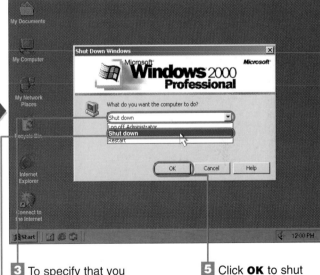

1 Click **Start**.

2 Click **Shut Down**.

■ The Shut Down Windows dialog box appears.

3 To specify that you want to shut down Windows, click this area.

4 Click **Shut down**.

5 Click **OK** to shut down your computer.

LOG OFF YOUR COMPUTER

If you share your computer with others, you can log off so another person can log on and use the computer.

Make sure you save your information and close your programs before logging off.

LOG OFF YOUR COMPUTER

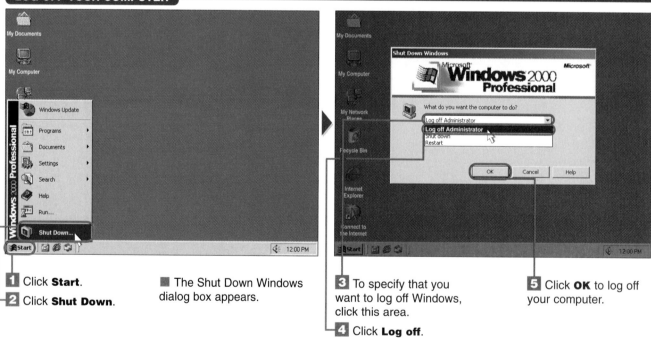

1 Click **Start**.

2 Click **Shut Down**.

■ The Shut Down Windows dialog box appears.

3 To specify that you want to log off Windows, click this area.

4 Click **Log off**.

5 Click **OK** to log off your computer.

20

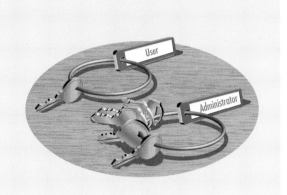

Why do I need to enter a user name and password each time I log on to a computer or network?

The user name and password you enter determines the type of access you will have on the computer or network. For example, if you log on as a user, you may not have permission to perform some tasks, such as installing hardware. If you log on as an administrator, you will have permission to perform any task.

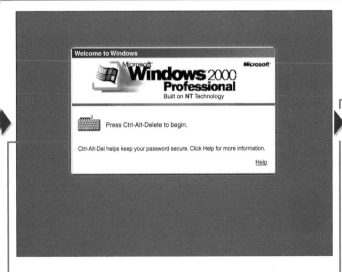

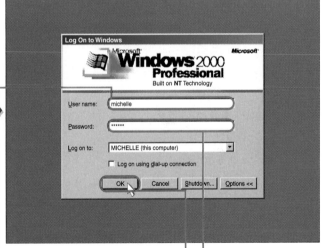

■ The Welcome to Windows dialog box appears.

6 To log on as a different user, press and hold down the `Ctrl` and `Alt` keys as you press the `Delete` key.

■ The Log On to Windows dialog box appears.

7 To enter a different user name, drag the mouse I over the current name until the text is highlighted. Then type a new name.

8 Click this area and then type the password.

9 Click **OK** to log on to the network.

LOCK YOUR COMPUTER

If you are leaving your desk for a short period of time, you can lock your computer so other people cannot access your information.

LOCK YOUR COMPUTER

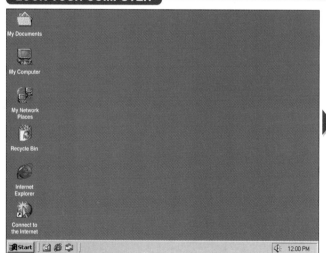

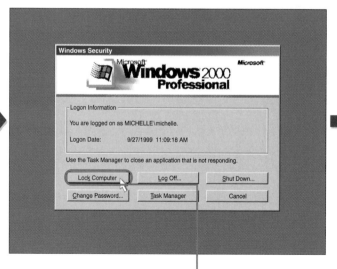

1 Press and hold down the `Ctrl` and `Alt` keys as you press the `Delete` key.

■ The Windows Security dialog box appears.

2 Click **Lock Computer**.

Can I hide my information without locking my computer?

Yes. You can turn off your monitor or set up a screen saver to hide the contents of your screen. Hiding the contents of your screen will not prevent others from accessing information on your computer. To set up a screen saver, see page 126.

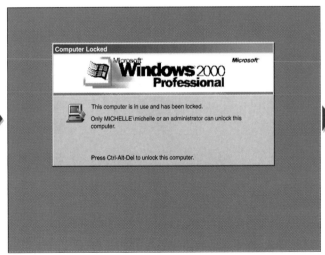

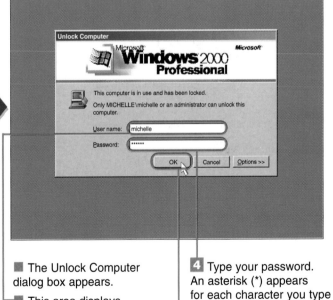

■ The Computer Locked dialog box appears.

3 When you return to your desk and want to unlock the computer, press and hold down the `Ctrl` and `Alt` keys as you press the `Delete` key.

■ The Unlock Computer dialog box appears.

■ This area displays your user name.

4 Type your password. An asterisk (*) appears for each character you type to prevent others from seeing your password.

5 Click **OK**.

GETTING HELP

If you do not know how to perform a task, you can use the Help feature to get information.

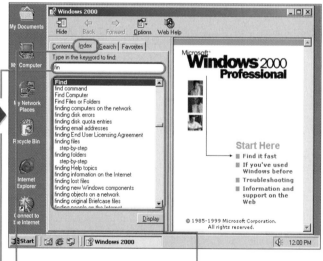

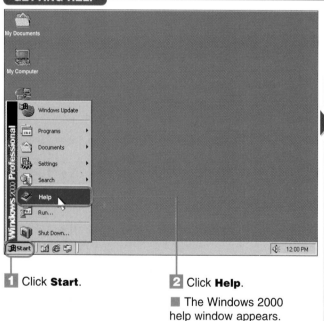

1 Click **Start**.

2 Click **Help**.

■ The Windows 2000 help window appears.

3 Click the **Index** tab to display an alphabetical list of help topics.

4 To search for a help topic of interest, click this area and then type the first few letters of the topic.

■ This area displays help topics beginning with the letters you typed.

24

How can I use the Help feature to find information on a topic of interest?

The **Contents** tab lets you browse through help topics by subject.

The **Index** tab lets you view an alphabetical list of help topics.

The **Search** tab lets you view all the help topics that contain a word of interest.

The **Favorites** tab lets you create a list of help topics you frequently use.

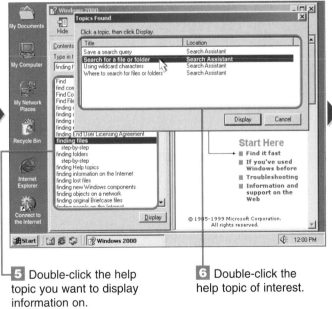

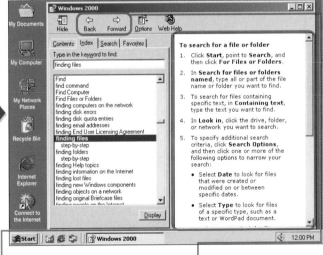

5 Double-click the help topic you want to display information on.

■ The Topics Found dialog box may appear, displaying a list of related help topics.

6 Double-click the help topic of interest.

■ The information on the help topic appears in this area.

■ You can click **Back** or **Forward** to move through the help topics you have viewed.

USING THE CALCULATOR

Windows provides a calculator you can use to perform calculations.

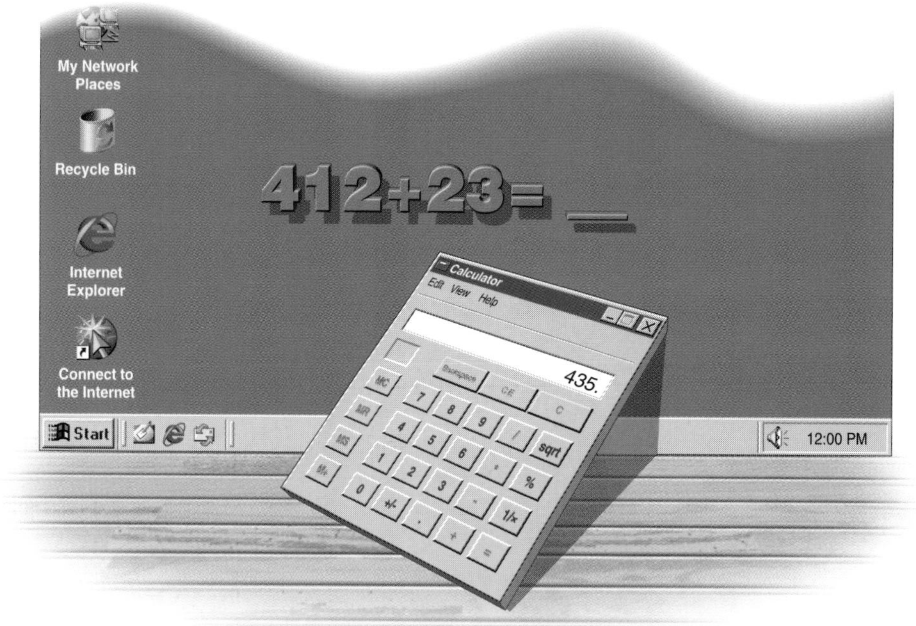

USING THE CALCULATOR

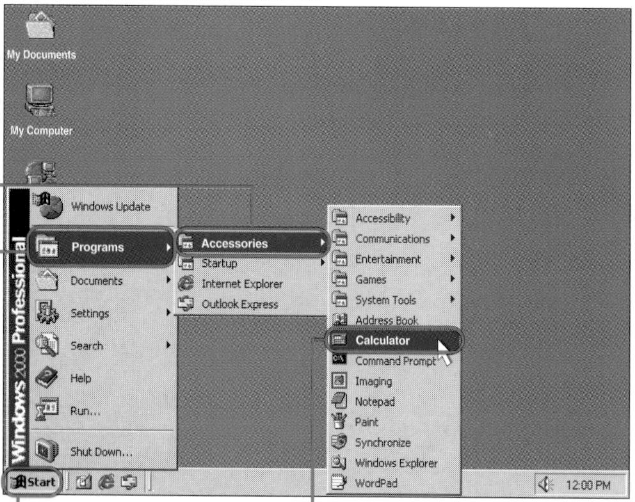

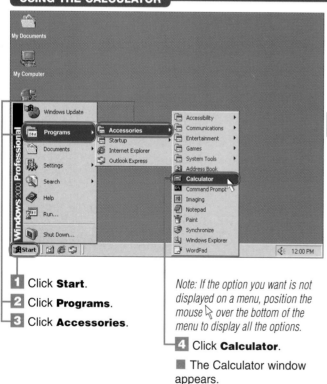

1 Click **Start**.

2 Click **Programs**.

3 Click **Accessories**.

Note: If the option you want is not displayed on a menu, position the mouse over the bottom of the menu to display all the options.

4 Click **Calculator**.

■ The Calculator window appears.

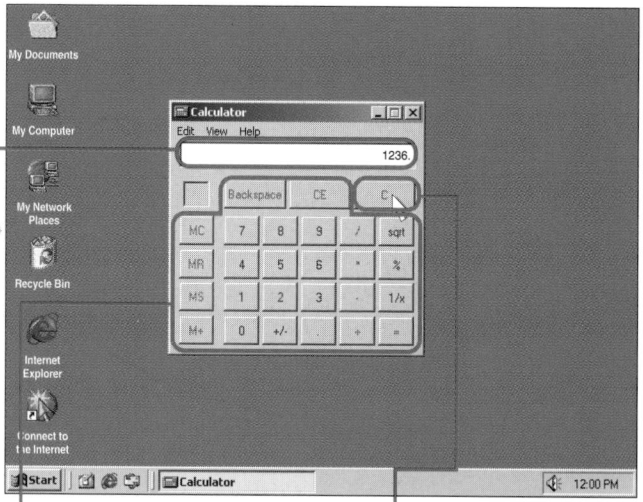

5 To enter information into the Calculator, click each button as you would press the buttons on a handheld calculator.

■ This area displays the numbers you enter and the result of each calculation.

6 You can click C to start a new calculation at any time.

Can I enter numbers using the keys on the right side of my keyboard?

To use the number keys on the right side of your keyboard, the Num Lock light must be on. To turn the light on, press the Num Lock key.

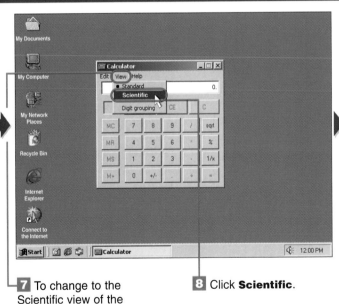

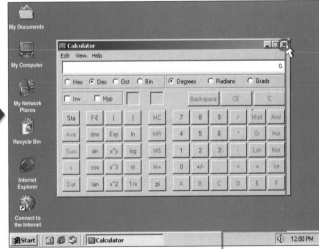

7 To change to the Scientific view of the Calculator, click **View**.

8 Click **Scientific**.

■ The Scientific view of the Calculator appears. You can use this view to perform more complex calculations, such as averages and exponents.

Note: To return to the Standard view, perform steps 7 and 8, selecting ***Standard*** *in step 8.*

9 When you finish using the Calculator, click ⊠ to close the Calculator window.

USING NOTEPAD

Notepad is a program you can use to take notes or create simple documents.

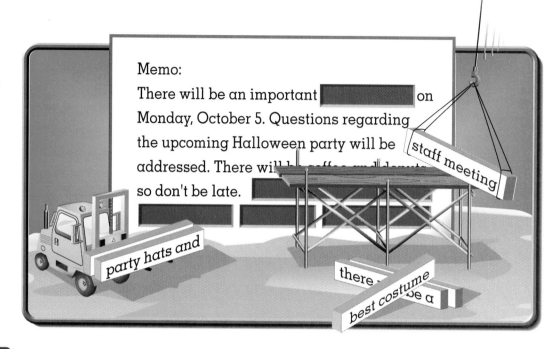

Memo:

There will be an important [ ] on Monday, October 5. Questions regarding the upcoming Halloween party will be addressed. There will be coffee and donuts so don't be late.

staff meeting

party hats and

there will be a best costume

USING NOTEPAD

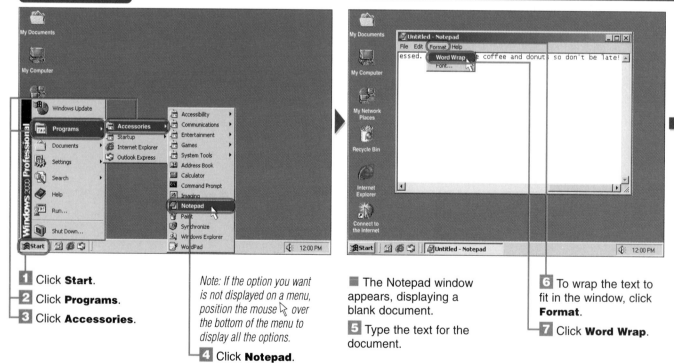

1 Click **Start**.

2 Click **Programs**.

3 Click **Accessories**.

Note: If the option you want is not displayed on a menu, position the mouse ⤷ over the bottom of the menu to display all the options.

4 Click **Notepad**.

■ The Notepad window appears, displaying a blank document.

5 Type the text for the document.

6 To wrap the text to fit in the window, click **Format**.

7 Click **Word Wrap**.

Can I quickly enter the current time and date in a Notepad document?

To enter the current time and date in your document, press the F5 key. Notepad will automatically place the time and date at the location of the insertion point.

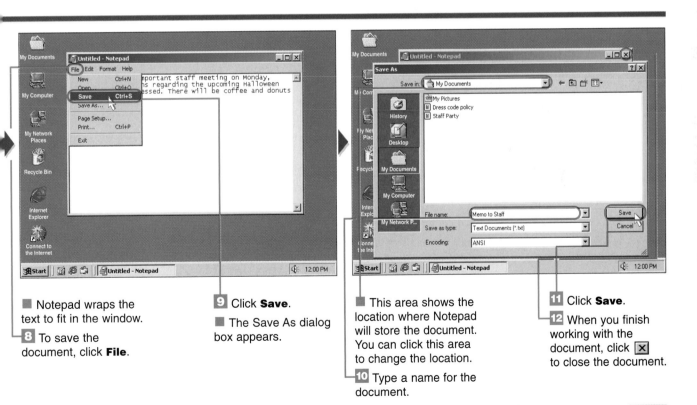

■ Notepad wraps the text to fit in the window.

8 To save the document, click **File**.

9 Click **Save**.

■ The Save As dialog box appears.

■ This area shows the location where Notepad will store the document. You can click this area to change the location.

10 Type a name for the document.

11 Click **Save**.

12 When you finish working with the document, click ✕ to close the document.

START A COMMAND PROMPT WINDOW

You can work with MS-DOS commands and programs in Windows.

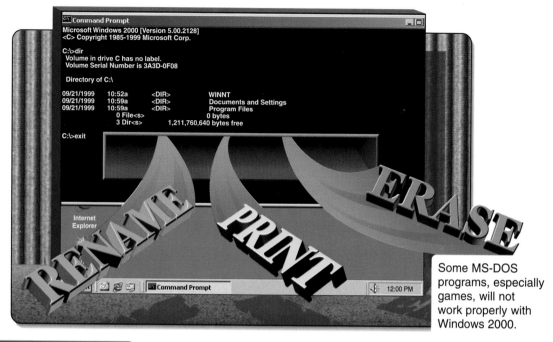

Some MS-DOS programs, especially games, will not work properly with Windows 2000.

START A COMMAND PROMPT WINDOW

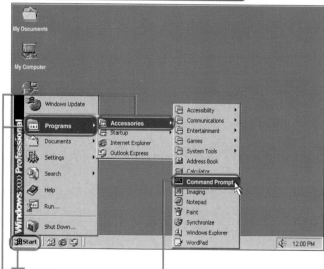

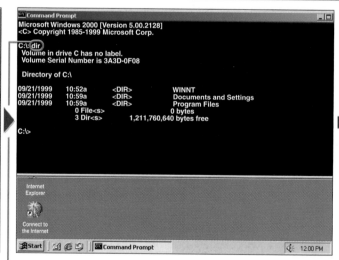

1 Click **Start**.

2 Click **Programs**.

3 Click **Accessories**.

Note: If the option you want is not displayed on a menu, position the mouse ⍗ over the bottom of the menu to display all the options.

4 Click **Command Prompt**.

■ The Command Prompt window appears.

■ You can enter MS-DOS commands and start MS-DOS programs in the window. In this example, we enter the **dir** command to list the contents of the current directory.

5 To fill the entire screen with the command prompt, hold down the **Alt** key and then press the **Enter** key.

30

How can I get help information for MS-DOS commands?

In the Command Prompt window, type **help** and then press the Enter key to display a list of MS-DOS commands that you can use.

C:\>help

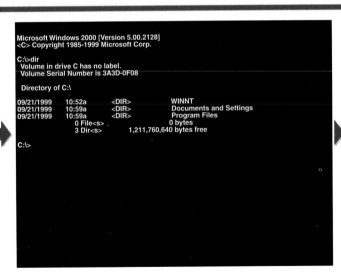

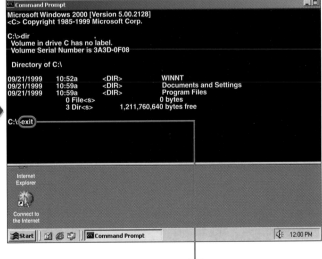

■ The command prompt fills the entire screen.

6 To return the command prompt to a window, hold down the Alt key and then press the Enter key.

■ The command prompt returns to a window.

7 When you finish using the Command Prompt window, type **exit** and then press the Enter key to close the window.

CHAPTER 2

Create Documents

In this chapter you will learn how to use the WordPad program to create documents quickly and efficiently.

Dear Kevin:

ool celebrates its 20th

START WORDPAD

WordPad allows you to create simple documents, such as letters and memos.

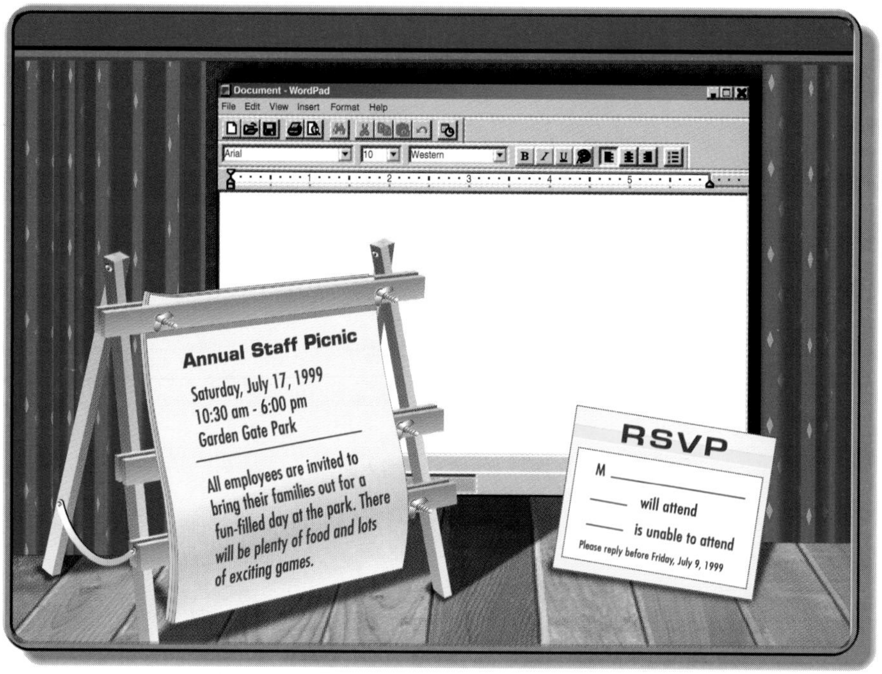

START WORDPAD

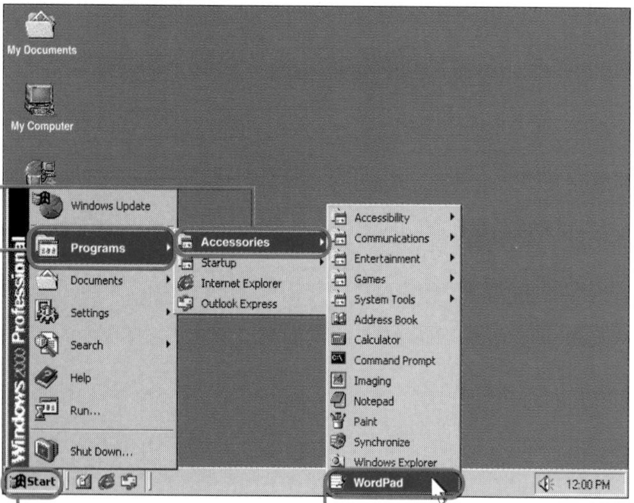

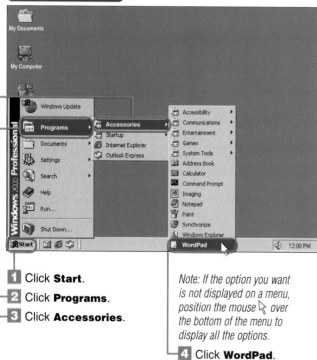

1 Click **Start**.

2 Click **Programs**.

3 Click **Accessories**.

Note: If the option you want is not displayed on a menu, position the mouse over the bottom of the menu to display all the options.

4 Click **WordPad**.

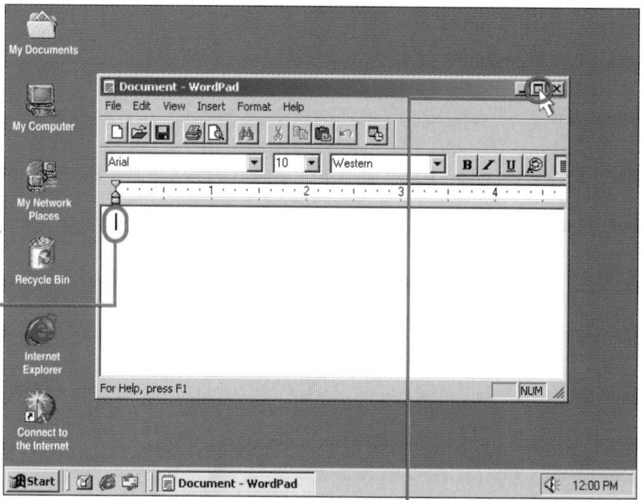

■ The WordPad window appears with a new, blank document.

■ The flashing line on your screen, called the insertion point, indicates where the text you type will appear.

5 Click ☐ to enlarge the WordPad window to fill your screen.

? Does WordPad offer all the features I need?

WordPad is a simple program that offers only basic word processing features. If you need more advanced features, you can purchase a more powerful word processor, such as Microsoft Word or Corel WordPerfect. These programs include features, such as tables, graphics, a spell checker and a thesaurus.

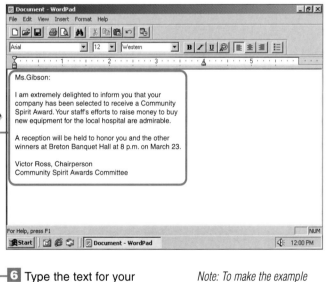

6 Type the text for your document.

■ When you reach the end of a line, WordPad automatically moves the text to the next line. You need to press the Enter key only when you want to start a new line or paragraph.

Note: To make the example easier to read, the font size has been changed. To change the font size, see page 45.

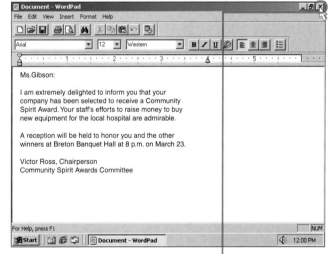

When you finish using WordPad, you can exit the program.

1 Before exiting WordPad, save any changes you made to the document. To save your changes, see page 40.

2 Click X to exit WordPad.

EDIT TEXT

You can easily add new text to your document and remove text you no longer need.

INSERT TEXT

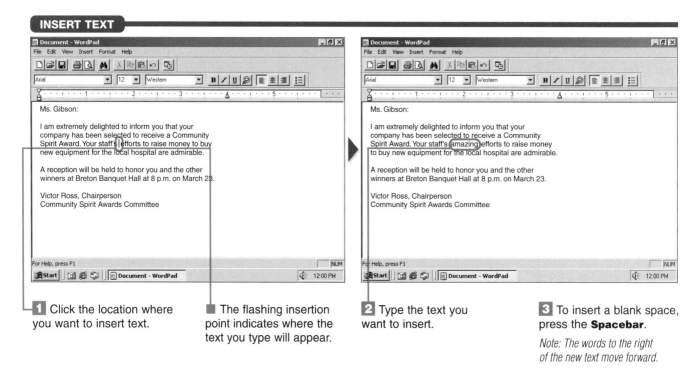

1 Click the location where you want to insert text.

■ The flashing insertion point indicates where the text you type will appear.

2 Type the text you want to insert.

3 To insert a blank space, press the **Spacebar**.

Note: The words to the right of the new text move forward.

How do I cancel changes I made?

WordPad remembers the last changes you made to your document. If you regret a change, you can cancel the change by using the Undo feature.

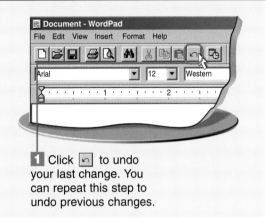

1 Click 🔄 to undo your last change. You can repeat this step to undo previous changes.

DELETE TEXT

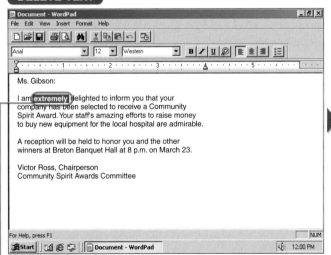

1 To select the text you want to delete, drag the mouse I over the text until the text is highlighted.

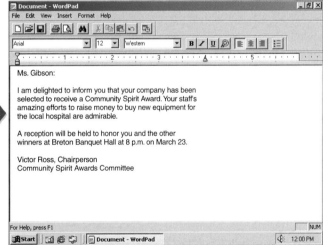

2 Press the Delete key to remove the text.

■ To delete one character at a time, click to the left of the first character you want to delete. Press the Delete key for each character you want to remove.

MOVE TEXT

You can reorganize your document by moving text from one location to another.

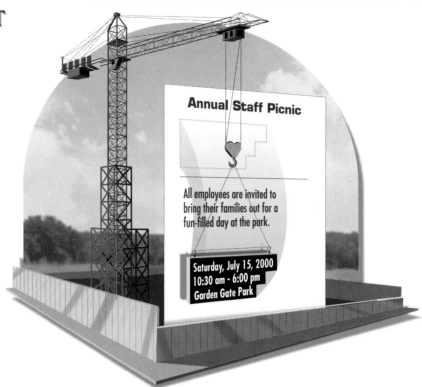

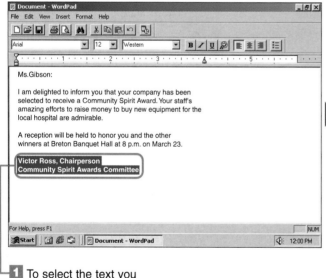

1 To select the text you want to move, drag the mouse I over the text until the text is highlighted.

2 Click [✂] to move the text.

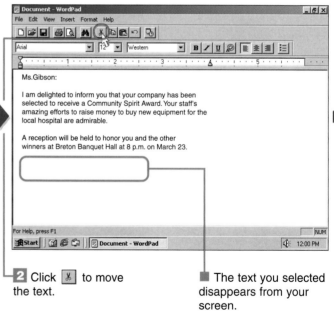

■ The text you selected disappears from your screen.

Can I copy text in a document?

To copy text, perform the steps below, except click 🖻 in step **2**.

If you plan to make major changes to a paragraph, you may want to copy the paragraph before you begin. This gives you two copies of the paragraph—the original paragraph and a paragraph you can change.

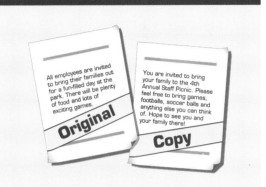

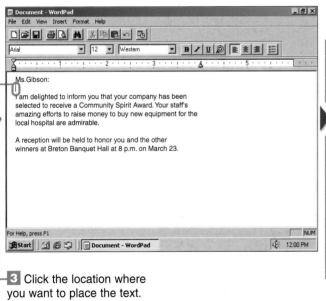

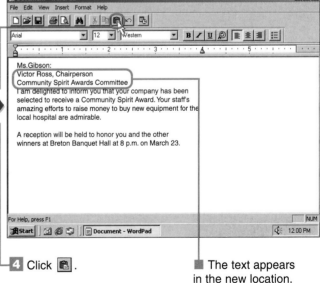

3 Click the location where you want to place the text. The flashing insertion point indicates where the text will appear.

4 Click 🖻.

■ The text appears in the new location.

SAVE A DOCUMENT

You should save your
document to store it
for future use. This
lets you later retrieve
the document for
reviewing or editing.

You should regularly
save changes you
make to a document to
avoid losing your work.

SAVE A DOCUMENT

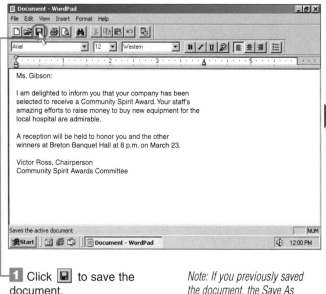

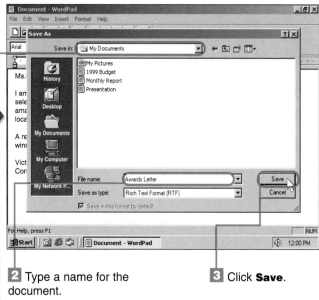

1 Click 🖫 to save the
document.

■ The Save As dialog
box appears.

*Note: If you previously saved
the document, the Save As
dialog box will not appear since
you have already named the
document.*

2 Type a name for the
document.

■ This area shows the
location where WordPad
will store the document.
You can click this area
to change the location.

3 Click **Save**.

You can produce a
paper copy of the
document displayed
on your screen.

PRINT A DOCUMENT

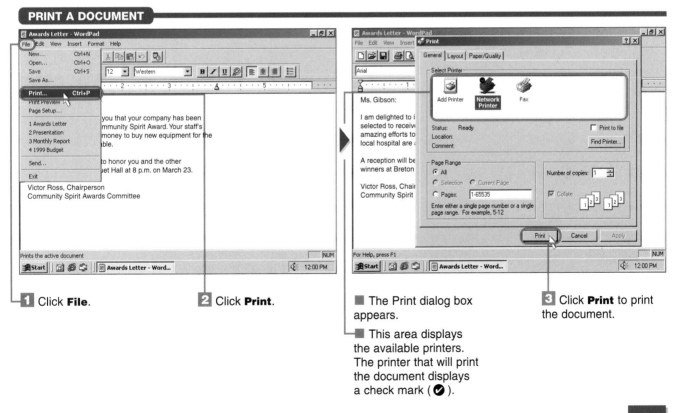

1 Click **File**.

2 Click **Print**.

■ The Print dialog box
appears.

■ This area displays
the available printers.
The printer that will print
the document displays
a check mark (✔).

3 Click **Print** to print
the document.

OPEN A DOCUMENT

You can open a saved document and display the document on your screen. This allows you to view and make changes to the document.

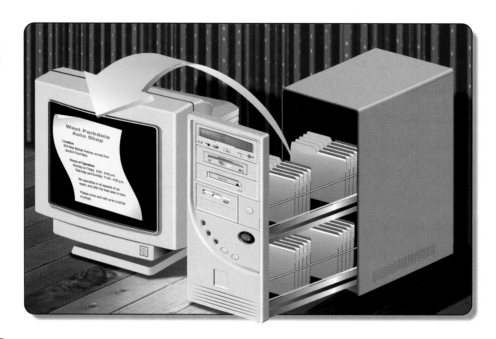

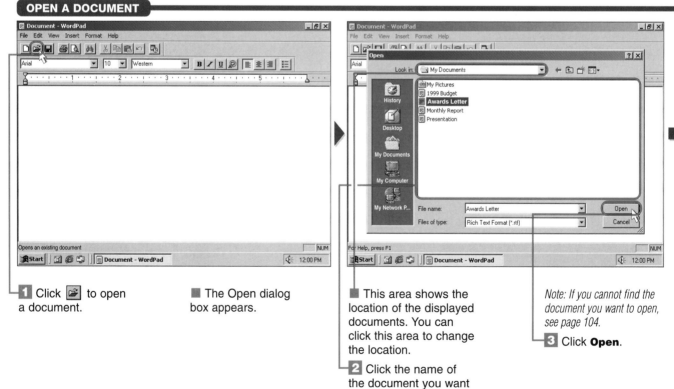

1 Click 🗁 to open a document.

■ The Open dialog box appears.

■ This area shows the location of the displayed documents. You can click this area to change the location.

2 Click the name of the document you want to open.

Note: If you cannot find the document you want to open, see page 104.

3 Click **Open**.

Can I work with two WordPad documents at the same time?

WordPad lets you work with only one document at a time. If you are currently working with a document, save the document before opening another. For information on saving a document, see page 40.

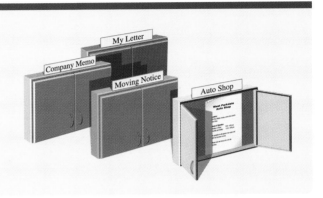

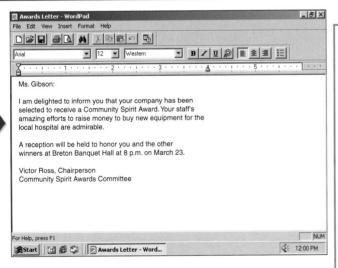

■ WordPad opens the document and displays it on your screen. You can now review and make changes to the document.

QUICKLY OPEN A DOCUMENT

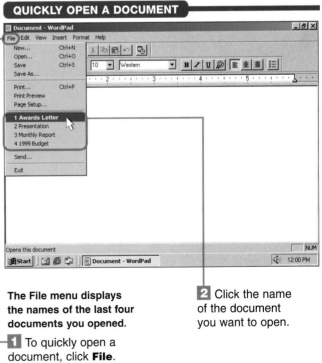

The File menu displays the names of the last four documents you opened.

1 To quickly open a document, click **File**.

2 Click the name of the document you want to open.

CHANGE FONT TYPE

You can enhance the appearance of your document by changing the design of the text.

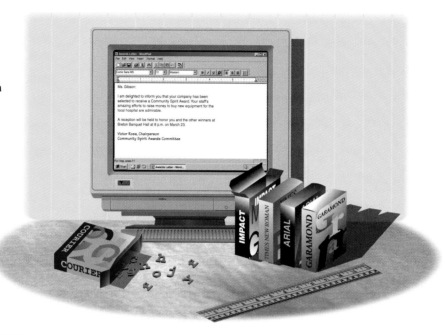

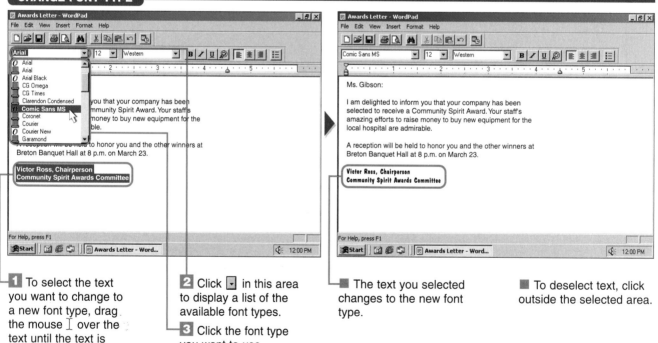

1 To select the text you want to change to a new font type, drag the mouse I over the text until the text is highlighted.

2 Click ▾ in this area to display a list of the available font types.

3 Click the font type you want to use.

■ The text you selected changes to the new font type.

■ To deselect text, click outside the selected area.

You can increase
or decrease the
size of text in your
document.

36 point
28 point
24 point
14 point
10 point
8 point

CHANGE FONT SIZE

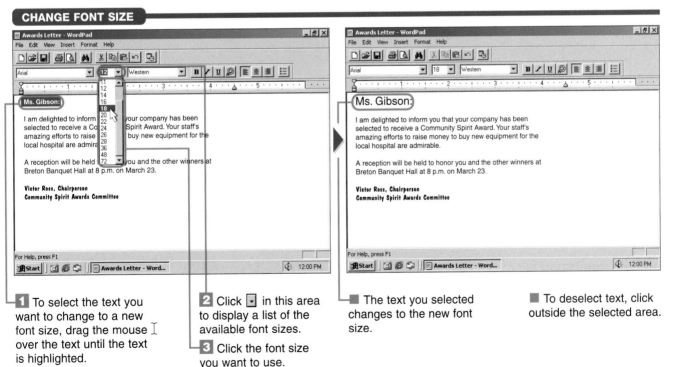

1 To select the text you want to change to a new font size, drag the mouse I over the text until the text is highlighted.

2 Click ⬇ in this area to display a list of the available font sizes.

3 Click the font size you want to use.

■ The text you selected changes to the new font size.

■ To deselect text, click outside the selected area.

BOLD, ITALIC AND UNDERLINE

You can use the Bold, Italic and Underline features to emphasize text in your document.

BOLD, ITALIC AND UNDERLINE

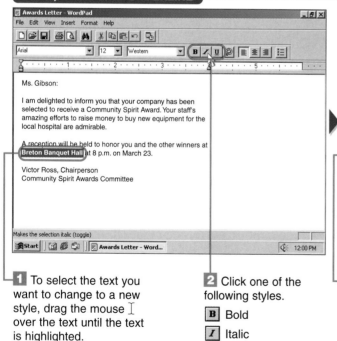

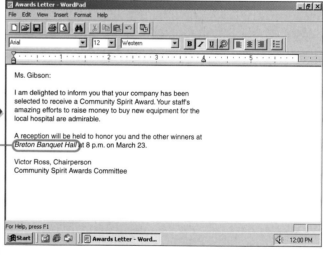

1 To select the text you want to change to a new style, drag the mouse I over the text until the text is highlighted.

2 Click one of the following styles.

B Bold

I Italic

U Underline

■ The text you selected appears in the new style.

■ To deselect text, click outside the selected area.

■ To remove a bold, italic or underline style, repeat steps **1** and **2**.

You can enhance
the appearance of
your document by
aligning text in
different ways.

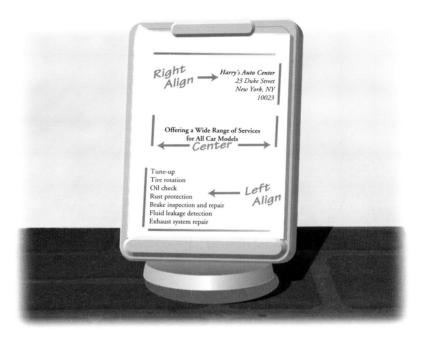

CHANGE ALIGNMENT OF TEXT

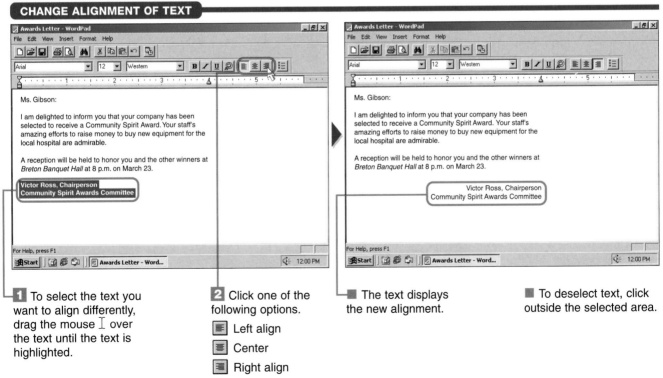

1 To select the text you want to align differently, drag the mouse I over the text until the text is highlighted.

2 Click one of the following options.

▤ Left align

▤ Center

▤ Right align

■ The text displays the new alignment.

■ To deselect text, click outside the selected area.

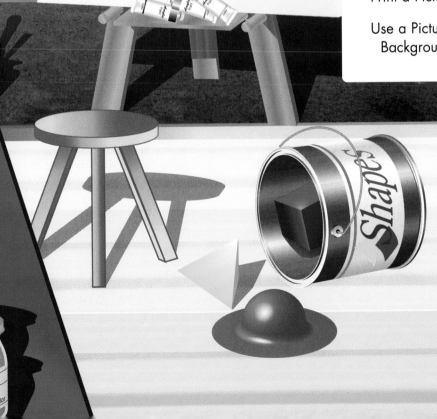

CHAPTER 3

Create Pictures

Learn how to use the Paint program to create your own pictures in this chapter.

START PAINT

You can use Paint
to draw pictures
and maps on your
computer.

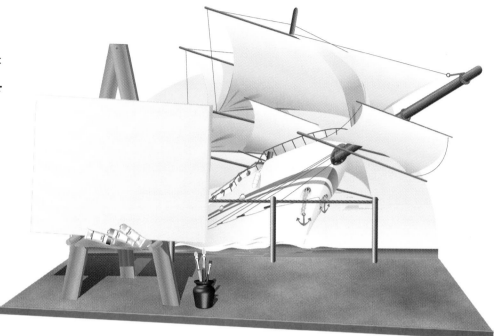

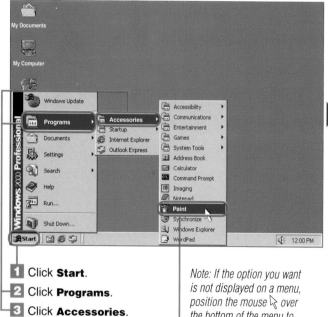

1 Click **Start**.

2 Click **Programs**.

3 Click **Accessories**.

*Note: If the option you want
is not displayed on a menu,
position the mouse ⬚ over
the bottom of the menu to
display all the options.*

4 Click **Paint**.

■ The Paint window
appears.

5 Click 🔲 to enlarge
the Paint window to fill
your screen.

50

What can I do with the pictures I draw in Paint?

You can place the pictures you draw in Paint in other programs. For example, you can add your company logo to a business letter you created in WordPad.

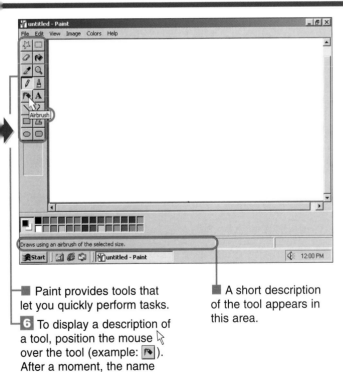

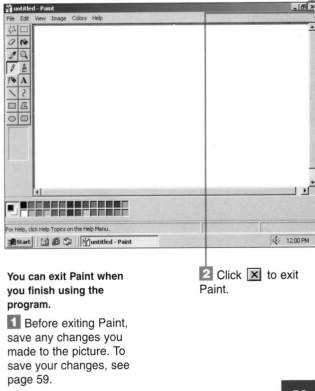

■ Paint provides tools that let you quickly perform tasks.

6 To display a description of a tool, position the mouse over the tool (example:). After a moment, the name of the tool appears.

■ A short description of the tool appears in this area.

You can exit Paint when you finish using the program.

1 Before exiting Paint, save any changes you made to the picture. To save your changes, see page 59.

2 Click ☒ to exit Paint.

DRAW SHAPES

You can draw shapes such as circles and squares in various colors.

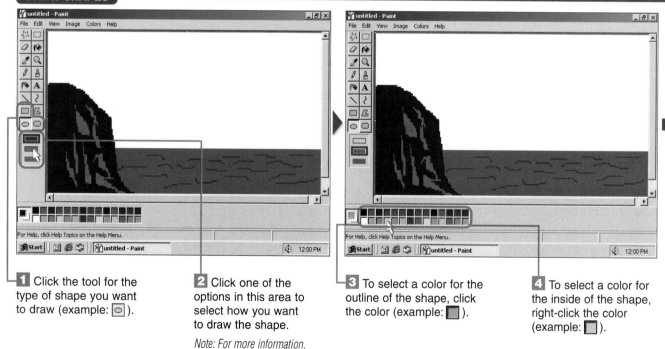

1 Click the tool for the type of shape you want to draw (example: ⊘).

2 Click one of the options in this area to select how you want to draw the shape.

Note: For more information, see the top of page 53.

3 To select a color for the outline of the shape, click the color (example: ■).

4 To select a color for the inside of the shape, right-click the color (example: ■).

52

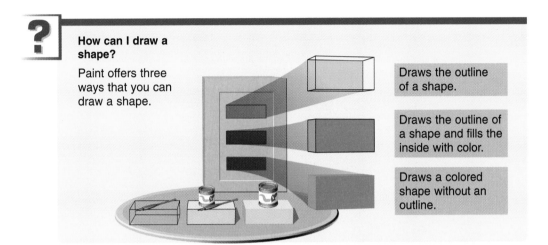

How can I draw a shape?

Paint offers three ways that you can draw a shape.

Draws the outline of a shape.

Draws the outline of a shape and fills the inside with color.

Draws a colored shape without an outline.

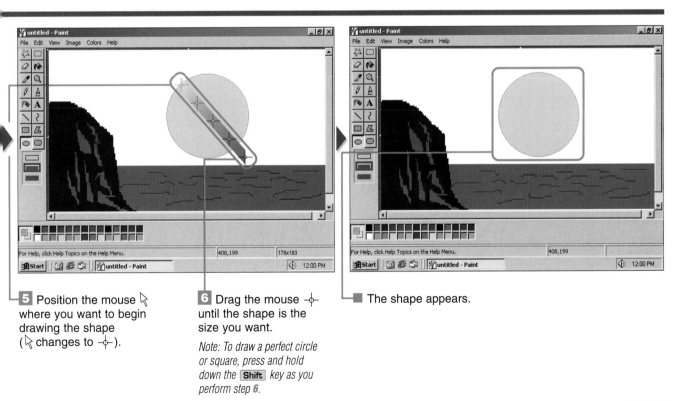

5 Position the mouse ⏴ where you want to begin drawing the shape (⏴ changes to ⊹).

6 Drag the mouse ⊹ until the shape is the size you want.

Note: To draw a perfect circle or square, press and hold down the **Shift** *key as you perform step* **6**.

■ The shape appears.

DRAW LINES

You can draw
straight, wavy
and curved lines
in various colors.

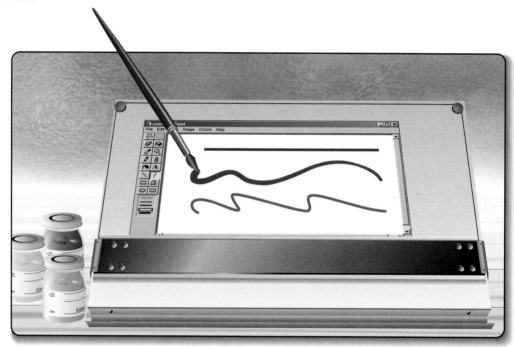

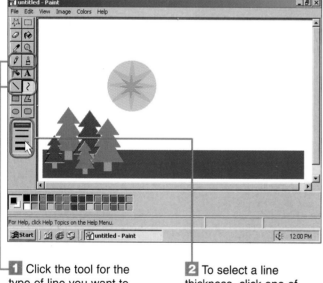

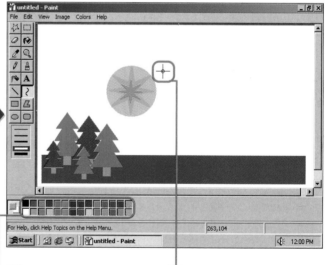

1 Click the tool for the
type of line you want to
draw (example: �).

*Note: For more information,
see the top of page 55.*

2 To select a line
thickness, click one of
the options in this area.

*Note: The ✏ tool does not
provide any line thickness
options. The ⃞ tool provides
a different set of options.*

3 To select a color for
the line, click the color
(example: ▨).

4 Position the mouse ▷
where you want to
begin drawing the line
(▷ changes to ✛, ✏ or ✛).

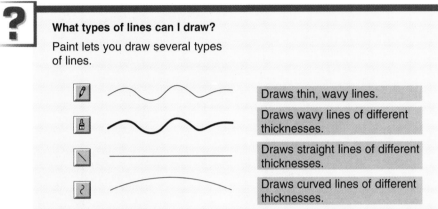

What types of lines can I draw?

Paint lets you draw several types of lines.

Draws thin, wavy lines.

Draws wavy lines of different thicknesses.

Draws straight lines of different thicknesses.

Draws curved lines of different thicknesses.

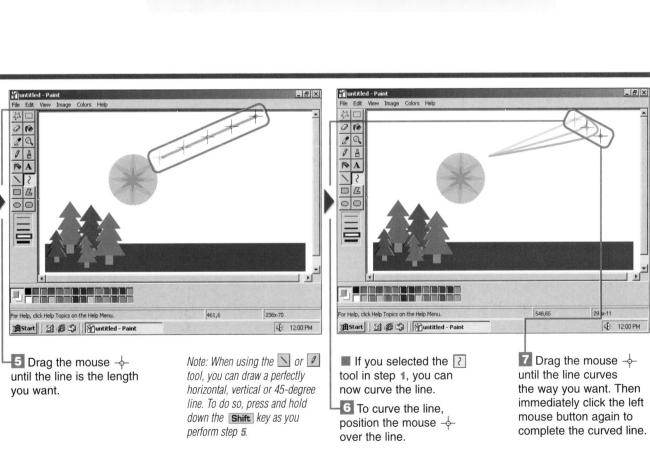

5 Drag the mouse until the line is the length you want.

Note: When using the ◥ or ◢ tool, you can draw a perfectly horizontal, vertical or 45-degree line. To do so, press and hold down the **Shift** *key as you perform step* **5***.*

■ If you selected the ◸ tool in step **1**, you can now curve the line.

6 To curve the line, position the mouse over the line.

7 Drag the mouse until the line curves the way you want. Then immediately click the left mouse button again to complete the curved line.

ADD TEXT

You can add text
to your picture,
such as a title or
explanation.

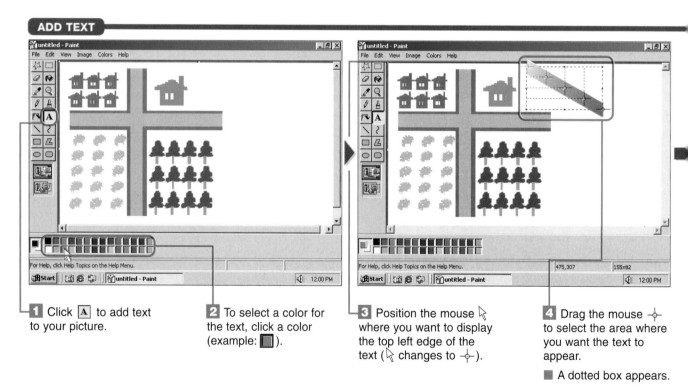

1 Click **A** to add text
to your picture.

2 To select a color for
the text, click a color
(example: ▓).

3 Position the mouse ▷
where you want to display
the top left edge of the
text (▷ changes to ✛).

4 Drag the mouse ✛
to select the area where
you want the text to
appear.

■ A dotted box appears.

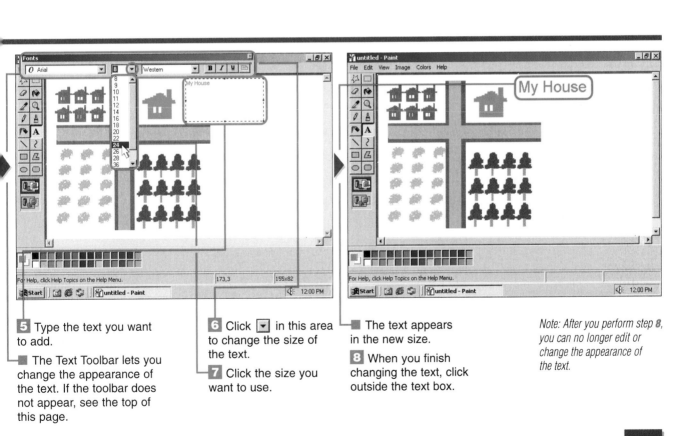

5 Type the text you want to add.

■ The Text Toolbar lets you change the appearance of the text. If the toolbar does not appear, see the top of this page.

6 Click ▼ in this area to change the size of the text.

7 Click the size you want to use.

■ The text appears in the new size.

8 When you finish changing the text, click outside the text box.

Note: After you perform step 8, you can no longer edit or change the appearance of the text.

57

ERASE PART OF A PICTURE

You can use the
Eraser tool to
remove part of
your picture.

When choosing a color
for the eraser, select a
color that matches the
background color of
your picture.

ERASE PART OF A PICTURE

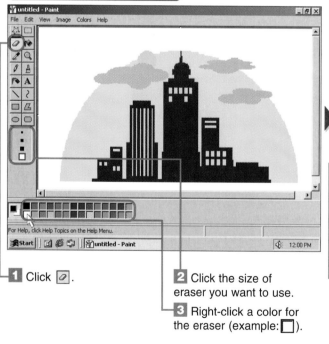

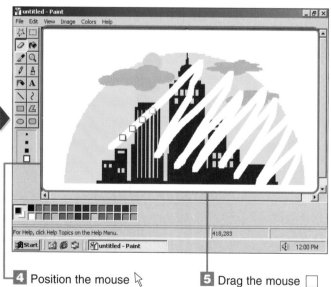

1 Click ⌀.

2 Click the size of
eraser you want to use.

3 Right-click a color for
the eraser (example: ☐).

4 Position the mouse ↖
where you want to start
erasing (↖ changes to ☐).

5 Drag the mouse ☐
over the area you want
to erase.

*Note: To immediately undo the
change, press and hold down
the* **Ctrl** *key and then press
the* **Z** *key.*

You should save your picture to store it for future use. This allows you to later review and make changes to the picture.

Corporation

You should regularly save changes you make to a picture to avoid losing your work.

SAVE A PICTURE

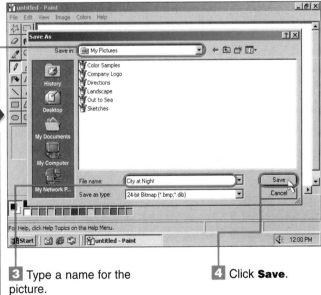

■1 Click **File**.

■2 Click **Save**.

■ The Save As dialog box appears.

Note: If you previously saved the picture, the Save As dialog box will not appear since you have already named the picture.

■3 Type a name for the picture.

■ This area shows the location where Paint will store the picture. You can click this area to change the location.

■4 Click **Save**.

OPEN A PICTURE

You can open a saved picture and display the picture on your screen. This allows you to view and make changes to the picture.

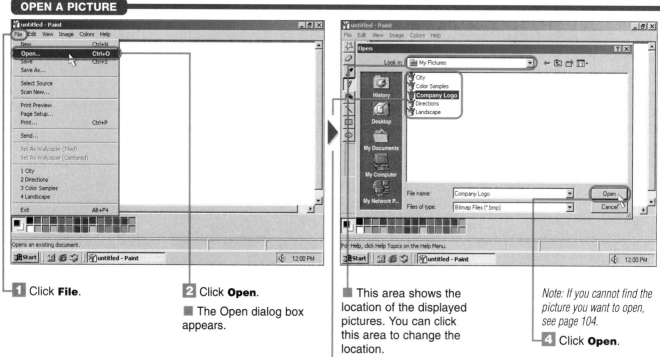

1 Click **File**.

2 Click **Open**.

■ The Open dialog box appears.

■ This area shows the location of the displayed pictures. You can click this area to change the location.

3 Click the name of the picture you want to open.

Note: If you cannot find the picture you want to open, see page 104.

4 Click **Open**.

60

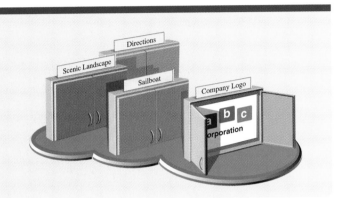

Can I work with two pictures at the same time?

Paint lets you work with only one picture at a time. If you are currently working with a picture, save the picture before opening another. For information on saving a picture, see page 59.

■ Paint opens the picture and displays it on your screen. You can now view and make changes to the picture.

QUICKLY OPEN A PICTURE

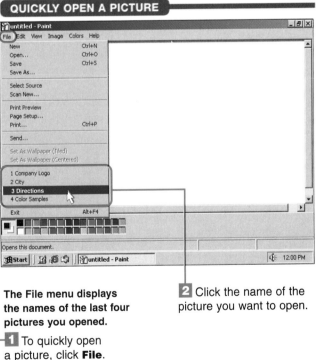

The File menu displays the names of the last four pictures you opened.

■1 To quickly open a picture, click **File**.

■2 Click the name of the picture you want to open.

PRINT A PICTURE

You can produce
a paper copy of a
picture you created.

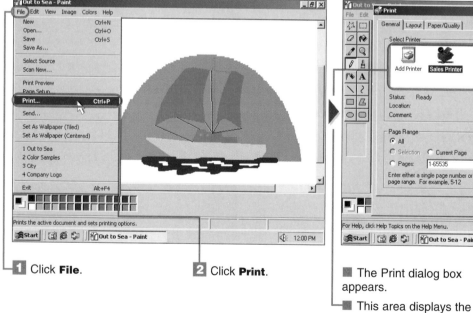

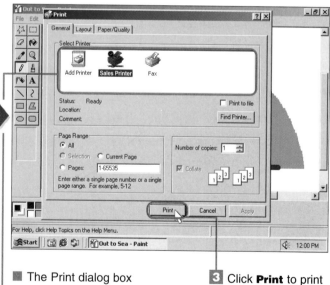

1 Click **File**.

2 Click **Print**.

■ The Print dialog box
appears.

■ This area displays the
available printers. The printer
that will print the picture
displays a check mark (●).

3 Click **Print** to print
the picture.

You can use a picture as the background for your desktop.

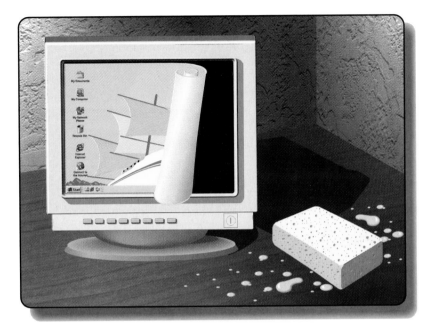

You must save a picture before you can use the picture as your desktop background. To save a picture, see page 59.

USE A PICTURE AS DESKTOP BACKGROUND

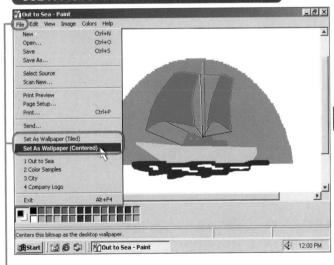

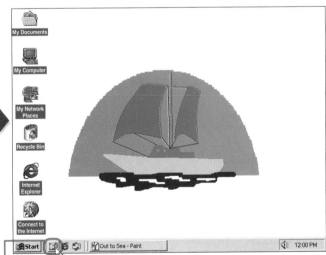

1 To use the displayed picture as your desktop background, click **File**.

2 Click the way you want the picture to appear on your desktop.

Tiled - Repeats picture to cover desktop

Centered - Displays picture centered on desktop

3 Click 🖳 to minimize all your open windows so you can clearly view the desktop.

■ The picture appears on your desktop.

■ To restore the original desktop background, see page 124.

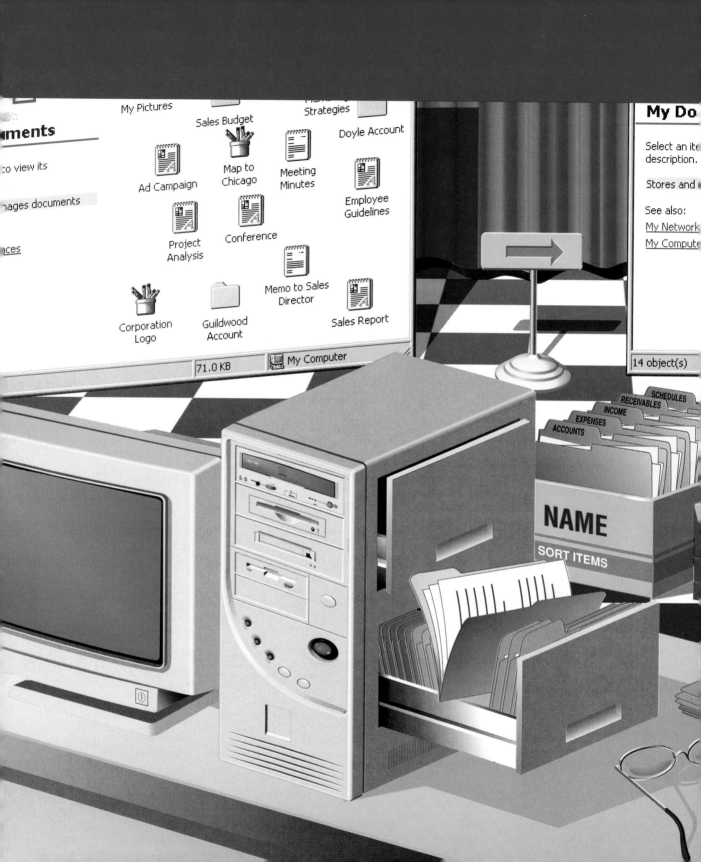

CHAPTER 4

View Files

This chapter shows you the ways you can view the files, folders and programs on your computer.

VIEW CONTENTS OF YOUR COMPUTER

You can easily
view the folders
and files stored
on your computer.

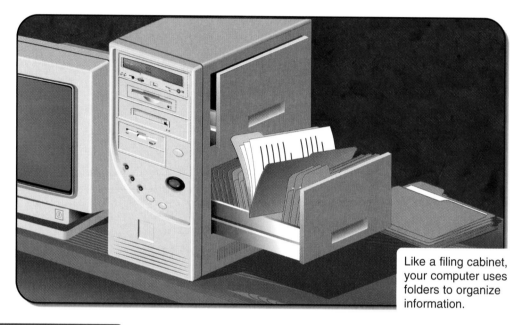

Like a filing cabinet,
your computer uses
folders to organize
information.

VIEW CONTENTS OF YOUR COMPUTER

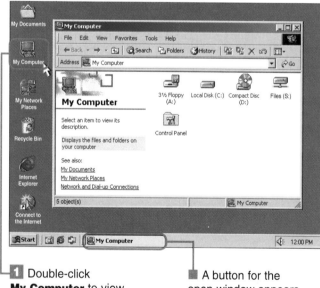

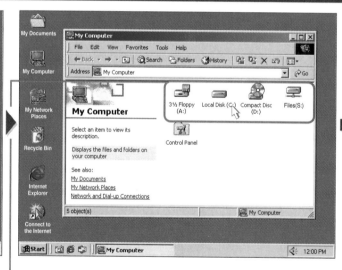

■1 Double-click
My Computer to view
the contents of your
computer.

■ The My Computer
window appears.

■ A button for the
open window appears
on the taskbar.

■ These items represent
drives on your computer
and the network.

■2 To display the
contents of a drive,
double-click the drive.

Note: If you want to view the
contents of a floppy or CD-ROM
drive, make sure you insert a
floppy disk or CD-ROM disc
before performing step **2**.

■ The contents of the
drive appear.

66

What do the icons in the My Computer window represent?

The My Computer window displays icons to represent drives on your computer and the network.

| Hard Drive on Your Computer | Floppy Drive | CD-ROM Drive | Drive on the Network |

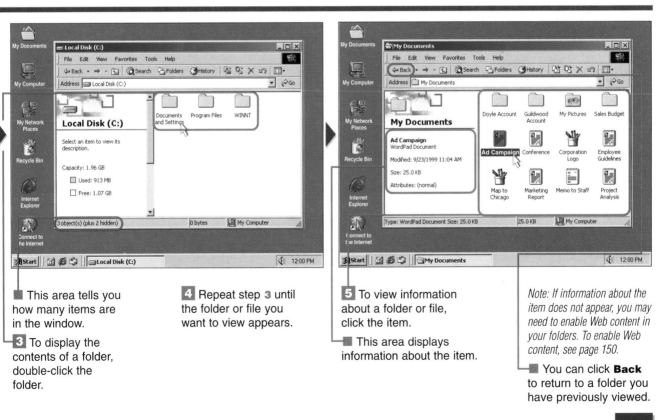

■ This area tells you how many items are in the window.

3 To display the contents of a folder, double-click the folder.

4 Repeat step **3** until the folder or file you want to view appears.

5 To view information about a folder or file, click the item.

■ This area displays information about the item.

Note: If information about the item does not appear, you may need to enable Web content in your folders. To enable Web content, see page 150.

■ You can click **Back** to return to a folder you have previously viewed.

CHANGE APPEARANCE OF ITEMS

You can change the
appearance of items
in a window. The
appearance you
select determines
the information
you will see in
the window.

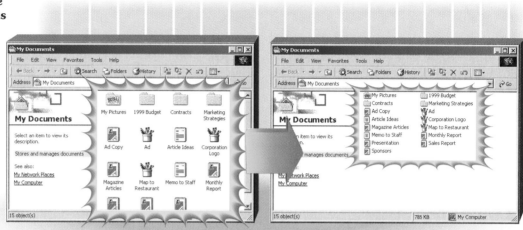

CHANGE APPEARANCE OF ITEMS

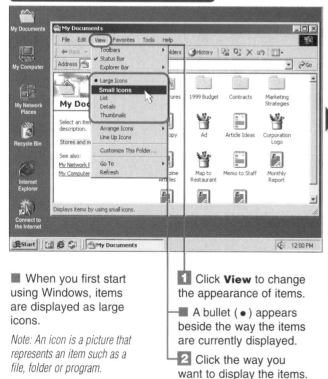

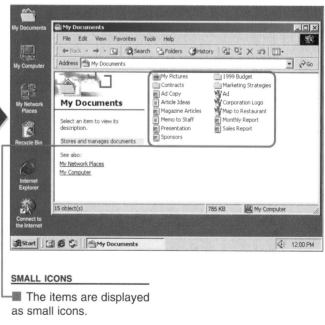

■ When you first start
using Windows, items
are displayed as large
icons.

Note: An icon is a picture that
represents an item such as a
file, folder or program.

1 Click **View** to change
the appearance of items.

■ A bullet (•) appears
beside the way the items
are currently displayed.

2 Click the way you
want to display the items.

SMALL ICONS

■ The items are displayed
as small icons.

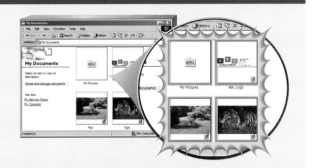

What is the Thumbnails view?

The Thumbnails view allows you to display a miniature version of each picture file in the window. Icons for other types of files are displayed in boxes. The Thumbnails view is not available in some windows.

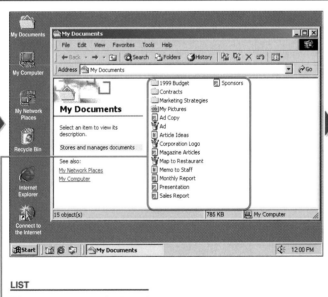

LIST

■ The items are displayed as small icons arranged in a list.

DETAILS

■ Information about each item is displayed, such as the name, size and type of item.

SORT ITEMS

You can sort the items displayed in a window. This can help you find files and folders more easily.

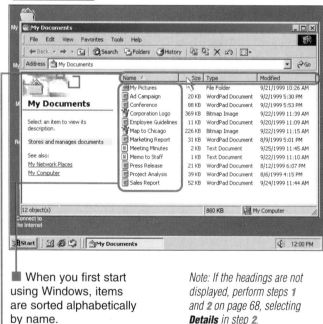

■ When you first start using Windows, items are sorted alphabetically by name.

1 Click the heading for the column you want to use to sort the items.

*Note: If the headings are not displayed, perform steps 1 and 2 on page 68, selecting **Details** in step 2.*

■ To sort the items in the reverse order, click the heading again.

SORT BY SIZE

■ The items are sorted by size.

How does Windows measure the size of files?

The size of each file is measured in kilobytes (KB). An average letter created in WordPad is approximately 5 KB.

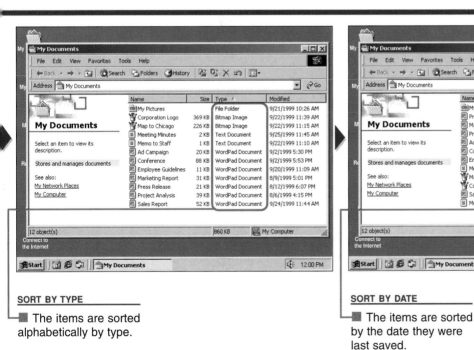

SORT BY TYPE

■ The items are sorted alphabetically by type.

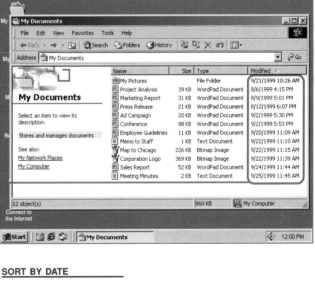

SORT BY DATE

■ The items are sorted by the date they were last saved.

ARRANGE ITEMS AUTOMATICALLY

You can have Windows automatically arrange items to fit neatly in a window.

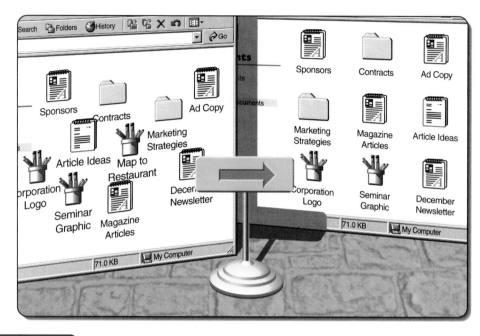

ARRANGE ITEMS AUTOMATICALLY

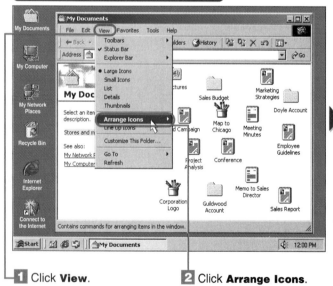

1 Click **View**.

2 Click **Arrange Icons**.

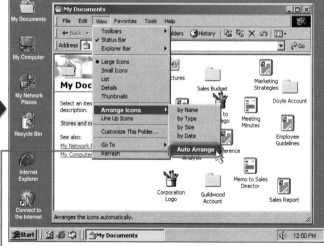

■ A check mark (✔) appears beside **Auto Arrange** when this feature is on.

3 Click **Auto Arrange** to turn this feature on.

*Note: If a check mark (✔) appears beside **Auto Arrange** and you want to leave this feature on, press the* Alt *key to close the menu.*

?

Why is the Auto Arrange feature not available?

The Auto Arrange feature is not available when items appear in the List or Details view. For information on changing the appearance of items, see page 68.

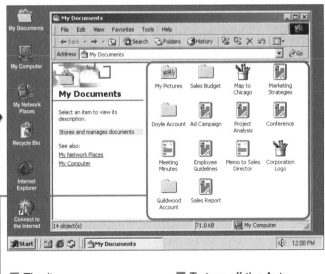

■ The items are automatically arranged in the window.

■ To turn off the Auto Arrange feature, repeat steps **1** to **3**.

■ When you change the size of a window and the Auto Arrange feature is on, Windows automatically rearranges the items to fit the new window size.

Note: To size a window, see page 13.

USING WINDOWS EXPLORER

Windows Explorer shows the location of every folder and file on your computer.

You can move, rename and delete files in Windows Explorer as you would in a My Computer window.

USING WINDOWS EXPLORER

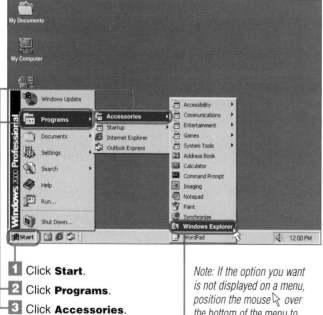

1 Click **Start**.

2 Click **Programs**.

3 Click **Accessories**.

Note: If the option you want is not displayed on a menu, position the mouse ⌖ over the bottom of the menu to display all the options.

4 Click **Windows Explorer**.

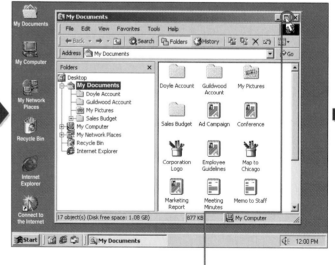

■ A window appears.

5 Click ▢ to enlarge the window to fill your screen.

Why don't the contents of some folders appear when I click the name of the folder?

Some folders contain important files that help keep your computer working properly. Windows does not automatically display the contents of these folders to prevent you from accidentally moving or deleting the files. To view the contents of the folder, click **Show Files** in the window.

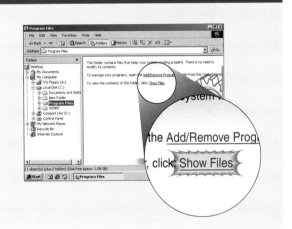

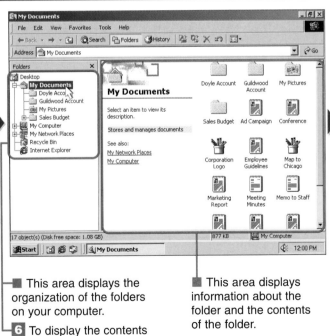

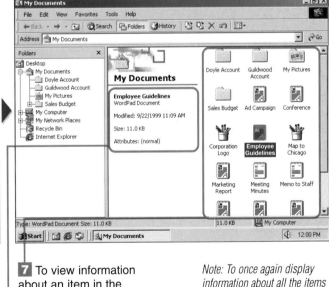

■ This area displays the organization of the folders on your computer.

6 To display the contents of a folder, click the name of the folder.

■ This area displays information about the folder and the contents of the folder.

Note: If information about the folder does not appear, you may need to enable Web content in your folders. To enable Web content, see page 150.

7 To view information about an item in the folder, click the item. The item is highlighted.

■ This area displays information about the item you selected.

Note: To once again display information about all the items in the folder, click a blank area on the right side of the window.

CONTINUED

USING WINDOWS EXPLORER

A folder may contain other folders. You can easily display or hide these folders at any time.

DISPLAY HIDDEN FOLDERS

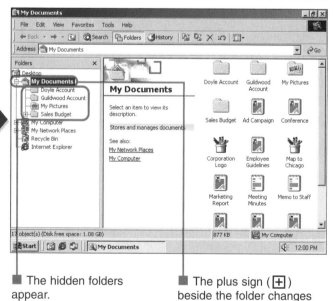

You can display hidden folders to view more of the information stored on your computer.

1 To display the hidden folders within a folder, click the plus sign (⊞) beside the folder.

■ The hidden folders appear.

■ The plus sign (⊞) beside the folder changes to a minus sign (⊟). This indicates that all the folders within the folder are now displayed.

How can I tell if a folder contains other folders?

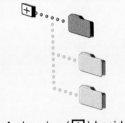

A plus sign (⊞) beside a folder indicates that all the folders it contains are hidden.

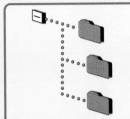

A minus sign (⊟) beside a folder indicates that all the folders it contains are displayed.

No sign beside a folder indicates that the folder does not contain any folders, although it may contain files.

HIDE FOLDERS

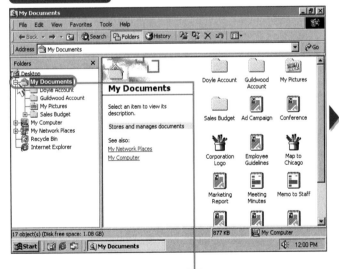

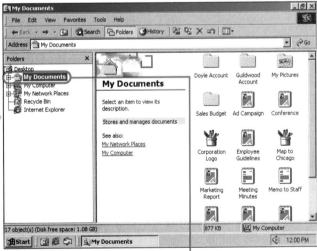

You can hide folders to reduce the number of folders displayed on your screen.

1 To hide the folders within a folder, click the minus sign (⊟) beside the folder.

■ The folders are hidden.

■ The minus sign (⊟) beside the folder changes to a plus sign (⊞). This indicates that all the folders within the folder are now hidden.

Annual Staff Picnic

Saturday, July 17, 1999
10:30 am - 6:00 pm
Garden Gate Park

All employees are invited to bring their families out for a fun-filled day at the park. There will be plenty of food and lots of exciting games.

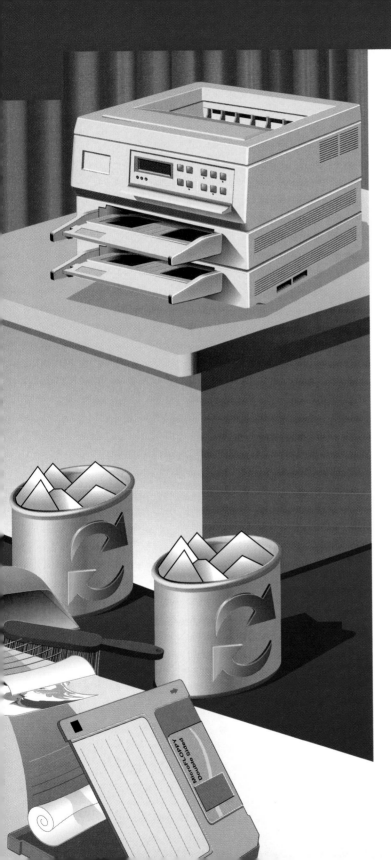

CHAPTER 5

Work With Files

This chapter teaches you how to manage your files efficiently. Learn how to move and copy files, create shortcuts, use the Briefcase feature and much more.

SELECT FILES

Before working with files, you must first select the files you want to work with. Selected files appear highlighted on your screen.

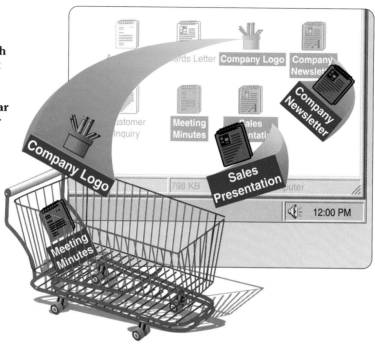

You can select folders the same way you select files. Selecting a folder will select all the files in the folder.

SELECT FILES

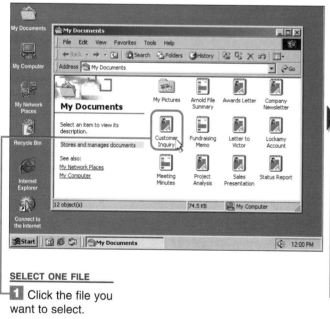

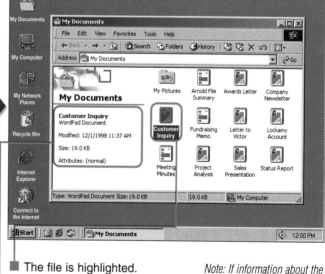

SELECT ONE FILE

1 Click the file you want to select.

■ The file is highlighted.

■ This area displays information about the file.

Note: If information about the file does not appear, you may need to enable Web content in your folders. To enable Web content, see page 150.

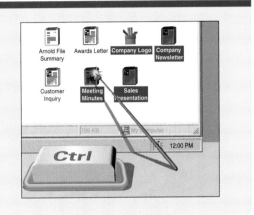

How do I deselect files?

To deselect all of the files in a window, click a blank area in the window.

To deselect one file from a group of selected files, press and hold down the `Ctrl` key as you click the file you want to deselect.

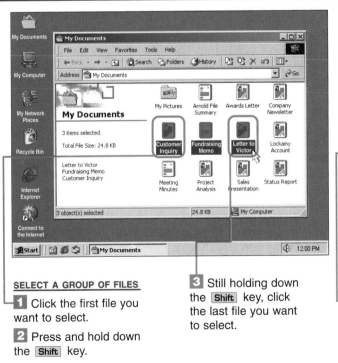

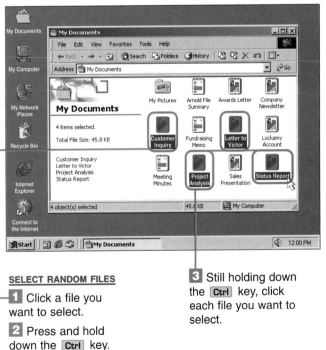

SELECT A GROUP OF FILES

1 Click the first file you want to select.

2 Press and hold down the `Shift` key.

3 Still holding down the `Shift` key, click the last file you want to select.

SELECT RANDOM FILES

1 Click a file you want to select.

2 Press and hold down the `Ctrl` key.

3 Still holding down the `Ctrl` key, click each file you want to select.

OPEN A FILE

You can open a file to display its contents on your screen. This lets you review and make changes to the file.

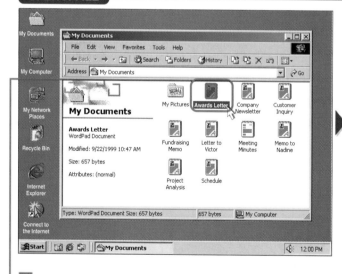

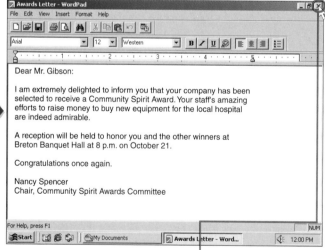

1 Double-click the file you want to open.

■ The file opens. You can review and make changes to the file.

2 When you finish working with the file, click ☒ to close the file.

OPEN A RECENTLY USED FILE

Windows remembers
the files you most
recently used. You
can quickly open
any of these files.

OPEN A RECENTLY USED FILE

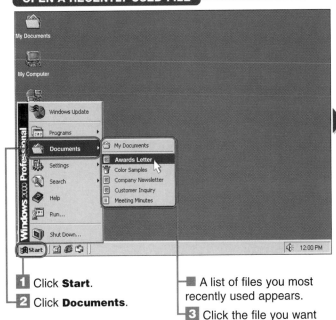

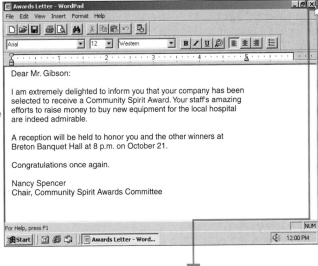

1 Click **Start**.

2 Click **Documents**.

■ A list of files you most
recently used appears.

3 Click the file you want
to open.

*Note: You can click **My Documents**
to open the My Documents folder.
Many programs automatically store
documents you create in this folder.*

■ The file opens. You
can review and make
changes to the file.

4 When you finish
working with the file,
click ☒ to close the file.

RENAME A FILE

You can give a file a new name to better describe the contents of the file. This can make the file easier to find.

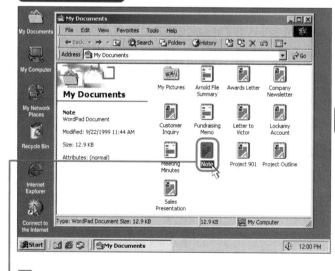

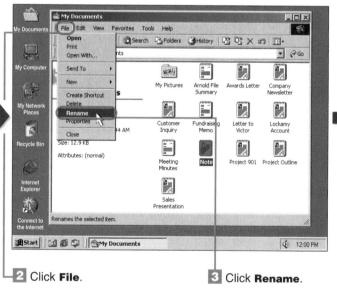

1 Click the file you want to rename.

2 Click **File**.

3 Click **Rename**.

Can I rename a folder?

You should only rename folders that you have created. To rename a folder, perform the steps below, selecting the folder you want to rename in step **1**.

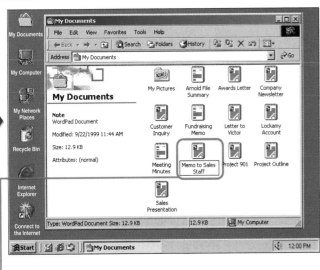

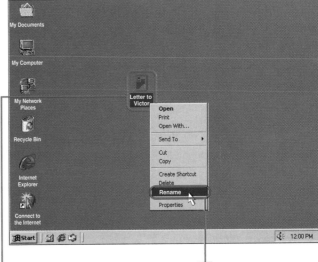

■ The name of the file appears in a box.

Note: A file name cannot contain the \ /:*?"< > or I characters.

4 Type a new name for the file and then press the `Enter` key.

You can easily rename a file on your desktop.

1 Right-click the file you want to rename. A menu appears.

2 Click **Rename**.

3 Type a new name and then press the `Enter` key.

CREATE A NEW FOLDER

You can create a new folder to help you better organize the information stored on your computer. Creating a folder is like placing a new folder in a filing cabinet.

CREATE A NEW FOLDER

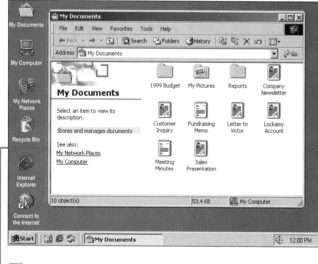

1 Display the contents of the folder where you want to place the new folder.

Note: To browse through the contents of your computer, see page 66.

2 Click **File**.

3 Click **New**.

4 Click **Folder**.

How can creating new folders help me organize the information on my computer?

You can create as many new folders as you need to develop a filing system that works for you. You can then organize your files by moving them to the new folders. To move files, see page 90.

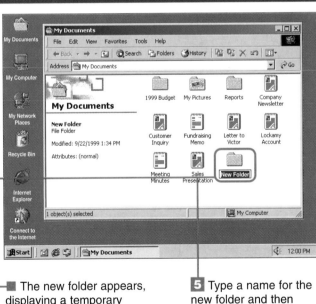

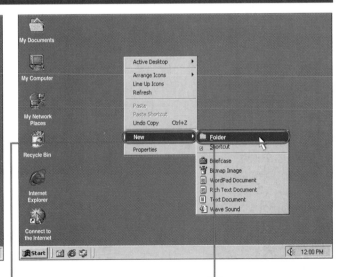

■ The new folder appears, displaying a temporary name (**New Folder**).

5 Type a name for the new folder and then press the **Enter** key.

Note: A folder name cannot contain the \ /:?"<> or | characters.*

You can create a new folder on your desktop.

1 Right-click an empty area on your desktop. A menu appears.

2 Click **New**.

3 Click **Folder**.

4 Type a name for the new folder and then press the **Enter** key.

CREATE A NEW FILE

You can instantly create, name and store a new file in the appropriate location without starting any programs.

You can focus on the organization of your files rather than the programs you need to accomplish your tasks.

CREATE A NEW FILE

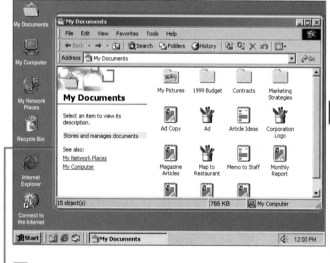

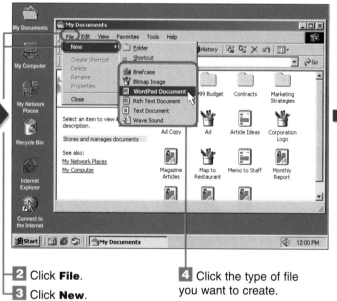

1 Display the contents of the folder where you want to place a new file.

2 Click **File**.

3 Click **New**.

4 Click the type of file you want to create.

? What types of files can I create?

The types of files you can create depend on the programs installed on your computer. By default, Windows allows you to create several types of files, such as images and text documents.

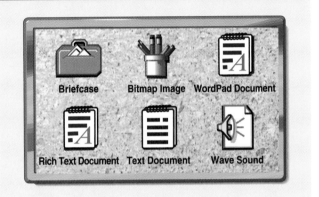

Briefcase   Bitmap Image   WordPad Document

Rich Text Document   Text Document   Wave Sound

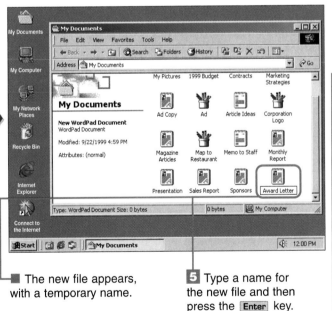

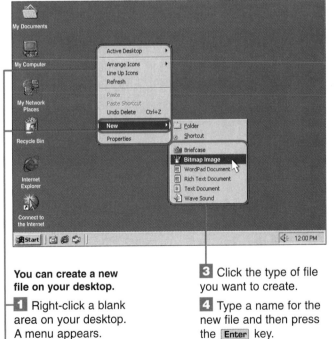

■ The new file appears, with a temporary name.

5 Type a name for the new file and then press the **Enter** key.

You can create a new file on your desktop.

1 Right-click a blank area on your desktop. A menu appears.

2 Click **New**.

3 Click the type of file you want to create.

4 Type a name for the new file and then press the **Enter** key.

MOVE AND COPY FILES

You can organize the files stored on your computer by moving or copying them to new locations.

Organizing files on your computer is similar to organizing files in a filing cabinet.

MOVE FILES

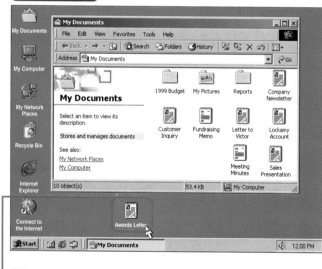

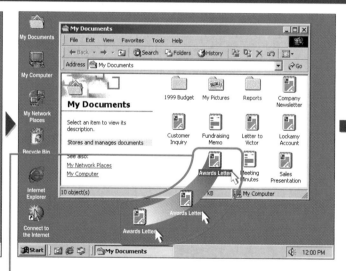

1 Position the mouse ↕ over the file you want to move.

■ To move more than one file, select all the files you want to move. Then position the mouse ↕ over one of the files.

Note: To select multiple files, see page 81.

2 Drag the file to a new location on your computer.

What is the difference between moving and copying a file?

Move a File

When you move a file, you place the file in a new location on your computer.

Copy a File

When you copy a file, you make an exact copy of the file and then place the copy in a new location. This lets you store the file in two locations.

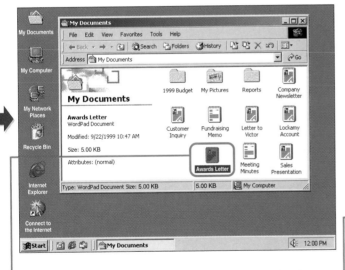

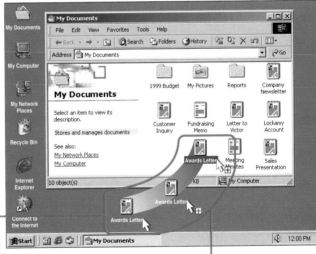

COPY FILES

■ The file moves to the new location.

Note: You can move folders the same way you move files. When you move a folder, all the files in the folder also move.

1 Position the mouse ⌖ over the file you want to copy.

2 Press and hold down the **Ctrl** key.

3 Still holding down the **Ctrl** key, drag the file to a new location.

COPY A FILE TO A FLOPPY DISK

You can make an exact copy of a file and then place the copy on a floppy disk. This is useful if you want to give a colleague a copy of the file.

COPY A FILE TO A FLOPPY DISK

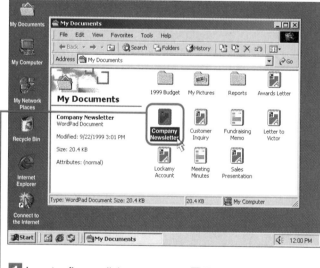

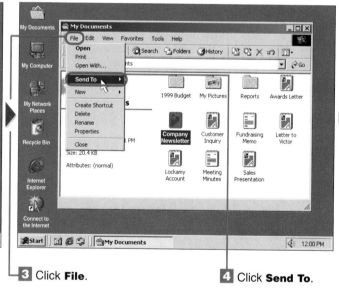

1 Insert a floppy disk into the floppy drive.

2 Click the file you want to copy to a floppy disk.

■ To copy more than one file, select all the files you want to copy.

Note: To select multiple files, see page 81.

3 Click **File**.

4 Click **Send To**.

How can I protect the information on my floppy disks?

You should keep floppy disks away from magnets, which can damage the information stored on the disks. Also be careful not to spill liquids, such as coffee or soda, on the disks.

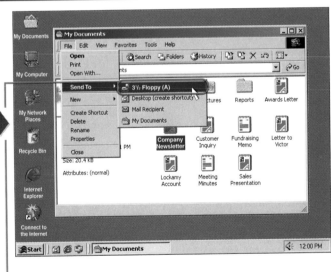

5 Click the drive that contains the floppy disk.

■ Windows places a copy of the file on the floppy disk.

Note: You can copy a folder to a floppy disk the same way you copy a file. When you copy a folder, all the files in the folder are also copied.

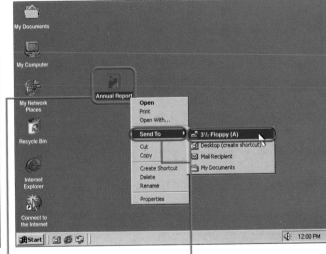

You can copy a file on your desktop to a floppy disk.

1 Insert a floppy disk into the floppy drive.

2 Right-click the file you want to copy to a floppy disk. A menu appears.

3 Click **Send To**.

4 Click the drive that contains the floppy disk.

DELETE A FILE

You can delete
a file you no
longer need.

Before you delete a file,
consider the value of your
work. Do not delete a file
unless you are certain you
no longer need the file.

DELETE A FILE

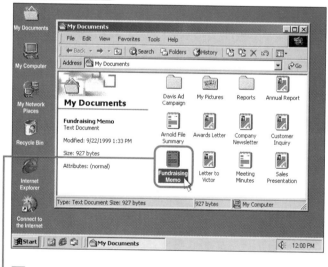

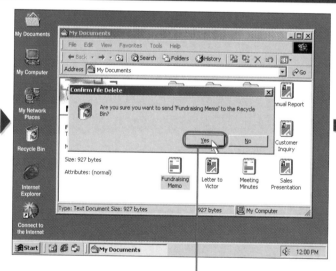

1 Click the file you
want to delete.

■ To delete more than
one file, select the files.

*Note: To select multiple files,
see page 81.*

2 Press the Delete key.

■ The Confirm File Delete
dialog box appears.

3 Click **Yes** to delete
the file.

Can I delete any file on my computer?

Make sure you only delete files that you have created. Do not delete any files that Windows or other programs require to operate.

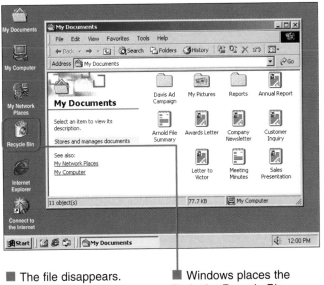

■ The file disappears.

■ Windows places the file in the Recycle Bin.

Note: To restore a file from the Recycle Bin, see page 96.

You can delete a folder and all the files it contains.

1 Click the folder you want to delete.

2 Press the **Delete** key.

■ The Confirm Folder Delete dialog box appears.

3 Click **Yes** to delete the folder.

RESTORE A DELETED FILE

The Recycle Bin stores all the files you have deleted. You can easily restore any of these files.

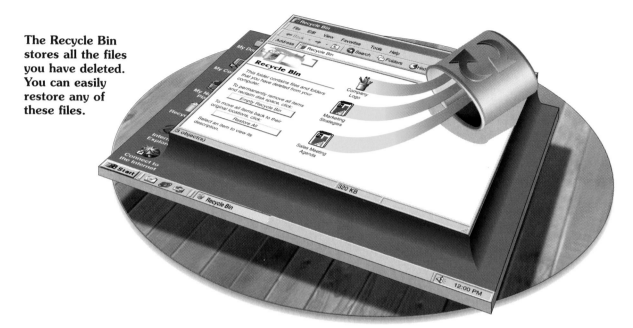

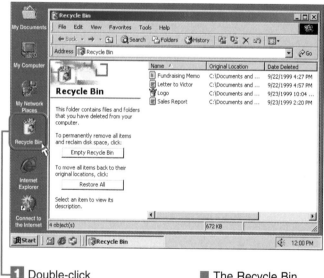

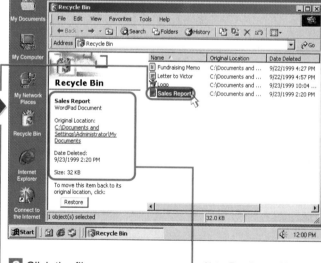

1 Double-click **Recycle Bin** to display all the files you have deleted.

■ The Recycle Bin window appears, displaying all the files you have deleted.

2 Click the file you want to restore.

■ To restore more than one file, select the files.

Note: To select multiple files, see page 81.

■ This area displays information about the file you selected.

How can I tell if the Recycle Bin contains deleted files?

The appearance of the Recycle Bin indicates whether or not the bin contains deleted files.

Contains deleted files

Does not contain deleted files

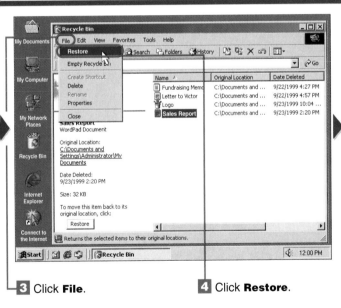

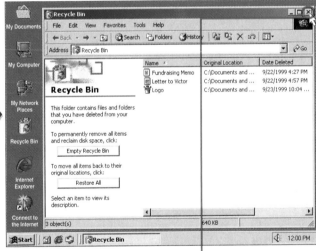

3 Click **File**.

4 Click **Restore**.

■ The file disappears from the Recycle Bin window. Windows places the file back in its original location.

5 Click ☒ to close the Recycle Bin window.

Note: You can restore folders the same way you restore files. When you restore a folder, all the files in the folder are also restored.

EMPTY THE RECYCLE BIN

You can create more free space on your computer by permanently removing all the files from the Recycle Bin.

EMPTY THE RECYCLE BIN

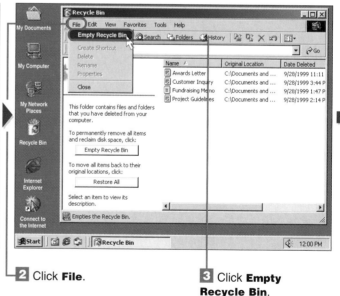

1 Double-click **Recycle Bin** to display all the files you have deleted.

■ The Recycle Bin window appears, displaying all the files you have deleted.

2 Click **File**.

3 Click **Empty Recycle Bin**.

? What if the Recycle Bin contains a file I may need?

Before emptying the Recycle Bin, make sure it does not contain files you may need in the future. To restore a file you may need, see page 96. Once you empty the Recycle Bin, the files are permanently removed from your computer and cannot be restored.

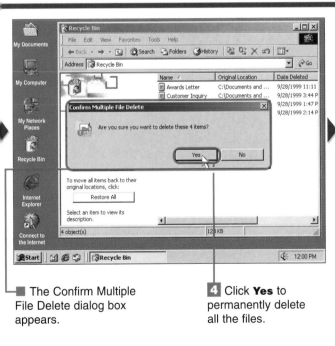

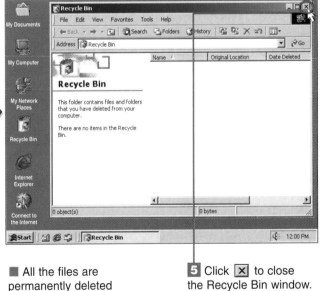

■ The Confirm Multiple File Delete dialog box appears.

4 Click **Yes** to permanently delete all the files.

■ All the files are permanently deleted from your computer.

5 Click ⊠ to close the Recycle Bin window.

PRINT A FILE

You can produce a paper copy of a file stored on your computer. Before printing, make sure your printer is turned on and contains paper.

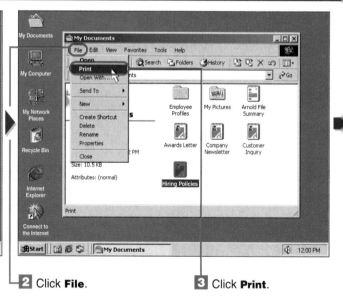

1 Click the file you want to print.

■ To print more than one file, select the files.

Note: To select multiple files, see page 81.

2 Click **File**.

3 Click **Print**.

What types of printers can I use to print my files?

Windows works with many types of printers. There are two common types of printers.

Ink-jet

An ink-jet printer produces documents that are suitable for routine business and personal use.

Laser

A laser printer is faster and produces higher-quality documents than an ink-jet printer, but is more expensive.

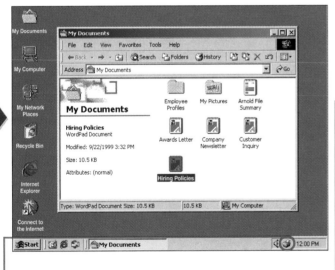

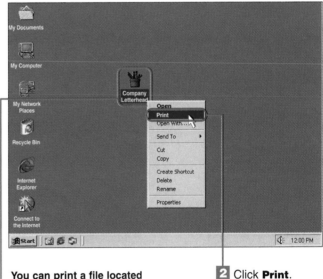

■ When you print a file, the printer icon (🖨) appears in this area. The icon disappears when the file has finished printing.

You can print a file located on your desktop.

1 Right-click the file you want to print. A menu appears.

2 Click **Print**.

VIEW FILES SENT TO THE PRINTER

You can view information about the files you sent to the printer.

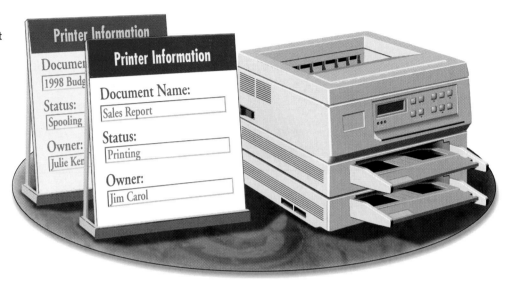

VIEW FILES SENT TO THE PRINTER

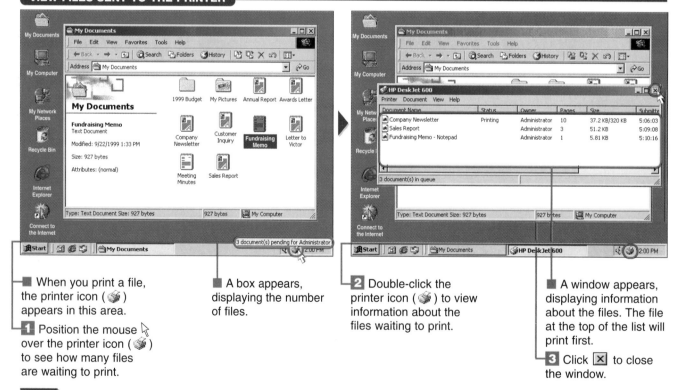

■ When you print a file, the printer icon (🖨) appears in this area.

1 Position the mouse over the printer icon (🖨) to see how many files are waiting to print.

■ A box appears, displaying the number of files.

2 Double-click the printer icon (🖨) to view information about the files waiting to print.

■ A window appears, displaying information about the files. The file at the top of the list will print first.

3 Click ☒ to close the window.

CANCEL PRINTING

You can stop a file from printing. This is useful if you want to make last-minute changes to the file.

CANCEL PRINTING

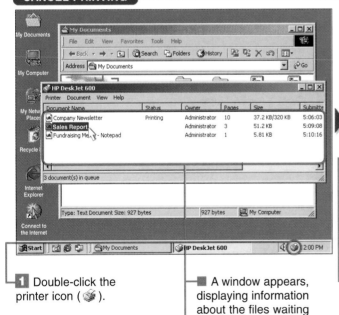

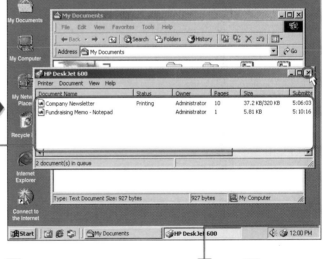

1 Double-click the printer icon ( ).

■ A window appears, displaying information about the files waiting to print.

2 Click the file you no longer want to print.

3 Press the Delete key and the file disappears from the list.

4 Click X to close the window.

SEARCH FOR FILES

If you cannot remember the exact name or location of a file you want to work with, you can have Windows search for the file.

SEARCH FOR FILES

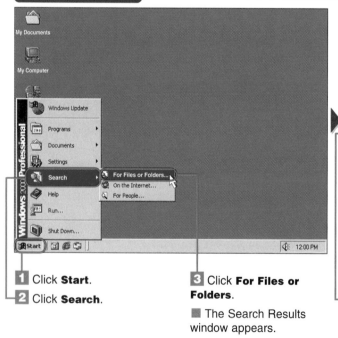

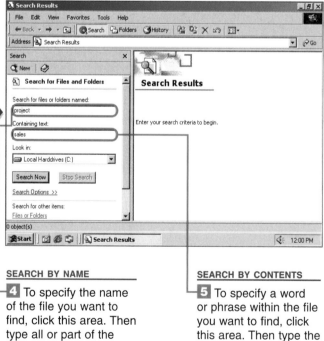

1 Click **Start**.

2 Click **Search**.

3 Click **For Files or Folders**.

■ The Search Results window appears.

SEARCH BY NAME

4 To specify the name of the file you want to find, click this area. Then type all or part of the name.

SEARCH BY CONTENTS

5 To specify a word or phrase within the file you want to find, click this area. Then type the word or phrase.

Can I search for a file if I know only part of the file name?

If you search for part of a file name, Windows will find all the files and folders with names that contain the word you specified. For example, searching for the word "report" will find every file or folder with a name containing the word "report".

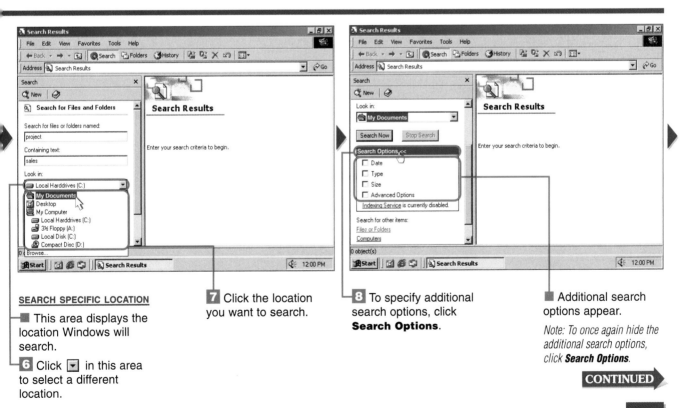

SEARCH SPECIFIC LOCATION

■ This area displays the location Windows will search.

6 Click ▼ in this area to select a different location.

7 Click the location you want to search.

8 To specify additional search options, click **Search Options**.

■ Additional search options appear.

Note: To once again hide the additional search options, click Search Options.

CONTINUED ▶

SEARCH FOR FILES

You can search for a file you worked with during a specific time period. You can also search for a specific type of file, such as files created in WordPad.

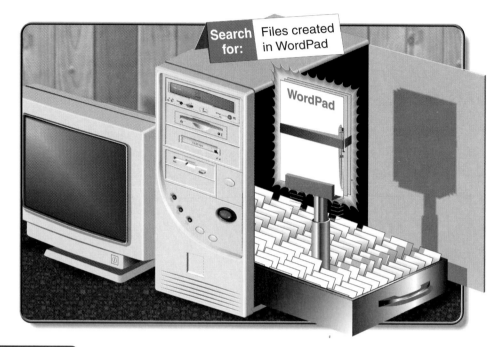

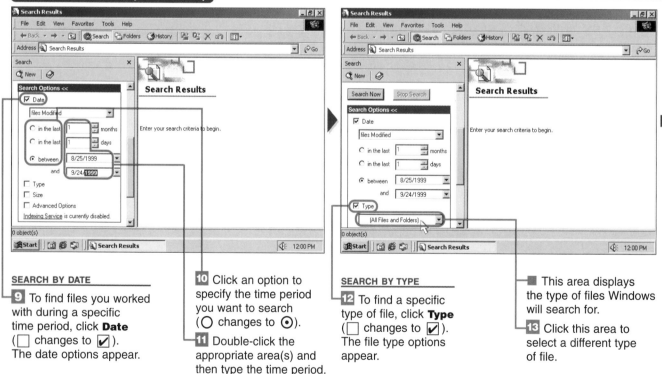

SEARCH BY DATE

9 To find files you worked with during a specific time period, click **Date** (☐ changes to ☑).
The date options appear.

10 Click an option to specify the time period you want to search (○ changes to ⊙).

11 Double-click the appropriate area(s) and then type the time period.

SEARCH BY TYPE

12 To find a specific type of file, click **Type** (☐ changes to ☑).
The file type options appear.

■ This area displays the type of files Windows will search for.

13 Click this area to select a different type of file.

How can I find all the programs on my computer?

To find all the programs on your computer, perform steps **1** to **8** starting on page 104. Then perform steps **12** to **15** below, selecting **Application** in step **14**.

WordPad

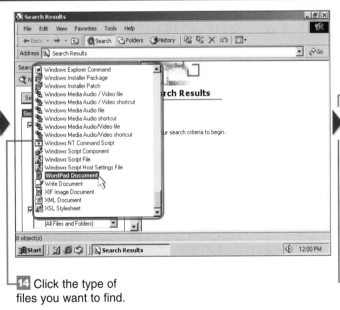

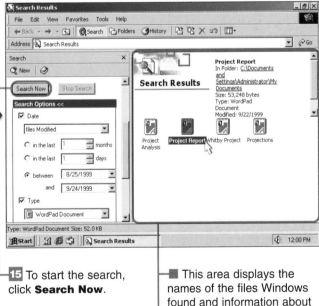

14 Click the type of files you want to find.

15 To start the search, click **Search Now**.

■ This area displays the names of the files Windows found and information about each file.

16 To open a file, double-click the name of the file.

ADD A SHORTCUT TO THE DESKTOP

You can add a
shortcut to the
desktop to provide
a quick way of
opening a file you
use regularly.

ADD A SHORTCUT TO THE DESKTOP

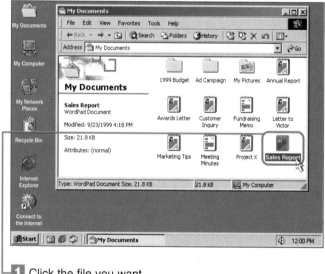

1 Click the file you want
to create a shortcut to.

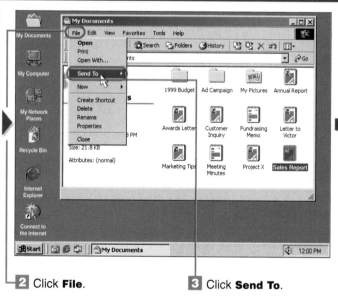

2 Click **File**.

3 Click **Send To**.

How do I rename or delete a shortcut?

You can rename or delete a shortcut the same way you would rename or delete any file. Renaming or deleting a shortcut does not affect the original file. For information on renaming a file, see page 84. For information on deleting a file, see page 94.

Rename

Delete

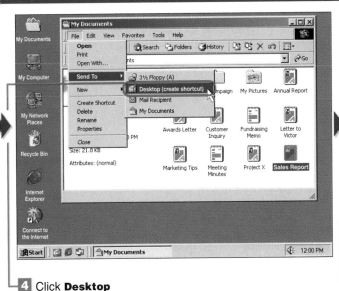

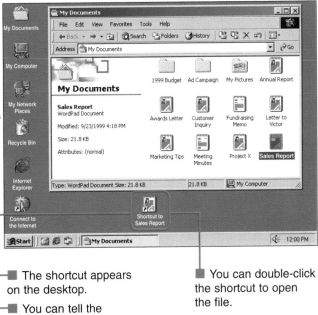

4 Click **Desktop (create shortcut)**.

■ The shortcut appears on the desktop.

■ You can tell the difference between the shortcut and the original file because the shortcut displays an arrow (🔼).

■ You can double-click the shortcut to open the file.

USING BRIEFCASE

Briefcase lets you work with files while you are away from the office. When you return, Briefcase will update all the files you have changed.

Briefcase is useful for working with office files on your home or portable computer.

TRANSFER FILES TO BRIEFCASE

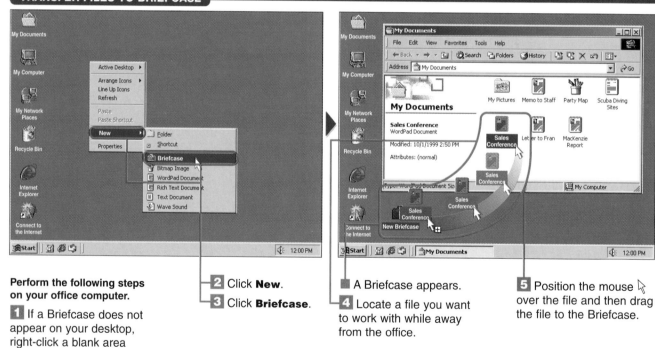

Perform the following steps on your office computer.

1 If a Briefcase does not appear on your desktop, right-click a blank area on your desktop. A menu appears.

2 Click **New**.

3 Click **Briefcase**.

■ A Briefcase appears.

4 Locate a file you want to work with while away from the office.

5 Position the mouse ⤡ over the file and then drag the file to the Briefcase.

Can I create more than one Briefcase?

You can create as many new Briefcases as you need. You may want to create a new Briefcase for each set of files you want to work with away from the office.

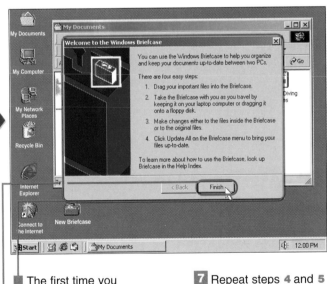

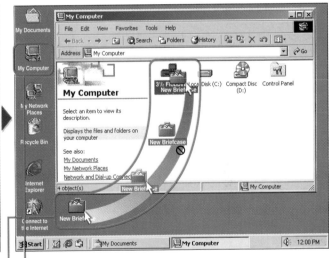

■ The first time you copy a file to a Briefcase, Windows displays a welcome message.

6 Click **Finish** to close the message.

7 Repeat steps **4** and **5** for each file you want to work with while away from the office.

8 Insert a floppy disk into a drive.

9 Double-click **My Computer**.

■ The My Computer window appears.

10 Position the mouse over the Briefcase and then drag the Briefcase to the drive containing the floppy disk.

■ Windows moves the Briefcase to the floppy disk. The Briefcase disappears from your screen.

11 Remove the floppy disk from the drive.

CONTINUED ▶

USING BRIEFCASE

When traveling or at home, you can work with Briefcase files as you would work with any files on your computer.

WORK WITH BRIEFCASE FILES

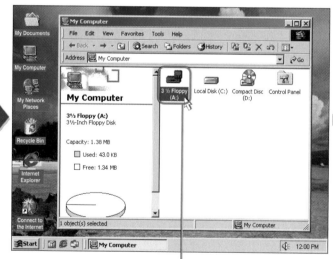

Perform the following steps on your home or portable computer.

 Insert the floppy disk containing the Briefcase into a floppy drive.

2 Double-click **My Computer**.

■ The My Computer window appears.

3 Double-click the drive containing the floppy disk.

Can I rename the files in a Briefcase?

Do not rename the files in a Briefcase or the original files on your office computer. If you rename the files, Briefcase will not be able to update the files.

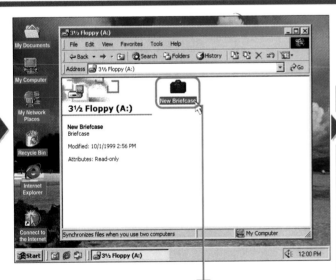

■ The contents of the floppy disk appear.

4 Double-click the Briefcase.

■ The contents of the Briefcase appear. You can open and edit the files in the Briefcase as you would open and edit any files.

5 When you finish working with the files, save and close the files.

6 Remove the floppy disk from the drive and return the disk to your office computer.

CONTINUED ▶

USING BRIEFCASE

When you return to
the office, you can
update the files you
have changed.

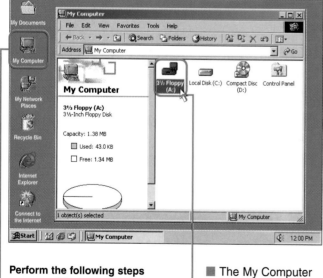

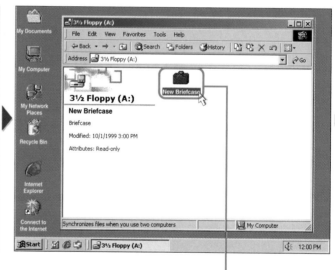

**Perform the following steps
on your office computer.**

1 Insert the floppy disk
containing the Briefcase
into the floppy drive.

2 Double-click **My Computer**.

■ The My Computer
window appears.

3 Double-click the
drive containing the
floppy disk.

■ The contents of the
floppy disk appear.

4 Double-click the
Briefcase.

How does Windows know which files need to be updated?

Windows compares the files in the Briefcase to the files on your office computer to decide which files need to be updated.

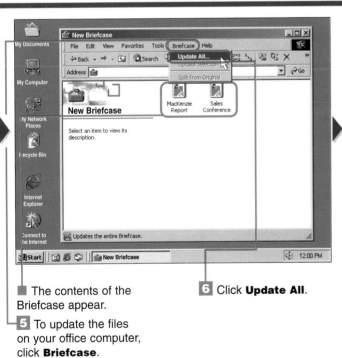

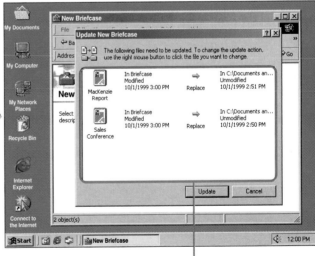

■ The contents of the Briefcase appear.

5 To update the files on your office computer, click **Briefcase**.

6 Click **Update All**.

■ The Update dialog box appears.

■ This area displays the name of each file that needs to be updated and the way Windows will update each file.

CONTINUED

USING BRIEFCASE

When using
Briefcase, you
can change the
way Windows
updates a file.

Replace office
file with Briefcase
file(⟹).

Do not update
the file (↘).

Replace Briefcase
file with office
file (⟸).

UPDATE BRIEFCASE FILES (CONTINUED)

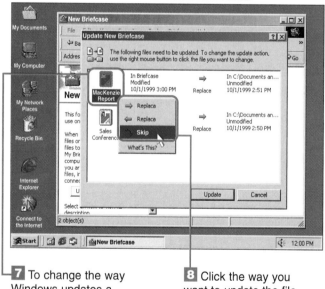

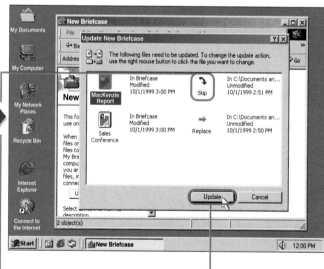

7 To change the way
Windows updates a
file, right-click the file.
A menu appears.

8 Click the way you
want to update the file.

■ Windows changes the
way it will update the file.

9 Click **Update**.

■ Windows updates
the files.

?

Can I use the Briefcase with a removable disk instead of a floppy disk?

You can use a Briefcase with a removable disk, such as a Zip® disk or Jaz® disk. A removable disk can store more information than a floppy disk, which allows you to store more files in the Briefcase.

DELETE A BRIEFCASE

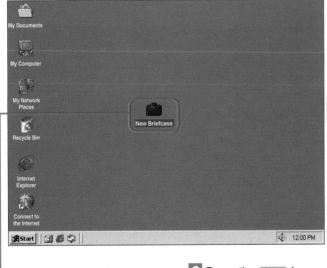

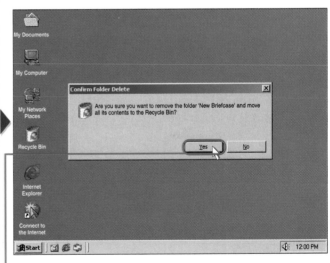

You can delete a Briefcase you no longer need.

1 Click the Briefcase you want to delete.

2 Press the `Delete` key.

■ A confirmation dialog box appears. Click **Yes** to confirm your change.

■ The Briefcase disappears from your screen. The original files on your computer are not deleted when you delete a Briefcase.

CHAPTER 6

Customize Windows

You can change Windows settings to suit your needs. Read this chapter to learn how to add wallpaper, set up a screen saver, add active desktop items and much more.

MOVE THE TASKBAR

You can move the
taskbar to a more
convenient location
on your screen.

MOVE THE TASKBAR

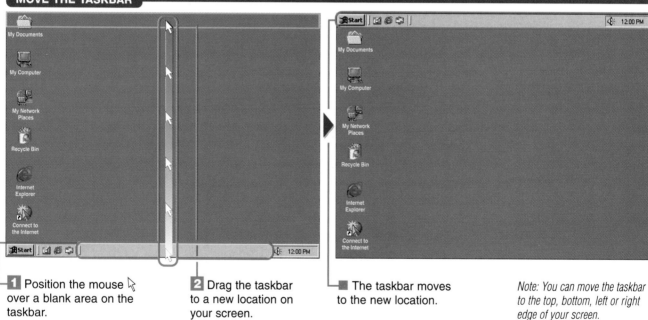

1 Position the mouse ▷
over a blank area on the
taskbar.

2 Drag the taskbar
to a new location on
your screen.

■ The taskbar moves
to the new location.

*Note: You can move the taskbar
to the top, bottom, left or right
edge of your screen.*

You can change the size of the taskbar so it can display more information.

SIZE THE TASKBAR

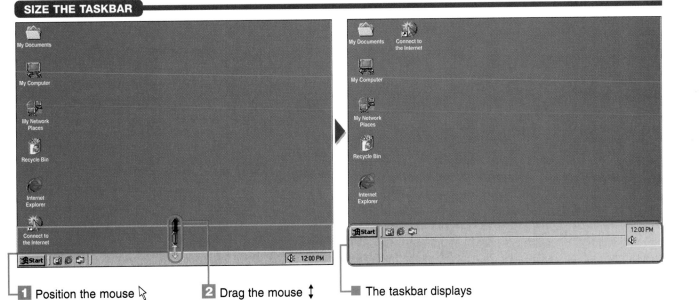

1 Position the mouse ⍺ over the edge of the taskbar (⍺ changes to ↕).

2 Drag the mouse ↕ until the taskbar displays the size you want.

■ The taskbar displays the new size.

CHANGE THE DATE AND TIME

You should make sure the correct date and time are set in your computer. Windows uses this information to determine when you create and update your documents.

CHANGE THE DATE AND TIME

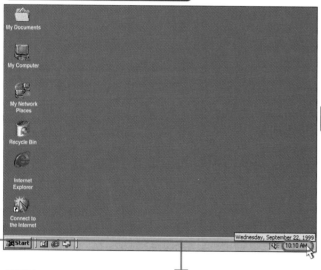

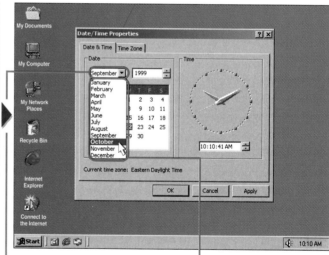

■ This area displays the time set in your computer.

1 To display the date set in your computer, position the mouse ⍉ over this area. A box appears, displaying the date.

2 To change the date or time set in your computer, double-click this area.

■ The Date/Time Properties dialog box appears.

■ This area displays the month set in your computer.

3 To change the month, click this area.

4 Click the correct month.

122

Will Windows keep track of the date and time even when I turn off my computer?

Your computer has a built-in clock that keeps track of the date and time even when you turn off the computer.

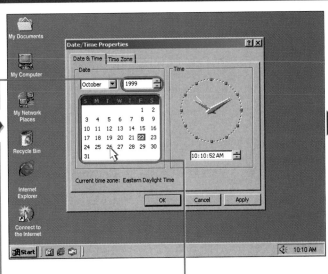

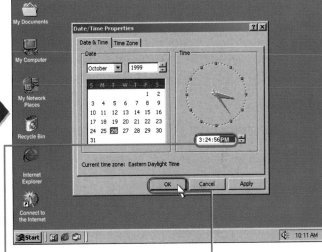

■ This area displays the year set in your computer.

5 To change the year, click ▲ or ▼ in this area until the correct year appears.

■ This area displays the days in the month. The current day is highlighted.

6 To change the day, click the correct day.

■ This area displays the time set in your computer.

7 To change the time, double-click the part of the time you want to change. Then type the correct information.

8 Click **OK** to confirm your changes.

ADD WALLPAPER

You can decorate your screen by adding wallpaper.

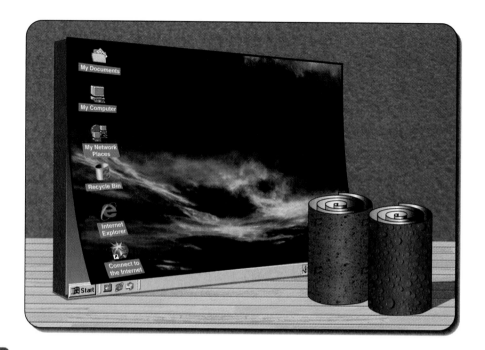

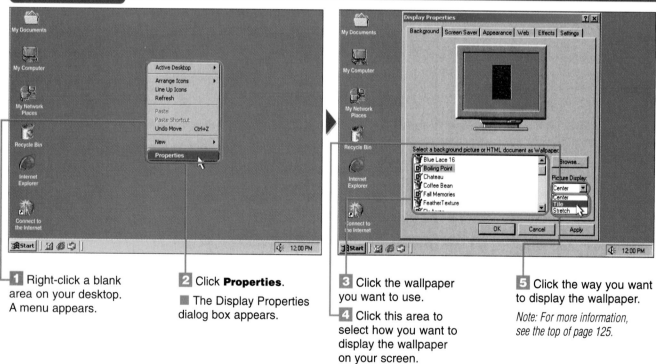

1 Right-click a blank area on your desktop. A menu appears.

2 Click **Properties**.

■ The Display Properties dialog box appears.

3 Click the wallpaper you want to use.

4 Click this area to select how you want to display the wallpaper on your screen.

5 Click the way you want to display the wallpaper.

Note: For more information, see the top of page 125.

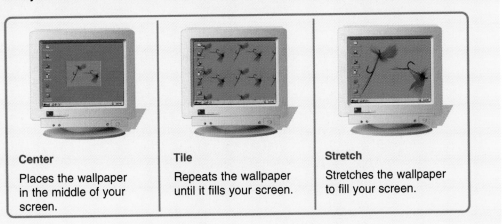

How can I display wallpaper on my screen?

Center

Places the wallpaper in the middle of your screen.

Tile

Repeats the wallpaper until it fills your screen.

Stretch

Stretches the wallpaper to fill your screen.

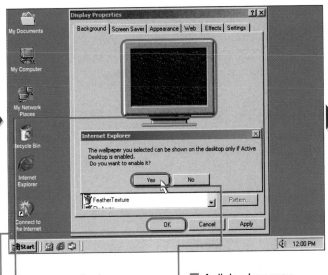

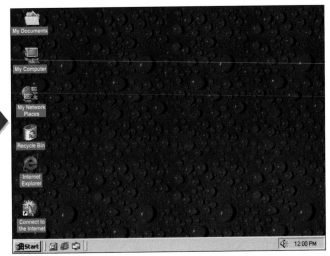

■ This area displays how the wallpaper will look on your screen.

6 Click **OK** to add the wallpaper to your screen.

■ A dialog box may appear if the wallpaper you selected requires you to enable the Active Desktop.

7 Click **Yes** to enable the Active Desktop.

Note: For information on the Active Desktop, see page 140.

■ The wallpaper appears on your screen.

■ To remove wallpaper from your screen, perform steps **1** to **3**, selecting **(None)** in step **3**. Then perform step **6**.

SET UP A SCREEN SAVER

A screen saver is a moving picture or pattern that appears on the screen when you do not use your computer for a period of time.

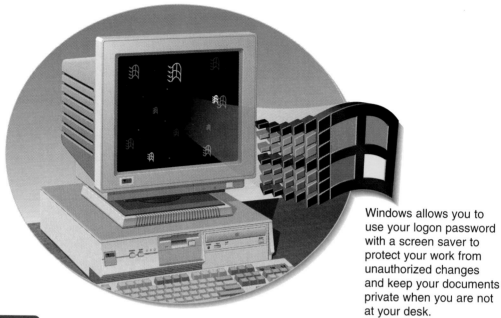

Windows allows you to use your logon password with a screen saver to protect your work from unauthorized changes and keep your documents private when you are not at your desk.

SET UP A SCREEN SAVER

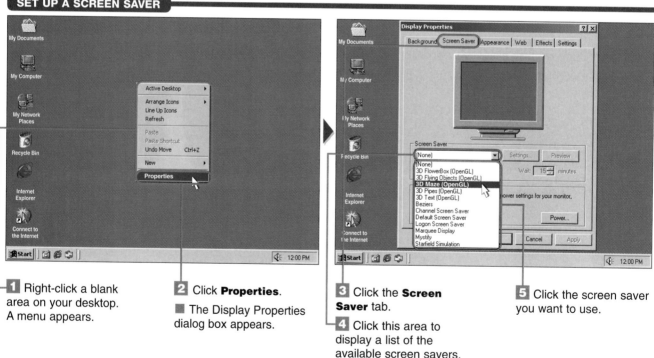

1 Right-click a blank area on your desktop. A menu appears.

2 Click **Properties**.

■ The Display Properties dialog box appears.

3 Click the **Screen Saver** tab.

4 Click this area to display a list of the available screen savers.

5 Click the screen saver you want to use.

How do I remove a screen saver that uses my logon password?

When you move the mouse or press a key to remove a screen saver from your screen, a dialog box appears, telling you the computer is locked. To unlock the computer and remove the screen saver from your screen, perform steps 3 and 4 on page 23.

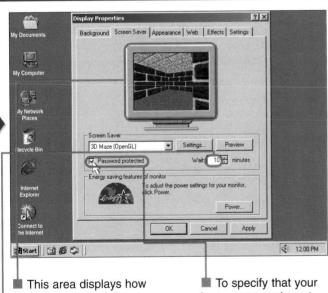

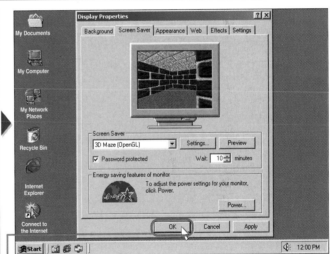

■ This area displays how the screen saver will look on your screen.

6 To change the length of time the computer must be inactive before the screen saver will appear, double-click this area. Then type a new number.

■ To specify that your logon password must be entered to remove the screen saver, click **Password protected** (☐ changes to ☑).

7 Click **OK** to confirm your changes.

■ The screen saver appears when you do not use your computer for the amount of time you specified.

■ You can move the mouse or press a key on the keyboard to remove the screen saver from your screen.

■ To turn off the screen saver, perform steps 1 to 5, selecting **(None)** in step 5. Then perform step 7.

CHANGE SCREEN COLORS

You can change the
colors displayed
on your screen to
personalize and
enhance Windows.

CHANGE SCREEN COLORS

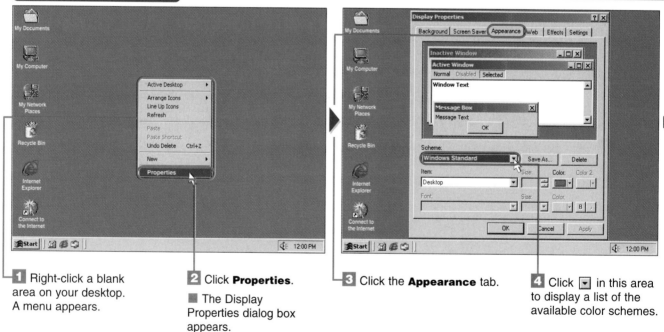

1 Right-click a blank
area on your desktop.
A menu appears.

2 Click **Properties**.

■ The Display
Properties dialog box
appears.

3 Click the **Appearance** tab.

4 Click ▼ in this area
to display a list of the
available color schemes.

What is the difference between the High Contrast, high color and VGA color schemes?

For information on changing the number of colors your computer displays, see page 132.

High Contrast schemes are designed for people with vision impairments.

High color schemes are designed for computers displaying more than 256 colors.

VGA schemes are designed for computers limited to 16 colors.

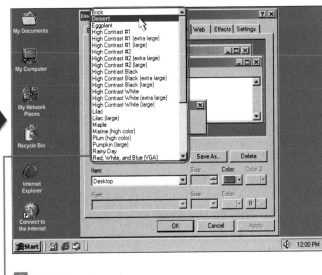

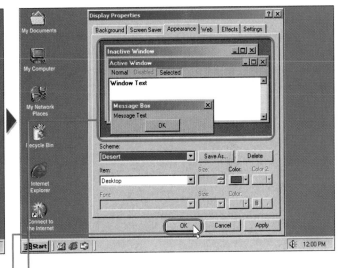

5 Click the color scheme you want to use.

■ This area displays how your screen will look with the color scheme you selected.

6 Click **OK** to change the color scheme.

■ To return to the original color scheme, perform steps **1** to **6**, selecting **Windows Standard** in step **5**.

CHANGE SCREEN RESOLUTION

You can change the amount of information that can fit on your screen.

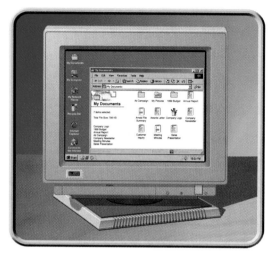

Lower resolutions display larger images on the screen. This lets you see information more clearly.

Higher resolutions display smaller images on the screen. This lets you display more information on the screen at once.

CHANGE SCREEN RESOLUTION

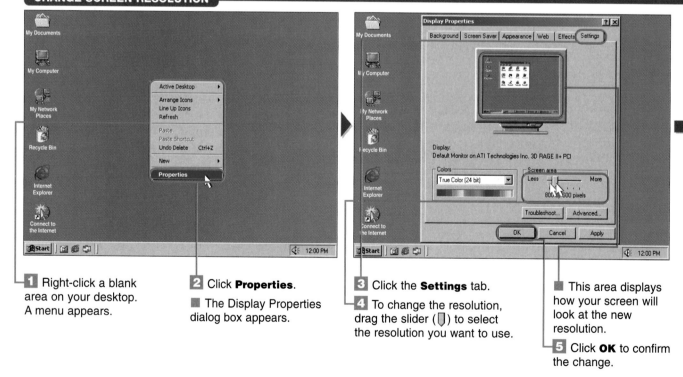

1 Right-click a blank area on your desktop. A menu appears.

2 Click **Properties**.

■ The Display Properties dialog box appears.

3 Click the **Settings** tab.

4 To change the resolution, drag the slider (⬛) to select the resolution you want to use.

■ This area displays how your screen will look at the new resolution.

5 Click **OK** to confirm the change.

What determines which screen resolutions are available on my computer?

Your monitor and video card determine which screen resolutions you can use.

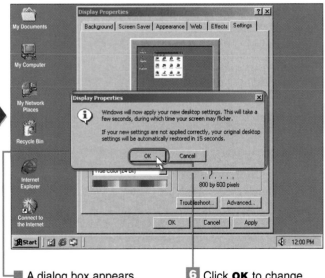

◾ A dialog box appears, stating that Windows will take a few seconds to change the screen resolution. Your screen may flicker during this time.

6 Click **OK** to change the resolution.

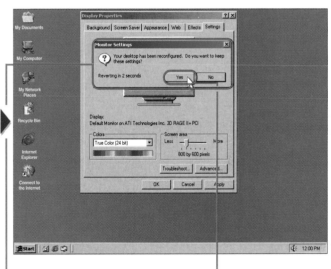

◾ Windows resizes the information on your screen.

◾ The Monitor Settings dialog box appears, asking if you want to keep the new screen resolution.

7 Click **Yes** to keep the screen resolution.

CHANGE COLOR DEPTH

You can change the number of colors displayed on your screen. More colors result in sharper images.

Your monitor and video card determine the maximum number of colors your screen can display.

CHANGE COLOR DEPTH

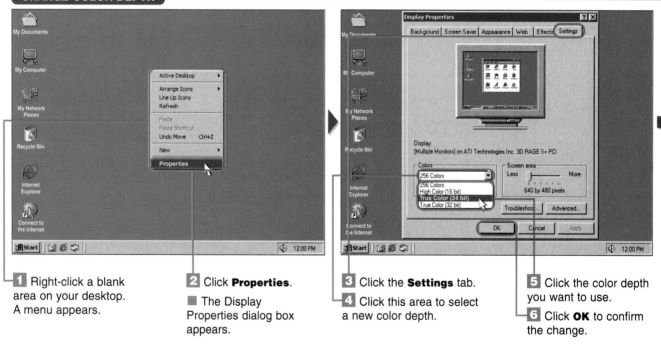

1 Right-click a blank area on your desktop. A menu appears.

2 Click **Properties**.

■ The Display Properties dialog box appears.

3 Click the **Settings** tab.

4 Click this area to select a new color depth.

5 Click the color depth you want to use.

6 Click **OK** to confirm the change.

**When would I change the
number of colors displayed
on my screen?**

You may want to display more
colors on your screen when
viewing photographs, playing
videos or playing games on
your computer.

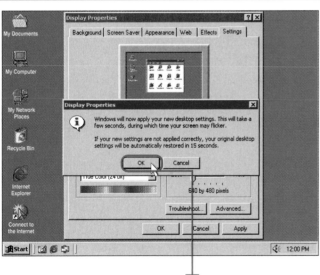

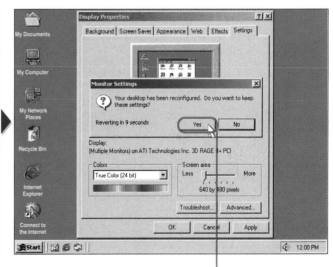

■ A dialog box appears,
stating that Windows will
take a few seconds to
change the color depth.
Your screen may flicker
during this time.

7 Click **OK** to change
the color depth.

■ Windows displays the
information on your screen
with the new color depth.

■ The Monitor Settings
dialog box appears, asking
if you want to keep the
new color depth.

8 Click **Yes** to keep
the color depth.

CHANGE MOUSE SETTINGS

You can change
the way your
mouse works to
suit your needs.

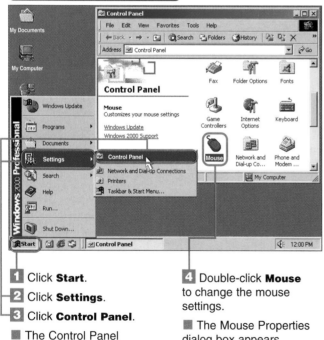

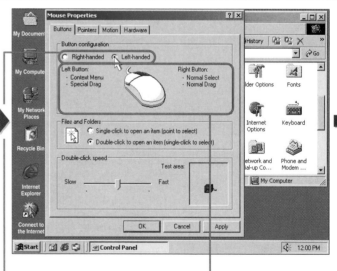

1 Click **Start**.

2 Click **Settings**.

3 Click **Control Panel**.

■ The Control Panel
window appears.

4 Double-click **Mouse**
to change the mouse
settings.

■ The Mouse Properties
dialog box appears.

SWITCH BUTTONS

5 To switch the functions
of the left and right mouse
buttons, click an option
to specify if you are
right-handed or left-handed
(○ changes to ⊙).

■ This area describes
the functions of the left
and right mouse buttons,
depending on the option
you selected.

How can I use the mouse to open and select files and folders?

Single-click

This option is useful for people who have trouble double-clicking. To open an item, click the left mouse button once. To select an item, position the mouse pointer over the item.

Double-click

This option is useful for experienced mouse users. To open an item, quickly click the left mouse button twice. To select an item, click the left mouse button once.

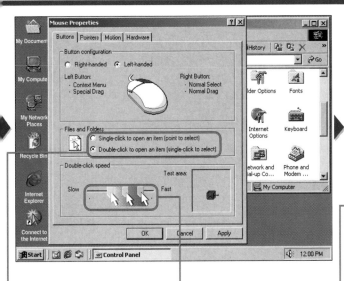

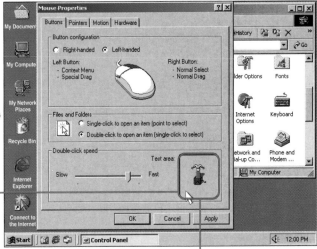

USE SINGLE-CLICK OR DOUBLE-CLICK

■6 To specify if you want to open items using a single-click or a double-click, click an option (○ changes to ⊙).

DOUBLE-CLICK SPEED

■7 To change the amount of time that can pass between two clicks of the mouse button for Windows to recognize a double-click, drag the slider (▯) to a new position.

■8 Double-click this area to test the double-click speed.

■ The jack-in-the-box appears if you clicked at the correct speed.

CONTINUED

CHANGE MOUSE SETTINGS

You can personalize your mouse by changing the way the mouse pointer moves on your screen. You can also change the appearance of the mouse pointers Windows displays.

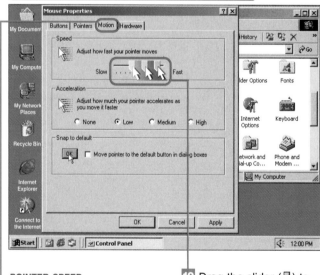

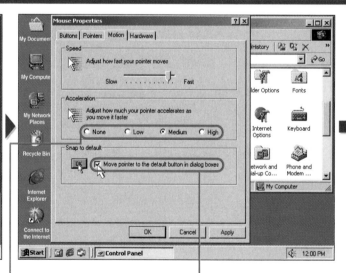

POINTER SPEED

9 To make the mouse pointer on your screen move faster or slower, click the **Motion** tab.

10 Drag the slider (⬇) to a new position to change the pointer speed.

POINTER ACCELERATION

11 To specify how fast the mouse pointer on your screen moves compared to how fast you move the mouse on your desk, click an option (○ changes to ◉).

SNAP TO DEFAULT

12 To have the mouse pointer automatically appear over the default button in many dialog boxes, click this option (☐ changes to ☑).

*Note: The default button in many dialog boxes is **OK**.*

Should I use a mouse pad?

A mouse pad provides a smooth surface for moving the mouse on your desk. A mouse pad reduces the amount of dirt that enters the mouse and protects your desk from scratches. Hard plastic mouse pads attract less dirt and provide a smoother surface than fabric mouse pads.

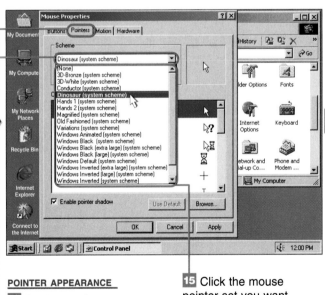

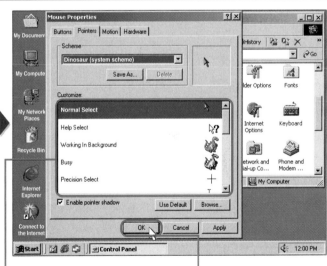

POINTER APPEARANCE

13 To change the appearance of the mouse pointers, click the **Pointers** tab.

14 Click this area to display a list of the mouse pointer sets.

15 Click the mouse pointer set you want to use.

■ This area displays the mouse pointers that make up the set you selected.

CONFIRM CHANGES

16 Click **OK** when you finish selecting all the mouse settings you want to change.

CHANGE DESKTOP ICONS

You can change the appearance of icons on your desktop to customize your computer.

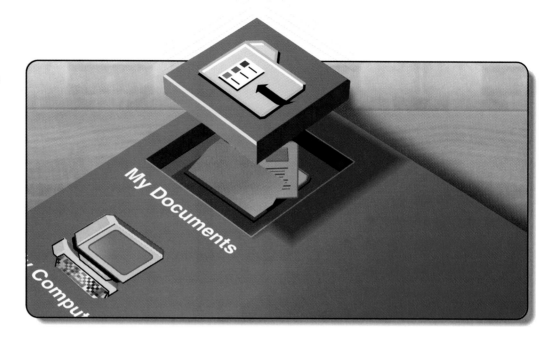

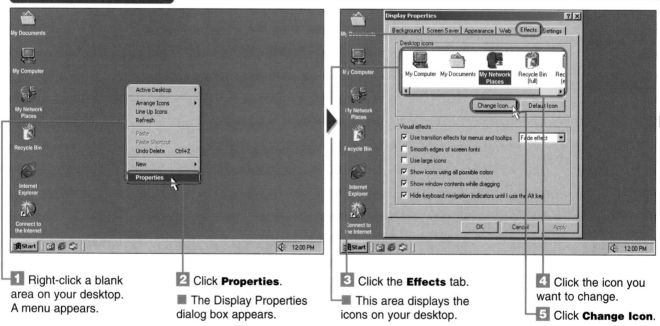

1 Right-click a blank area on your desktop. A menu appears.

2 Click **Properties**.

■ The Display Properties dialog box appears.

3 Click the **Effects** tab.

■ This area displays the icons on your desktop.

4 Click the icon you want to change.

5 Click **Change Icon**.

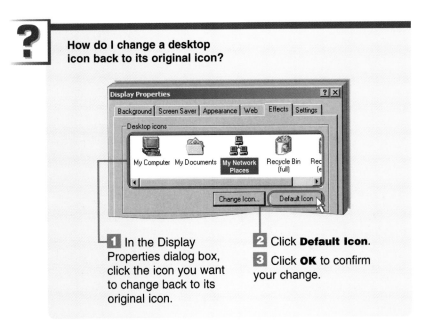

How do I change a desktop icon back to its original icon?

1 In the Display Properties dialog box, click the icon you want to change back to its original icon.

2 Click **Default Icon**.

3 Click **OK** to confirm your change.

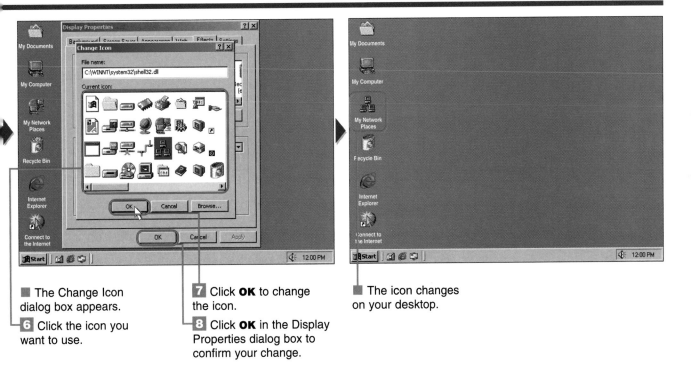

■ The Change Icon dialog box appears.

6 Click the icon you want to use.

7 Click **OK** to change the icon.

8 Click **OK** in the Display Properties dialog box to confirm your change.

■ The icon changes on your desktop.

ADD AN ACTIVE DESKTOP ITEM

You can add active
content from the Web
to your desktop. Active
content is information
that changes on your
screen, such as a stock
ticker or a weather map.

ADD AN ACTIVE DESKTOP ITEM

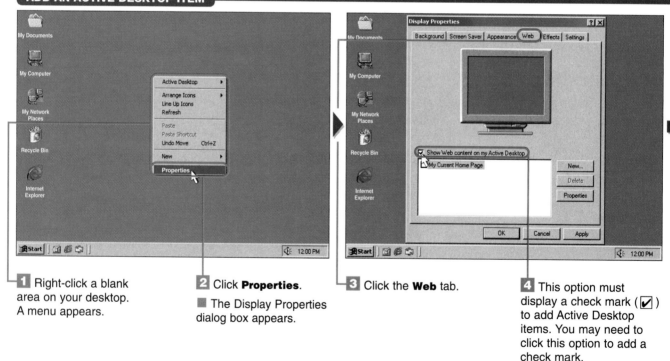

1 Right-click a blank
area on your desktop.
A menu appears.

2 Click **Properties**.

■ The Display Properties
dialog box appears.

3 Click the **Web** tab.

4 This option must
display a check mark (☑)
to add Active Desktop
items. You may need to
click this option to add a
check mark.

What is the My Current Home Page item?

The My Current Home Page item displays your home page on the desktop. Your home page is the Web page that appears when you start your Web browser. Windows automatically adds this Active Desktop item to your computer for you.

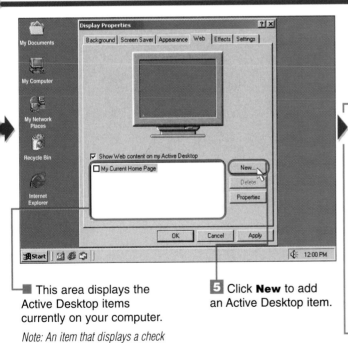

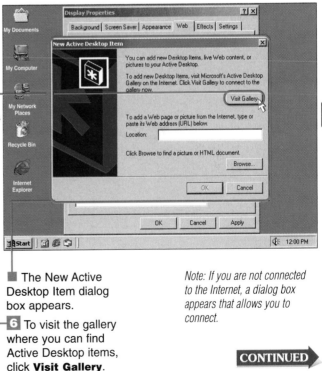

■ This area displays the Active Desktop items currently on your computer.

Note: An item that displays a check mark (✔) appears on your desktop.

5 Click **New** to add an Active Desktop item.

■ The New Active Desktop Item dialog box appears.

6 To visit the gallery where you can find Active Desktop items, click **Visit Gallery**.

Note: If you are not connected to the Internet, a dialog box appears that allows you to connect.

CONTINUED

ADD AN ACTIVE DESKTOP ITEM

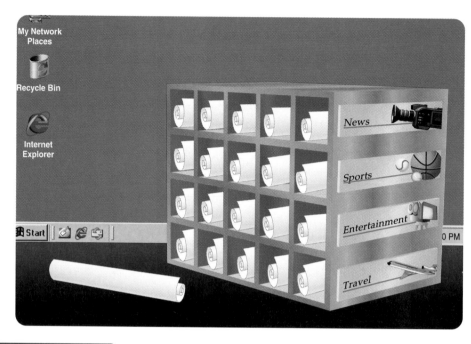

The gallery offers various items you can add to your desktop. The items are organized into categories such as news, sports, entertainment and travel.

ADD AN ACTIVE DESKTOP ITEM (CONTINUED)

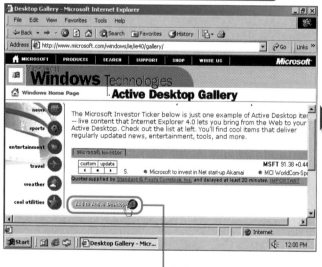

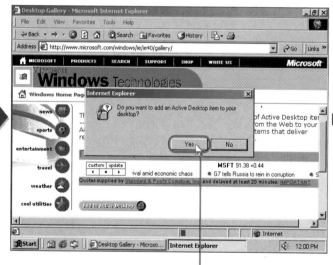

■ The Internet Explorer Web browser opens and the gallery appears.

Note: To maximize the window to fill your screen, click 🔲 *in the top right corner of the window.*

7 Follow the instructions on your screen to find an Active Desktop item of interest.

8 Click **Add to Active Desktop** to add the item to your desktop.

■ A dialog box appears, asking you if you want to add the Active Desktop item to your desktop.

9 Click **Yes** to add the item to your desktop.

142

Why did a Security Warning dialog box appear when I displayed the gallery?

If the Security Warning dialog box appears when you visit the Active Desktop Gallery, Microsoft needs to transfer information to your computer. Click **Yes** to transfer the information to your computer.

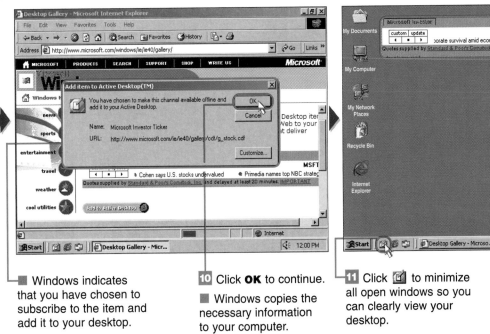

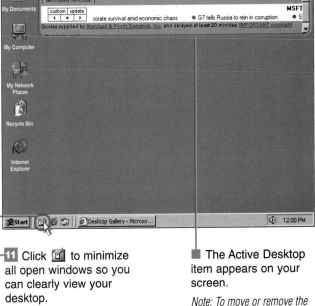

■ Windows indicates that you have chosen to subscribe to the item and add it to your desktop.

10 Click **OK** to continue.

■ Windows copies the necessary information to your computer.

11 Click 📷 to minimize all open windows so you can clearly view your desktop.

■ The Active Desktop item appears on your screen.

Note: To move or remove the item, see page 144.

WORK WITH ACTIVE DESKTOP ITEMS

You can temporarily remove an Active Desktop item you no longer want to appear on your desktop. You can redisplay the item at any time.

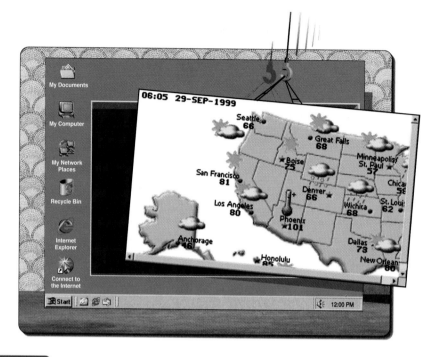

REMOVE OR DISPLAY AN ITEM

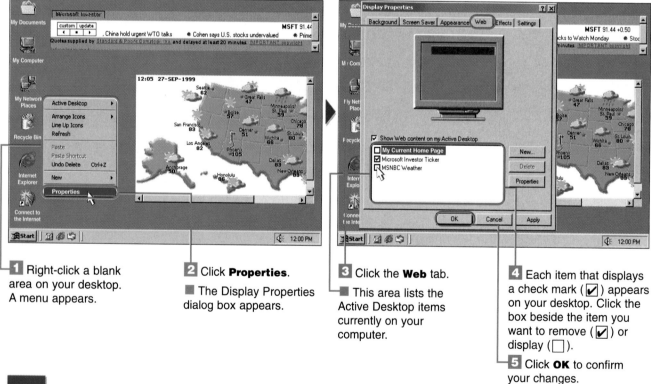

1 Right-click a blank area on your desktop. A menu appears.

2 Click **Properties**.

■ The Display Properties dialog box appears.

3 Click the **Web** tab.

■ This area lists the Active Desktop items currently on your computer.

4 Each item that displays a check mark (✔) appears on your desktop. Click the box beside the item you want to remove (✔) or display (☐).

5 Click **OK** to confirm your changes.

You can move an
Active Desktop item
to a new location on
your screen.

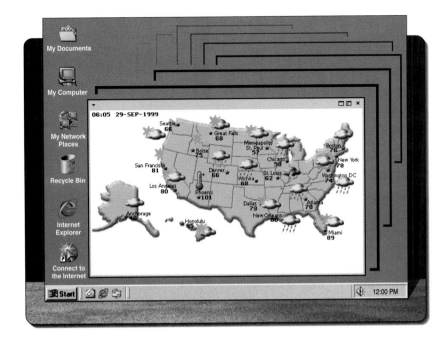

MOVE AN ITEM

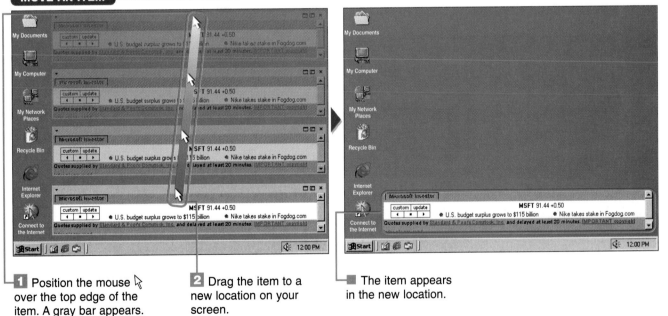

1 Position the mouse ▷ over the top edge of the item. A gray bar appears.

2 Drag the item to a new location on your screen.

■ The item appears in the new location.

ADD A PROGRAM TO THE START MENU

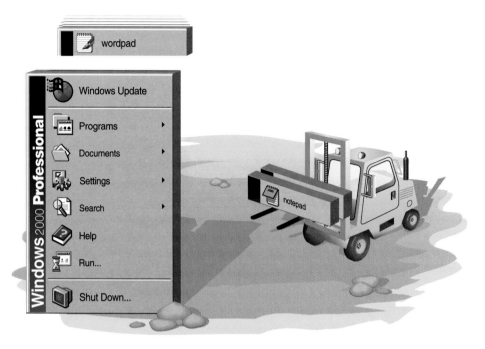

You can add your favorite programs to the Start menu so you can quickly open them.

ADD A PROGRAM TO THE START MENU

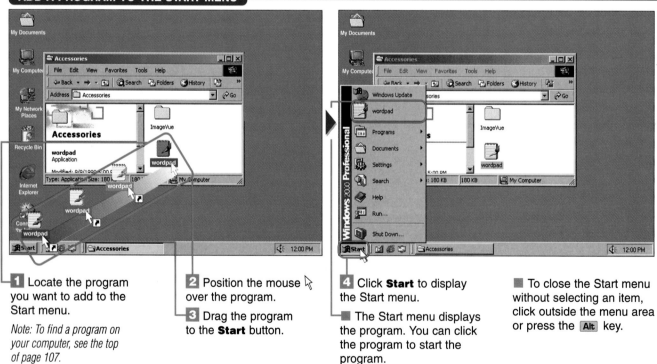

1 Locate the program you want to add to the Start menu.

Note: To find a program on your computer, see the top of page 107.

2 Position the mouse ⬉ over the program.

3 Drag the program to the **Start** button.

4 Click **Start** to display the Start menu.

■ The Start menu displays the program. You can click the program to start the program.

■ To close the Start menu without selecting an item, click outside the menu area or press the **Alt** key.

Can I add files and folders to the Start menu?

You can perform the steps on page 146 to add a file or folder to the Start menu. Adding files and folders you frequently use to the Start menu saves you the time of searching for them on your computer.

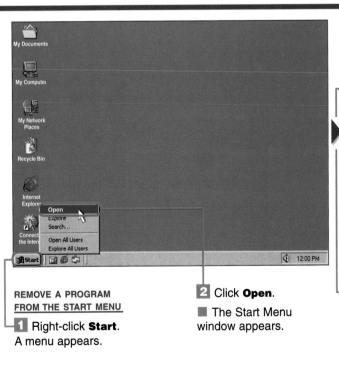

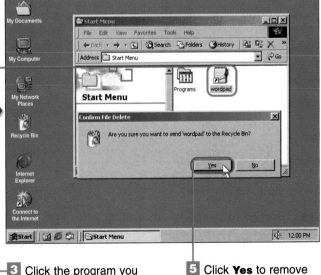

REMOVE A PROGRAM FROM THE START MENU

■1 Right-click **Start**. A menu appears.

■2 Click **Open**.

■ The Start Menu window appears.

■3 Click the program you no longer want to appear on the Start menu.

■4 Press the Delete key.

■ A confirmation dialog box appears.

■5 Click **Yes** to remove the program from the Start menu.

Note: Removing a program from the Start menu does not delete the program from your computer.

START A PROGRAM AUTOMATICALLY

If you use the same program every day, you can have the program start automatically every time you turn on your computer.

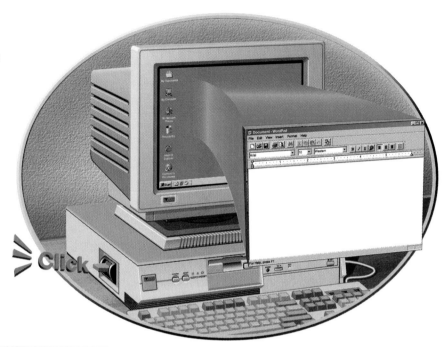

START A PROGRAM AUTOMATICALLY

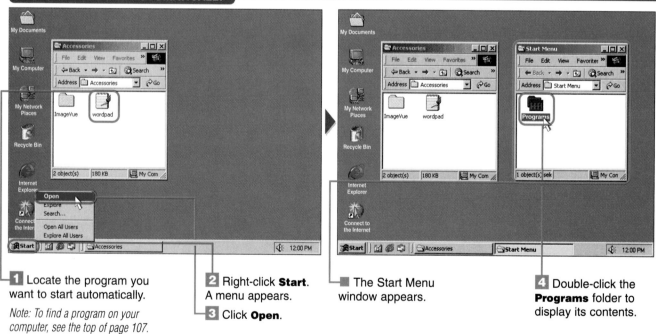

1 Locate the program you want to start automatically.

Note: To find a program on your computer, see the top of page 107.

2 Right-click **Start**. A menu appears.

3 Click **Open**.

■ The Start Menu window appears.

4 Double-click the **Programs** folder to display its contents.

How do I stop a program from starting automatically?

If you no longer want a program to start automatically, delete the shortcut for the program from the Startup folder. You can delete a shortcut the same way you delete a file. For information on deleting a file, see page 94. Deleting a shortcut from the Startup folder will not remove the program from your computer.

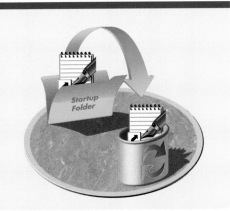

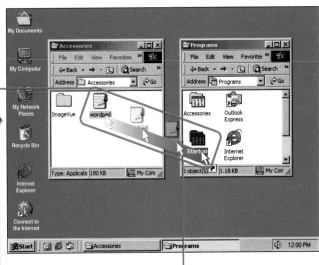

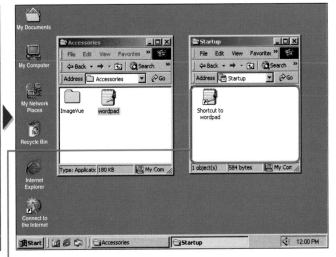

■ The contents of the Programs folder appear.

5 Position the mouse ⌕ over the program you want to start automatically.

6 Drag the program to the Startup folder.

7 Double-click the Startup folder to display its contents.

■ The contents of the Startup folder appear.

■ Windows placed a shortcut to the program in the folder.

Note: For information on shortcuts, see page 108.

■ The programs in the Startup folder start automatically every time you turn on your computer.

CHANGE FOLDER OPTIONS

You can choose how you want to display the contents of your folders.

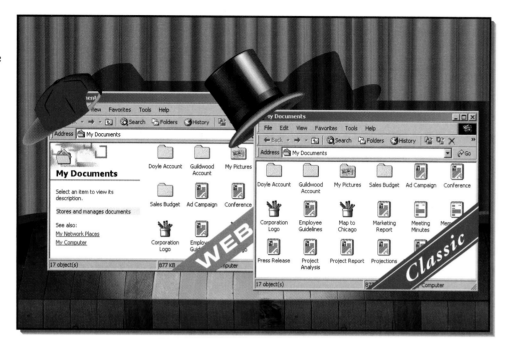

CHANGE FOLDER OPTIONS

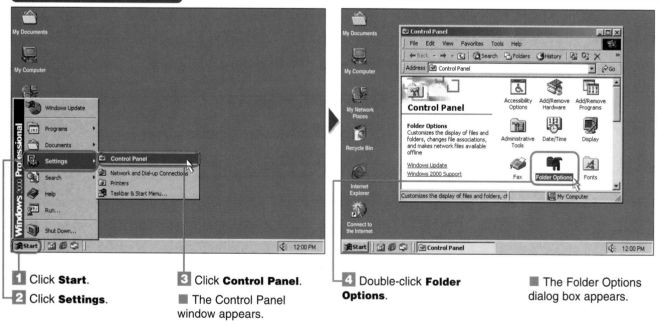

1 Click **Start**.

2 Click **Settings**.

3 Click **Control Panel**.

■ The Control Panel window appears.

4 Double-click **Folder Options**.

■ The Folder Options dialog box appears.

?

What is the difference between enabling Web content in my folders and using Windows classic folders?

When you enable Web content in your folders, Windows displays descriptive text and hyperlinks on the left side of each open folder. When you use Windows classic folders, your open folders do not display Web content.

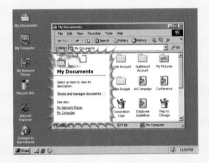

Web Content

Windows Classic

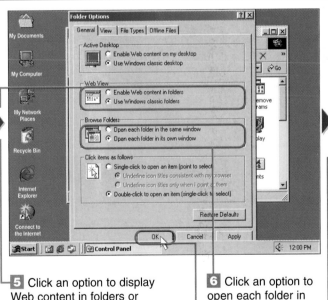

5 Click an option to display Web content in folders or use Windows classic folders (○ changes to ⊙).

Note: For more information, refer to the top of this page.

6 Click an option to open each folder in the same window or in its own window (○ changes to ⊙).

7 Click **OK** to confirm your changes.

■ Windows displays folders using the options you selected.

■ In this example, open folders display the Windows classic folder style.

■ If you chose to open each folder in its own window, you can double-click a folder in the current window to display the folder in a new window.

CREATE A NEW USER ON YOUR COMPUTER

If you share your computer with one or more people, you can create a new user account so each person can use their own personalized settings.

You must be logged on to your computer as an administrator to create a new user account. See page 20 to log on to a computer.

CREATE A NEW USER ON YOUR COMPUTER

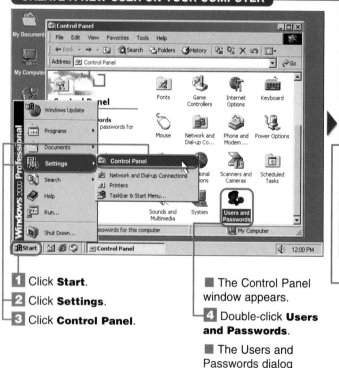

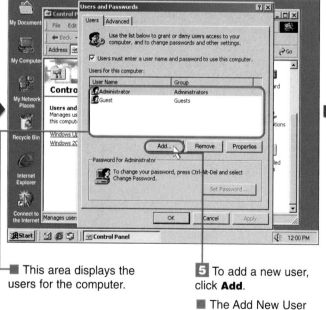

1 Click **Start**.

2 Click **Settings**.

3 Click **Control Panel**.

■ The Control Panel window appears.

4 Double-click **Users and Passwords**.

■ The Users and Passwords dialog box appears.

■ This area displays the users for the computer.

5 To add a new user, click **Add**.

■ The Add New User dialog box appears.

? **My computer is part of a network. Can I create a new user on the network?**

If your computer is part of a network, you must see your network administrator for information on adding a new user.

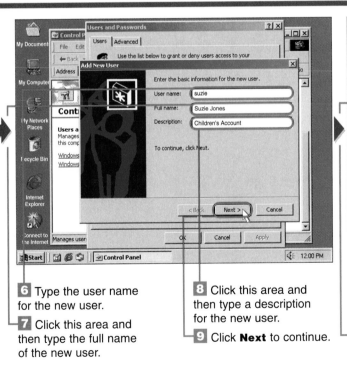

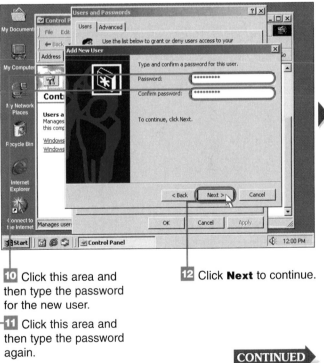

6 Type the user name for the new user.

7 Click this area and then type the full name of the new user.

8 Click this area and then type a description for the new user.

9 Click **Next** to continue.

10 Click this area and then type the password for the new user.

11 Click this area and then type the password again.

12 Click **Next** to continue.

CONTINUED

CREATE A NEW USER
ON YOUR COMPUTER

You can specify the type
of access you want to grant
a new user. The access
you grant determines the
type of tasks the user can
perform on the computer.

CREATE A NEW USER ON YOUR COMPUTER (CONTINUED)

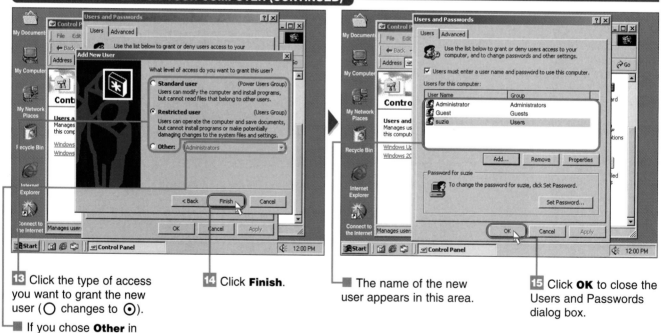

13 Click the type of access
you want to grant the new
user (○ changes to ⊙).

■ If you chose **Other** in
step **13**, you can click this
area to specify the type of
access you want to grant.

14 Click **Finish**.

■ The name of the new
user appears in this area.

15 Click **OK** to close the
Users and Passwords
dialog box.

DELETE A USER FROM YOUR COMPUTER

You can delete
a user you no
longer need.

You must be logged on
to your computer as an
administrator to delete a
user account. See page 20
to log on to a computer.

DELETE A USER FROM YOUR COMPUTER

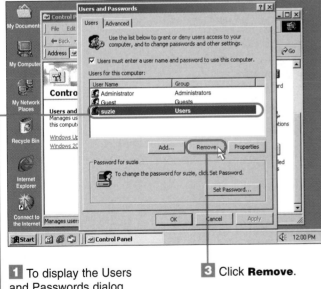

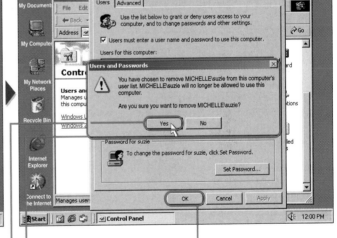

1 To display the Users
and Passwords dialog
box, perform steps **1** to **4**
on page 152.

2 Click the user you
want to remove.

3 Click **Remove**.

■ A confirmation dialog
box appears.

4 Click **Yes** to remove
the user from the computer.

■ The user is removed
from the users list.

5 Click **OK** to close the
Users and Passwords
dialog box.

CHANGE YOUR PASSWORD

You can change
the password you
use to log on to
your computer
or network at
any time.

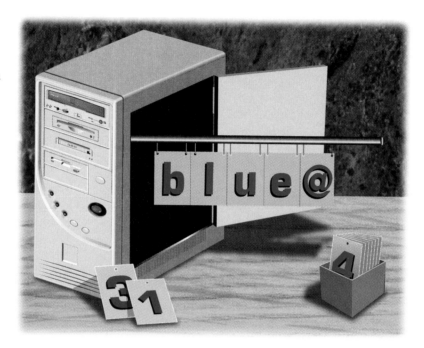

Frequently changing
your password makes
it more difficult for
other people to access
your computer.

CHANGE YOUR PASSWORD

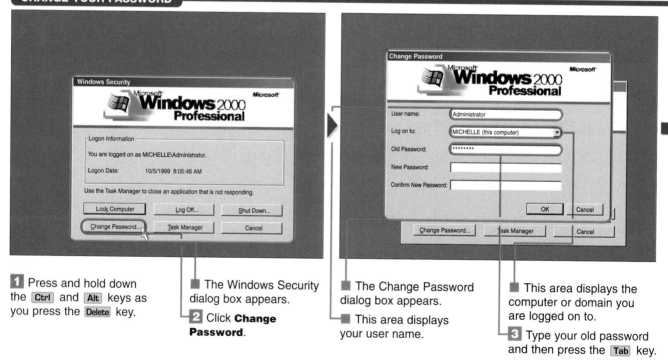

■ Press and hold down
the **Ctrl** and **Alt** keys as
you press the **Delete** key.

■ The Windows Security
dialog box appears.

2 Click **Change
Password**.

■ The Change Password
dialog box appears.

■ This area displays
your user name.

■ This area displays the
computer or domain you
are logged on to.

3 Type your old password
and then press the **Tab** key.

?

How do I pick a good password?

When choosing a password, do not use words that people can associate with you, such as your name or favorite sport. A good password connects two words or number sequences with a special character, like **blue@123**.

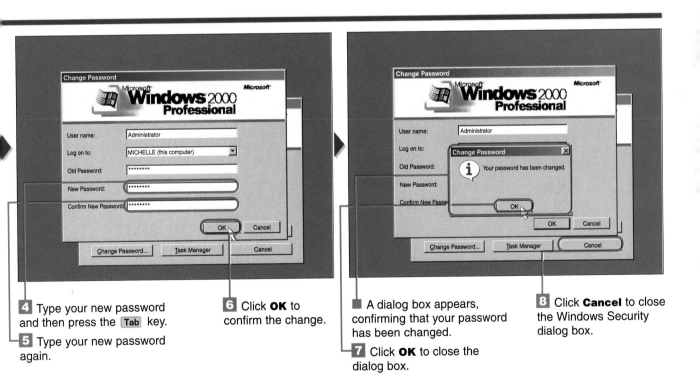

4 Type your new password and then press the `Tab` key.

5 Type your new password again.

6 Click **OK** to confirm the change.

■ A dialog box appears, confirming that your password has been changed.

7 Click **OK** to close the dialog box.

8 Click **Cancel** to close the Windows Security dialog box.

CHAPTER 7

Have Fun With Windows

In this chapter you will find out how to use Windows to play games, listen to music CDs, record sounds and more.

SOUNDS

CLASSICAL INSTRUMENTS

PLAY GAMES

Windows includes several games you can play on your computer. Games are a fun way to improve your mouse skills and hand-eye coordination.

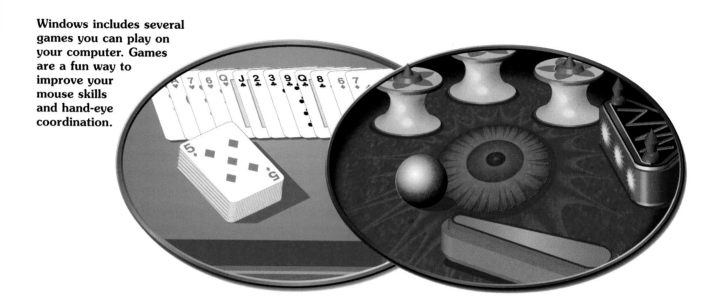

PLAY GAMES

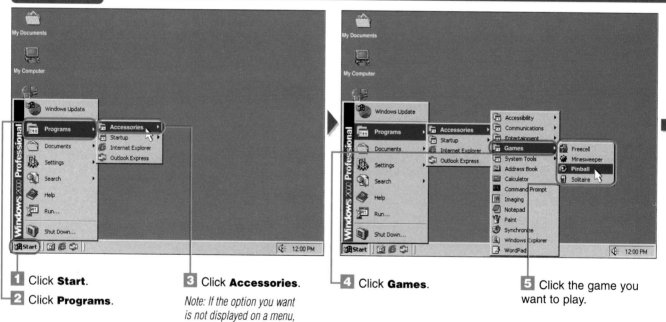

1 Click **Start**.

2 Click **Programs**.

3 Click **Accessories**.

Note: If the option you want is not displayed on a menu, position the mouse over the bottom of the menu to display all the options.

4 Click **Games**.

5 Click the game you want to play.

What other games are included with Windows?

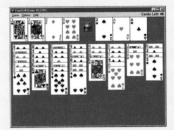

FreeCell

FreeCell is a single-player card game.

Minesweeper

Minesweeper is a strategy game in which you try to avoid being blown up by mines.

PINBALL

Pinball is similar to a pinball game you would find at an arcade. You launch a ball and then try to score as many points as possible.

SOLITAIRE

Solitaire is a classic card game that you play on your own. You try to put all the cards in order from ace to king in four stacks, one stack for each suit.

PLAY A MUSIC CD

You can use your computer to play music CDs while you work.

You need a CD-ROM drive, a sound card and speakers to play music CDs.

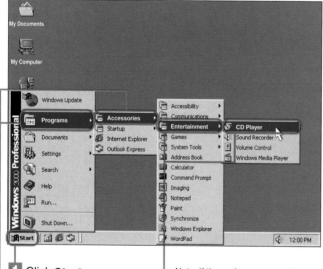

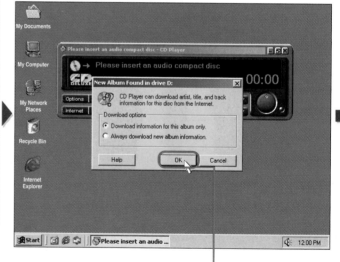

1 Click **Start**.

2 Click **Programs**.

3 Click **Accessories**.

Note: If the option you want is not displayed on a menu, position the mouse ▷ over the bottom of the menu to display all the options.

4 Click **Entertainment**.

5 Click **CD Player**.

■ The CD Player window appears.

6 Insert a music CD into the CD-ROM drive.

■ A dialog box may appear, asking if you want to download information about the CD from the Internet, such as the name of the artist and each song.

7 To have CD Player download information about the CD, click **OK**.

Note: If you are not connected to the Internet, a dialog box appears that allows you to connect.

162

Can I listen to music privately?

You can listen to music privately by plugging a headset into your CD-ROM drive.

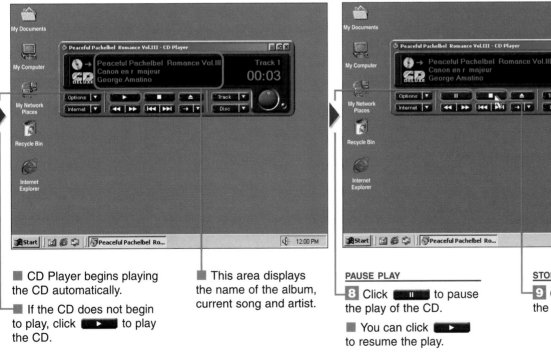

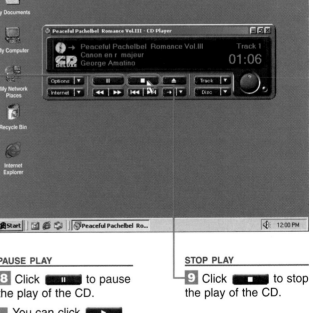

■ CD Player begins playing the CD automatically.

■ If the CD does not begin to play, click to play the CD.

■ This area displays the name of the album, current song and artist.

PAUSE PLAY

8 Click to pause the play of the CD.

■ You can click to resume the play.

STOP PLAY

9 Click to stop the play of the CD.

CONTINUED

PLAY A MUSIC CD

You can switch
between the
songs on a CD.

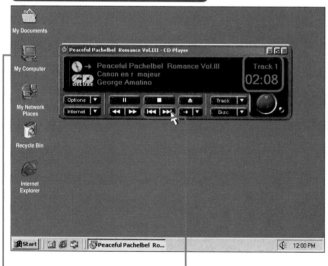

PLAY ANOTHER SONG

■ This area displays
which song is currently
playing and the amount
of time the song has
played.

10 Click one of the
following options to play
another song on the CD.

◄◄ Play the previous song

►►► Play the next song

CLOSE CD PLAYER

11 When you finish
listening to a CD, click
▲ to eject the CD.

12 Click ☒ to close
the CD Player window.

ADJUST THE VOLUME

You can easily adjust
the volume of sound
coming from your
speakers.

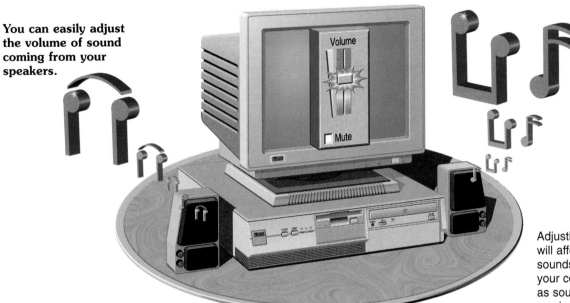

Adjusting the volume
will affect all the
sounds you play on
your computer, such
as sound from a
music CD or video.

ADJUST THE VOLUME

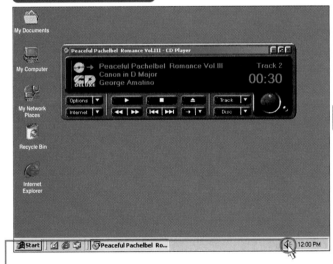

1 Click 🔊 to display
the Volume control.

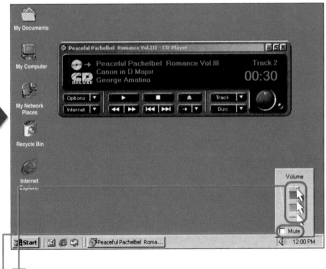

2 Drag the slider (▭)
up or down to increase or
decrease the volume.

3 Click this option to turn off
the volume (☐ changes to ☑).
The speaker icon (🔊) changes
to 🔇 on the taskbar.

*Note: You can repeat step 3
to once again turn on the
volume.*

■ To hide the Volume
control, click outside
the box.

PLAY VIDEOS

You can play
videos on your
computer.

Windows can play
different types of
videos, including videos
with the .avi, .qt and
.mpg extensions
(example: film.avi).

PLAY VIDEOS

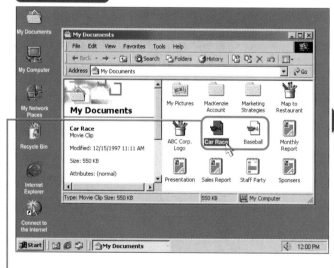

1 Double-click the
video you want to play.

■ The Windows Media
Player window appears
and the video starts to play.

2 Click one of these
options to pause (⏸)
or stop (⏹) the play
of the video.

3 Click ▶ to once
again play the video.

?

Where can I get videos?

You can purchase videos at computer stores or obtain videos on the Internet. To quickly find a variety of videos on the Internet, click **Media Guide** in the Windows Media Player window. Windows will open your Web browser and display a Web page with links to many videos on the Web.

■ This area displays the current position in the video and the total length of the video.

4 To move through the video, position the mouse over the slider ( ) and then drag the slider to a new location.

5 When you finish playing the video, click ☒ to close the window.

ASSIGN SOUNDS TO PROGRAM EVENTS

You can have Windows play sound effects when you perform certain tasks on your computer.

For example, you can hear a phone ring when you receive a fax or music when you exit Windows.

ASSIGN A SOUND SCHEME

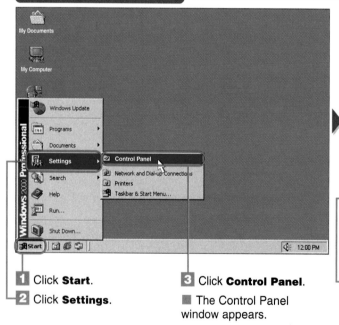

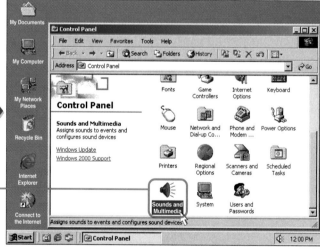

1 Click **Start**.

2 Click **Settings**.

3 Click **Control Panel**.

■ The Control Panel window appears.

4 Double-click **Sounds and Multimedia**.

■ The Sounds and Multimedia Properties dialog box appears.

? **What do I need to hear sounds on my computer?**

You need a sound card and speakers on your computer to hear sounds. If your sound card and speakers are set up properly, you will hear a short musical introduction each time Windows starts.

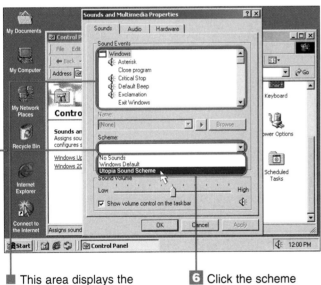

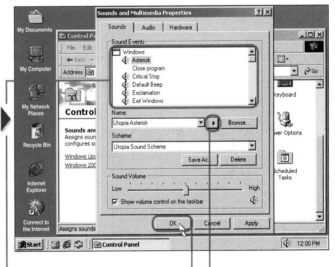

■ This area displays the events to which you can assign sounds.

5 Click this area to display a list of the available sound schemes. Each scheme will change the sounds for many events at once.

6 Click the scheme you want to use.

*Note: A dialog box may appear, asking if you want to save the previous scheme. Click **No** to continue without saving.*

■ A speaker icon (🔊) appears beside each event that will play a sound.

7 To hear the sound an event will play, click the event.

8 Click ▶ to hear the sound.

Note: To adjust the volume of the sound, see page 165.

9 Click **OK** to confirm your selection.

ASSIGN SOUNDS TO PROGRAM EVENTS

You can assign a sound to an event performed on your computer.

You may want to hear your favorite cartoon character each time you close a program or a sigh of relief when you restore a window.

ASSIGN A SOUND TO ONE EVENT

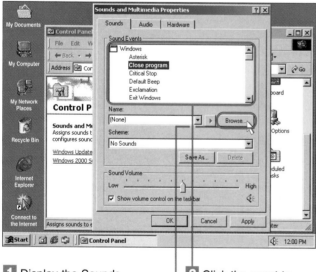

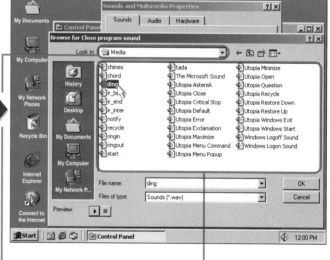

1 Display the Sounds and Multimedia Properties dialog box.

Note: To display the Sounds and Multimedia Properties dialog box, perform steps 1 to 4 on page 168.

2 Click the event to which you want to assign a sound.

3 Click **Browse** to find the sound you want to use on your computer.

■ The Browse dialog box appears.

■ This area shows the location of the displayed sound files. You can click this area to change the location.

4 Click the sound you want to hear every time the event occurs.

Where can I get more sounds?

You can purchase sounds at computer stores or get sounds on the Internet. Make sure you use sounds with the .wav extension, such as **wolfhowl.wav**.

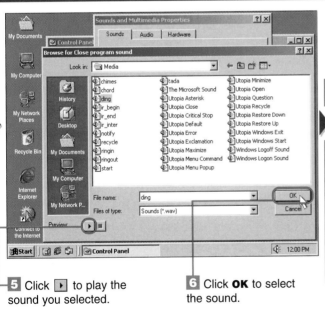

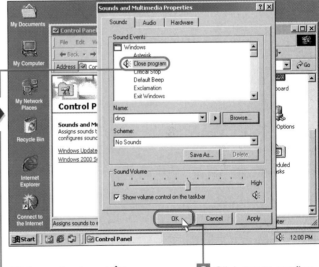

5 Click ▶ to play the sound you selected.

6 Click **OK** to select the sound.

■ A speaker icon (🔊) appears beside the event.

7 To assign sounds to other events, repeat steps **2** to **6** for each event.

8 Click **OK** to confirm your changes.

You can use Sound Recorder to record your own sounds.

You need a sound card and speakers to record and play sounds.

RECORD SOUNDS

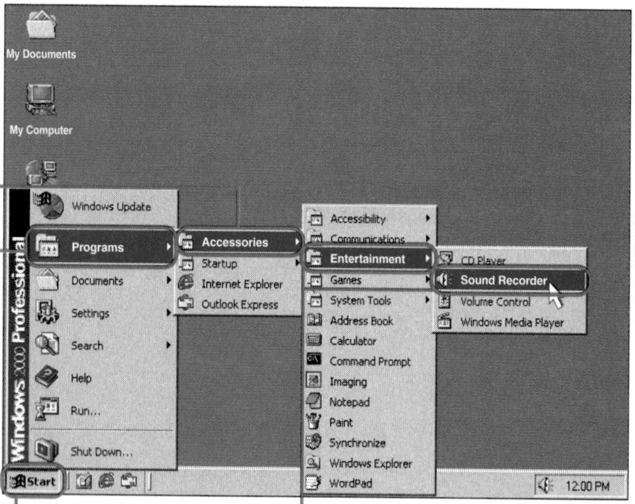

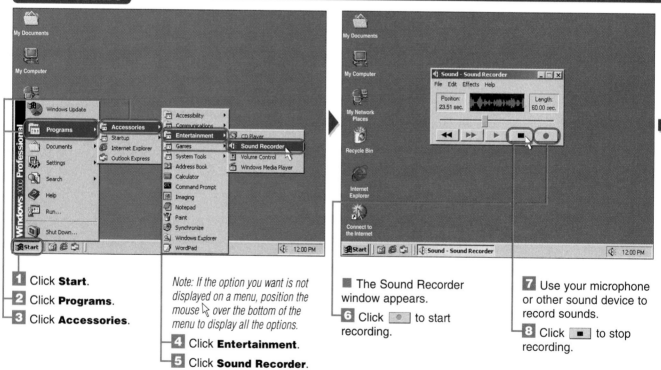

1 Click **Start**.

2 Click **Programs**.

3 Click **Accessories**.

Note: If the option you want is not displayed on a menu, position the mouse over the bottom of the menu to display all the options.

4 Click **Entertainment**.

5 Click **Sound Recorder**.

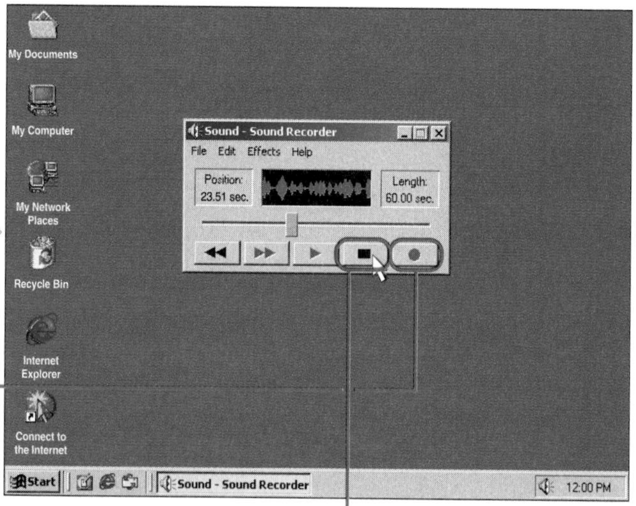

■ The Sound Recorder window appears.

6 Click to start recording.

7 Use your microphone or other sound device to record sounds.

8 Click to stop recording.

What devices can I use to record sounds?

You can record sounds from a microphone, CD player, stereo, VCR or any other sound device connected to your computer.

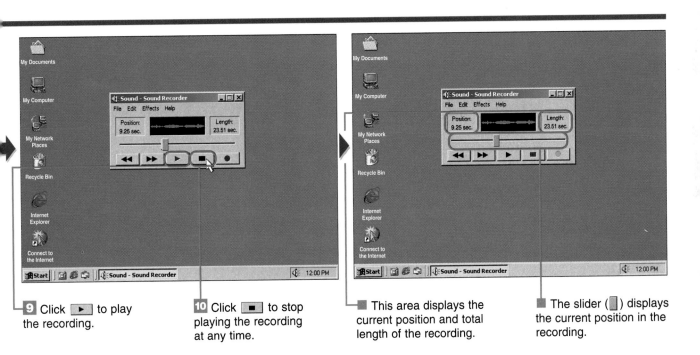

9 Click ► to play the recording.

10 Click ■ to stop playing the recording at any time.

■ This area displays the current position and total length of the recording.

■ The slider (▯) displays the current position in the recording.

CONTINUED

RECORD SOUNDS

Sound Recorder offers several sound effects you can use to change your recording.

You can adjust the volume, change the speed, add an echo or play a recording in reverse.

RECORD SOUNDS (CONTINUED)

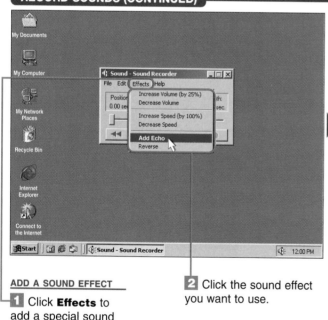

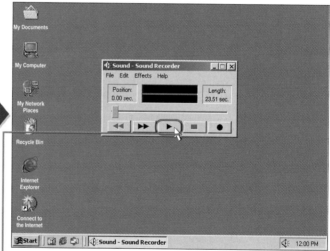

ADD A SOUND EFFECT

1 Click **Effects** to add a special sound effect to the recording.

2 Click the sound effect you want to use.

3 Click ▶ to play the recording and hear the sound effect.

■ You can repeat steps **1** and **2** for each sound effect you want to use.

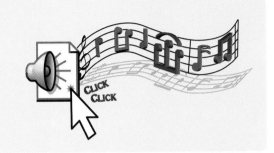

How can I play a recording I created?

Sound files you created in Sound Recorder display a specific icon (🔊). You can double-click the icon to play the recording.

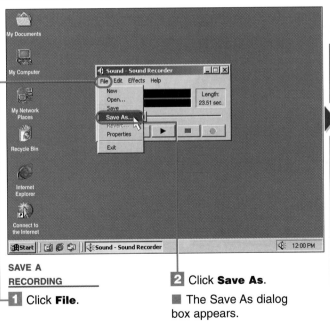

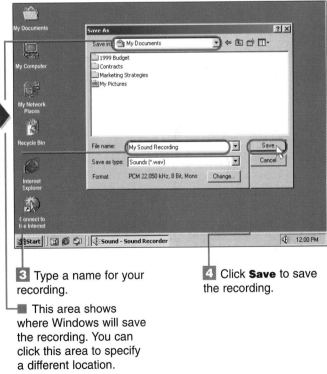

SAVE A RECORDING

1 Click **File**.

2 Click **Save As**.

■ The Save As dialog box appears.

3 Type a name for your recording.

■ This area shows where Windows will save the recording. You can click this area to specify a different location.

4 Click **Save** to save the recording.

CHAPTER 8

Optimize Your Computer

Find out how to use Windows to enhance your computer's performance in this chapter. Learn how to detect and repair disk errors, schedule tasks, install programs and much more.

FORMAT A FLOPPY DISK

You must format a floppy disk before you can use the disk to store information.

Floppy disks you buy at computer stores are usually formatted. You may want to later format a disk to erase the information it contains and prepare the disk for storing new information.

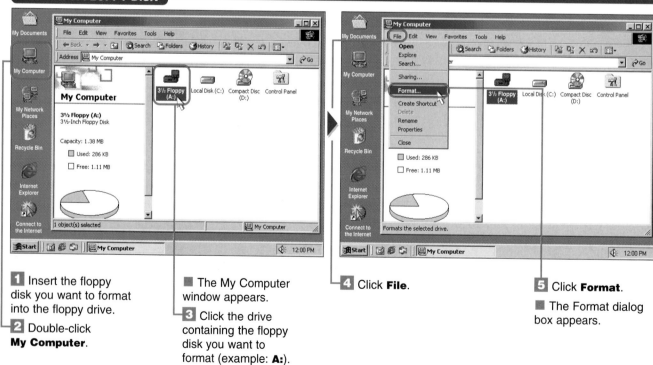

1 Insert the floppy disk you want to format into the floppy drive.

2 Double-click **My Computer**.

■ The My Computer window appears.

3 Click the drive containing the floppy disk you want to format (example: **A:**).

4 Click **File**.

5 Click **Format**.

■ The Format dialog box appears.

178

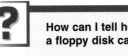

How can I tell how much information a floppy disk can store?

Double-Density Disk

A 3.5-inch floppy disk that has one hole can store 720 KB of information.

High-Density Disk

A 3.5-inch floppy disk that has two holes and displays the HD symbol can store 1.44 MB of information.

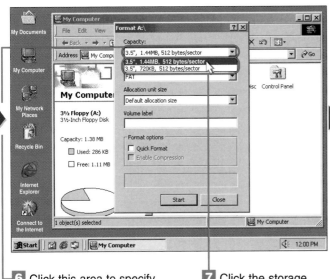

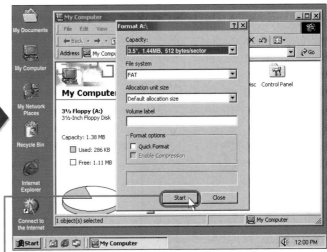

6 Click this area to specify how much information the floppy disk can store.

7 Click the storage capacity of the floppy disk.

8 Click **Start** to start formatting the floppy disk.

CONTINUED

FORMAT A FLOPPY DISK

Before formatting
a floppy disk, make
sure the disk does not
contain information you
may need. Formatting
a floppy disk will
permanently remove
all the information
on the disk.

FORMAT A FLOPPY DISK (CONTINUED)

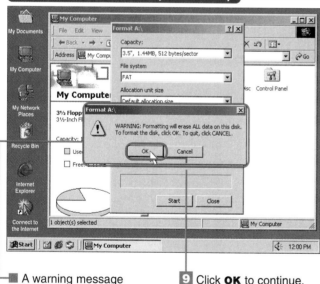

■ A warning message
appears, indicating that
formatting the floppy disk
will erase all the data on
the disk.

9 Click **OK** to continue.

■ This area displays the
progress of the format.

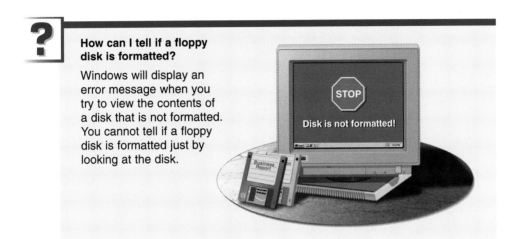

How can I tell if a floppy disk is formatted?

Windows will display an error message when you try to view the contents of a disk that is not formatted. You cannot tell if a floppy disk is formatted just by looking at the disk.

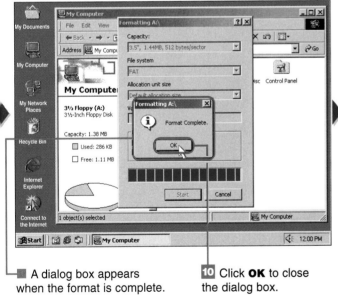

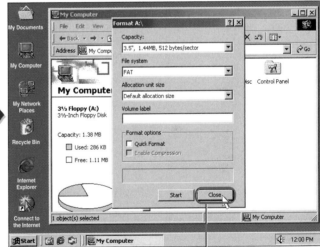

■ A dialog box appears when the format is complete.

10 Click **OK** to close the dialog box.

■ To format another floppy disk, insert the disk and then repeat steps **6** to **10** starting on page 179.

11 Click **Close** to close the Format dialog box.

VIEW AMOUNT OF DISK SPACE

You can view the
amount of used
and free space
on a disk.

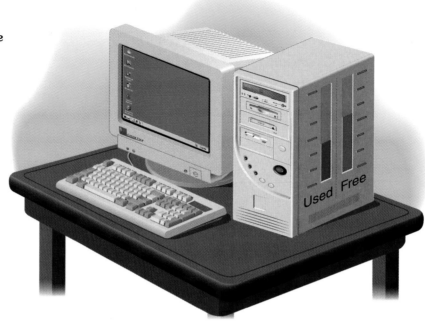

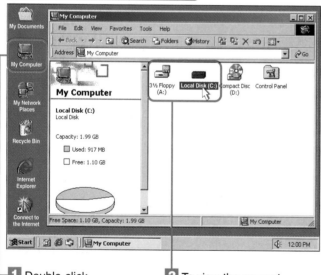

1 Double-click
My Computer.

■ The My Computer
window appears.

2 To view the amount
of space on a disk,
click the disk of interest
(example: **C:**).

*Note: To view the amount of
space on a floppy disk, you
must first insert the disk into
the floppy drive.*

3 Click **File**.

4 Click **Properties**.

■ The Properties dialog
box appears.

182

How can I increase the amount of free space on my hard disk?

Delete files you no longer need. See page 94 to delete files.

Use Disk Cleanup to remove unnecessary files from your computer. See page 188 to use Disk Cleanup.

Copy files you rarely use to a floppy disk and then delete the files from your computer. See page 92 to copy files to a floppy disk.

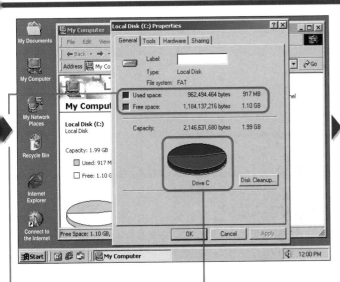

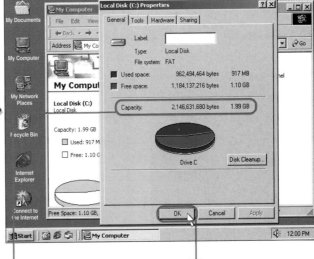

■ This area displays the amount of used and free space on the disk in bytes, megabytes (MB) and gigabytes (GB).

■ A pie chart visually indicates the amount of used and free space on the disk.

■ This area displays the total disk storage space, in both bytes and gigabytes (GB).

5 When you finish viewing the information, click **OK** to close the Properties dialog box.

DETECT AND REPAIR DISK ERRORS

You can improve the performance of your computer by checking for hard disk errors. Windows will attempt to automatically repair any disk errors it finds.

The hard disk is the primary device a computer uses to store information.

You must be logged on to your computer or network as an administrator to detect and repair disk errors. See page 20 to log on to a computer or network.

DETECT AND REPAIR DISK ERRORS

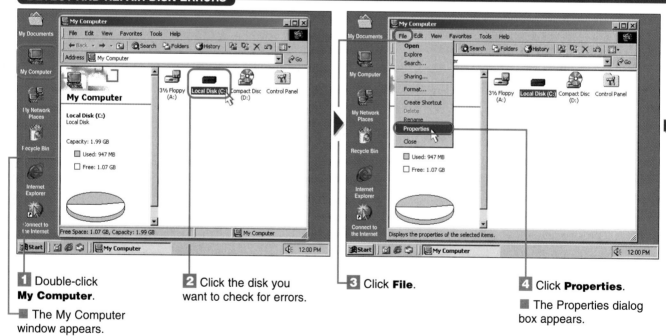

1 Double-click **My Computer**.

■ The My Computer window appears.

2 Click the disk you want to check for errors.

3 Click **File**.

4 Click **Properties**.

■ The Properties dialog box appears.

?

Can I work with files on my computer while Windows checks for disk errors?

You should not have any files open while Windows checks for disk errors. If you have files open, Windows may not be able to check the disk properly. Open files may also increase the time it takes for Windows to complete the check.

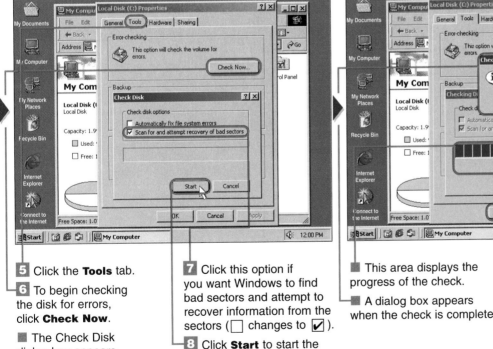

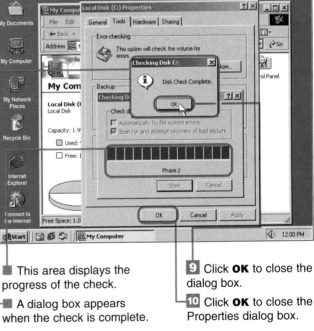

5 Click the **Tools** tab.

6 To begin checking the disk for errors, click **Check Now**.

■ The Check Disk dialog box appears.

7 Click this option if you want Windows to find bad sectors and attempt to recover information from the sectors (☐ changes to ☑).

8 Click **Start** to start the check.

■ This area displays the progress of the check.

■ A dialog box appears when the check is complete.

9 Click **OK** to close the dialog box.

10 Click **OK** to close the Properties dialog box.

DEFRAGMENT YOUR HARD DISK

You can improve
the performance
of your computer
by defragmenting
your hard disk.

You must be logged on to
your computer or network
as an administrator to
defragment a hard disk.
See page 20 to log on to
a computer or network.

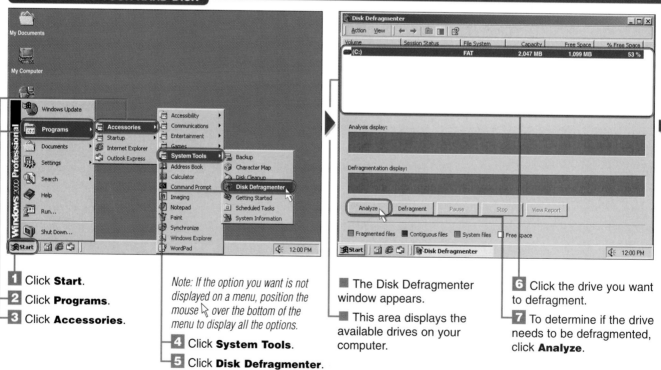

1 Click **Start**.

2 Click **Programs**.

3 Click **Accessories**.

*Note: If the option you want is not
displayed on a menu, position the
mouse ⟍ over the bottom of the
menu to display all the options.*

4 Click **System Tools**.

5 Click **Disk Defragmenter**.

■ The Disk Defragmenter
window appears.

■ This area displays the
available drives on your
computer.

6 Click the drive you want
to defragment.

7 To determine if the drive
needs to be defragmented,
click **Analyze**.

186

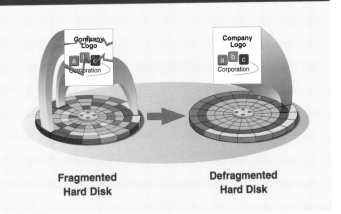

Why would I need to defragment my hard disk?

A fragmented hard disk stores parts of a file in many different locations. Your computer must search many areas on the disk to retrieve a file. You can use Disk Defragmenter to place all the parts of a file in one location. This reduces the time your computer will spend locating the file.

Fragmented Hard Disk

Defragmented Hard Disk

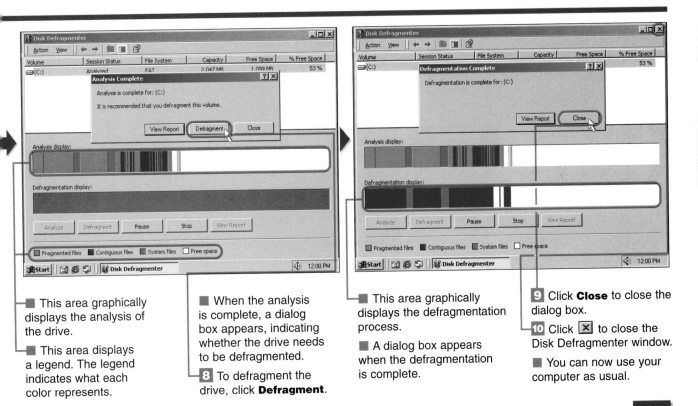

■ This area graphically displays the analysis of the drive.

■ This area displays a legend. The legend indicates what each color represents.

■ When the analysis is complete, a dialog box appears, indicating whether the drive needs to be defragmented.

8 To defragment the drive, click **Defragment**.

■ This area graphically displays the defragmentation process.

■ A dialog box appears when the defragmentation is complete.

9 Click **Close** to close the dialog box.

10 Click ✕ to close the Disk Defragmenter window.

■ You can now use your computer as usual.

USING DISK CLEANUP

Disk Cleanup will remove unnecessary files from your computer to free up disk space.

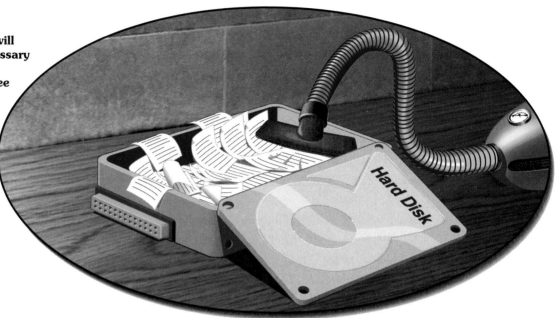

USING DISK CLEANUP

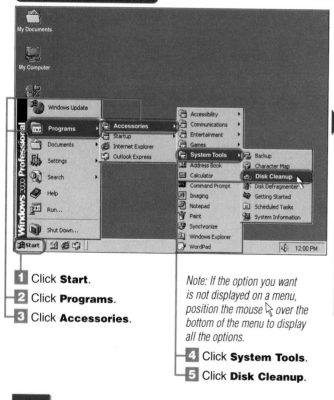

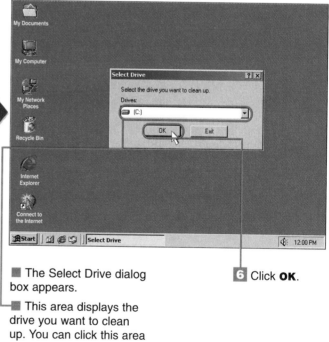

1 Click **Start**.

2 Click **Programs**.

3 Click **Accessories**.

Note: If the option you want is not displayed on a menu, position the mouse ⇩ over the bottom of the menu to display all the options.

4 Click **System Tools**.

5 Click **Disk Cleanup**.

■ The Select Drive dialog box appears.

■ This area displays the drive you want to clean up. You can click this area to select a different drive.

6 Click **OK**.

What types of files can Disk Cleanup remove?

Downloaded Program Files

Information transferred from the Internet when you view certain Web pages.

Temporary Internet Files

Web pages stored on your computer for quick viewing.

Recycle Bin

Files you have deleted.

Offline Files

Copies of files on the network you have made available offline. For information on making files available offline, see page 244.

Temporary Offline Files

Copies of files you have recently used on the network.

Catalog files for the Content Indexer

Files created to speed up searches on your computer.

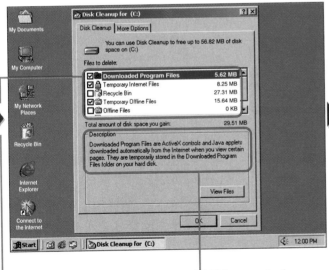

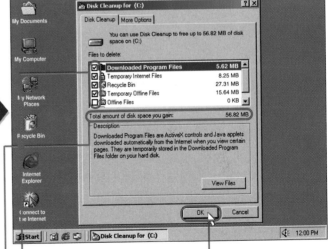

■ The Disk Cleanup dialog box appears.

■ This area displays the types of files you can remove and the amount of disk space taken up by each file type.

■ This area displays a description of the highlighted file type.

7 Windows will remove the files for each file type that displays a check mark (☑). You can click the box (☐) beside a file type to add or remove the check mark.

■ This area displays the total space Windows will free up from the file types you selected.

8 Click **OK** to remove the files.

■ A confirmation dialog box appears. Click **Yes** to permanently delete the files.

SCHEDULE TASKS

You can use Task Scheduler to have Windows automatically perform tasks on a regular basis. This is useful for running computer maintenance programs such as Disk Cleanup.

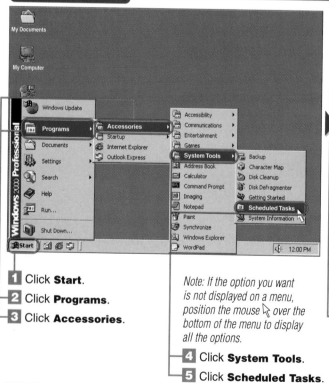

1 Click **Start**.

2 Click **Programs**.

3 Click **Accessories**.

Note: If the option you want is not displayed on a menu, position the mouse ⟨ over the bottom of the menu to display all the options.

4 Click **System Tools**.

5 Click **Scheduled Tasks**.

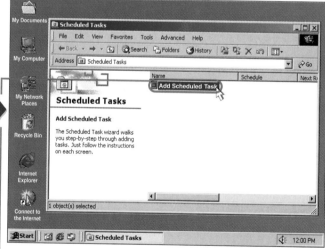

■ The Scheduled Tasks window appears.

6 Double-click **Add Scheduled Task** to schedule a new program.

■ The Scheduled Task Wizard appears.

How does Task Scheduler know when to start a program?

Task Scheduler uses the date and time set in your computer to determine when to start a scheduled task. Before you schedule a task, make sure this information is correct. See page 122 to change the date and time set in your computer.

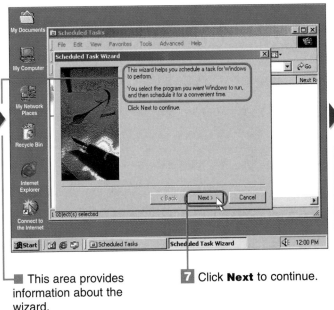

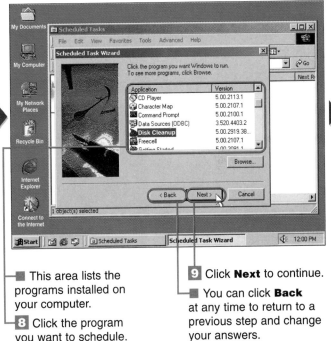

■ This area provides information about the wizard.

7 Click **Next** to continue.

■ This area lists the programs installed on your computer.

8 Click the program you want to schedule.

9 Click **Next** to continue.

■ You can click **Back** at any time to return to a previous step and change your answers.

CONTINUED ▶

SCHEDULE TASKS

You can specify the date and time you want Task Scheduler to start a program. Schedule a program during a time when your computer will be turned on.

SCHEDULE TASKS (CONTINUED)

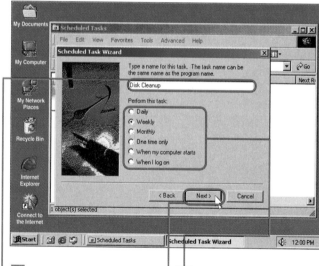

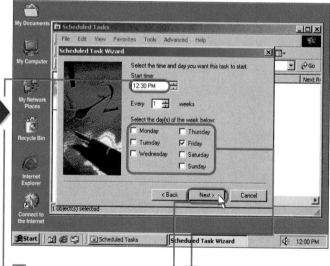

10 Windows provides a name for the program. To use a different name, type the name.

11 Click an option to specify when you want the program to run (○ changes to ⊙).

12 Click **Next** to continue.

13 To specify when you want the program to run, click the part of the time you want to change and then type a new time.

Note: The options available in this screen depend on the option you selected in step 11.

14 Click each day of the week you want the program to run (☐ changes to ☑).

15 Click **Next** to continue.

Can I remove a task so it will no longer run automatically?

To remove a task so Windows will no longer run the task automatically, click the program in the Scheduled Tasks window and then press the Delete key. Then click **Yes** to confirm the deletion. Deleting a program from Task Scheduler does not remove the program from your computer.

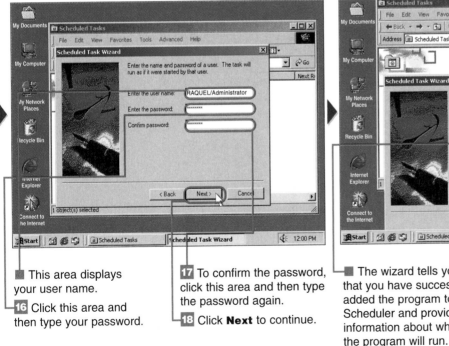

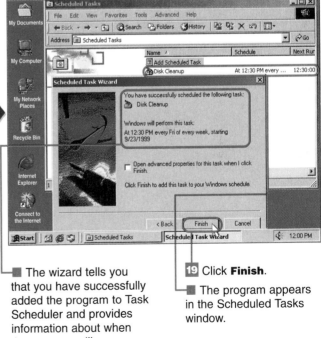

■ This area displays your user name.

16 Click this area and then type your password.

17 To confirm the password, click this area and then type the password again.

18 Click **Next** to continue.

■ The wizard tells you that you have successfully added the program to Task Scheduler and provides information about when the program will run.

19 Click **Finish**.

■ The program appears in the Scheduled Tasks window.

ADD FONTS TO YOUR COMPUTER

You can add fonts
to your computer
to give you more
choices when
creating documents.

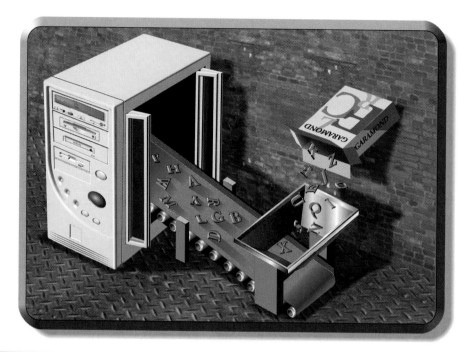

ADD FONTS TO YOUR COMPUTER

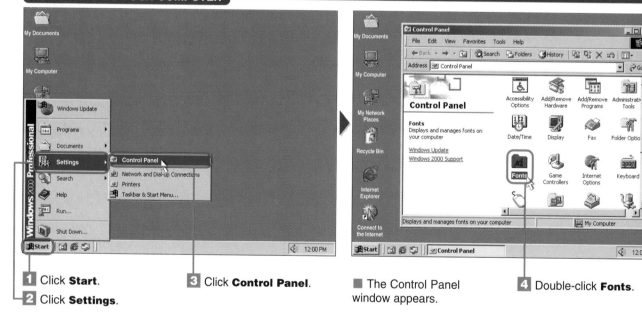

1 Click **Start**.

2 Click **Settings**.

3 Click **Control Panel**.

■ The Control Panel
window appears.

4 Double-click **Fonts**.

Where can I get fonts?

You can purchase fonts wherever computer software is sold. You can also find fonts on the Internet. Some fonts on the Internet are compressed. You can use a program such as WinZip to decompress the fonts so you can add them to your computer. WinZip is available on the Web at www.winzip.com.

Fonts are available at the following Web sites:

www.fontface.com

www.fontage.com

www.tyworld.com

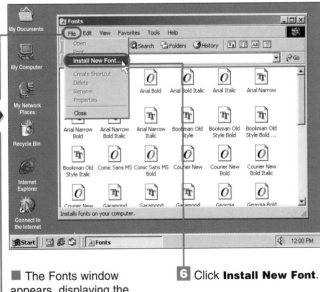

■ The Fonts window appears, displaying the fonts installed on your computer.

5 Click **File**.

6 Click **Install New Font**.

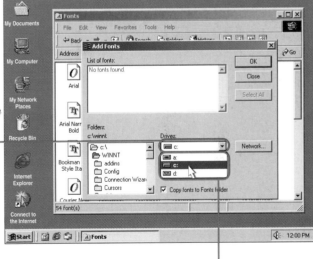

■ The Add Fonts dialog box appears.

7 Click this area to select the drive containing the fonts you want to add.

8 Click the drive containing the fonts.

CONTINUED

ADD FONTS TO YOUR COMPUTER

When you add fonts to your computer, you will be able to use the fonts in all your programs.

ADD FONTS TO YOUR COMPUTER (CONTINUED)

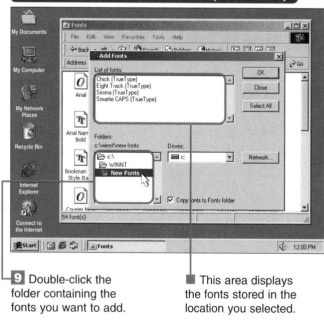

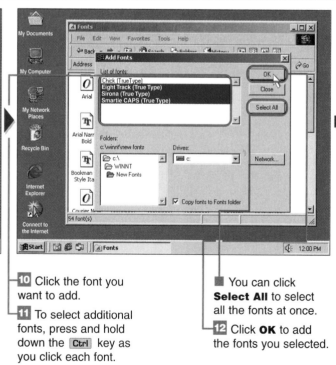

9 Double-click the folder containing the fonts you want to add.

■ This area displays the fonts stored in the location you selected.

10 Click the font you want to add.

11 To select additional fonts, press and hold down the **Ctrl** key as you click each font.

■ You can click **Select All** to select all the fonts at once.

12 Click **OK** to add the fonts you selected.

?

What types of fonts are available on my computer?

TrueType Fonts

A TrueType font will print exactly as it appears on your screen.

OpenType Fonts

OpenType fonts use the same technology as TrueType fonts. Most of the fonts included with Windows are OpenType fonts.

System Fonts

Windows often uses system fonts to display text in menus and dialog boxes.

Printer Fonts

Most printers include built-in fonts that are stored in the printer's memory. A printer font may not print as it appears on your screen. Printer fonts do not appear in the Fonts window.

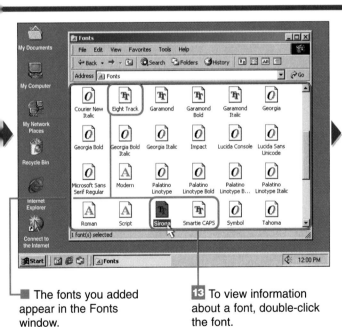

■ The fonts you added appear in the Fonts window.

13 To view information about a font, double-click the font.

■ A window appears, displaying information about the font you selected and samples of the font in various sizes.

14 When you finish reviewing the information, click **Done** to close the window.

INSTALL A PROGRAM

You can add a new program to your computer. Programs come on a CD-ROM disc or floppy disks.

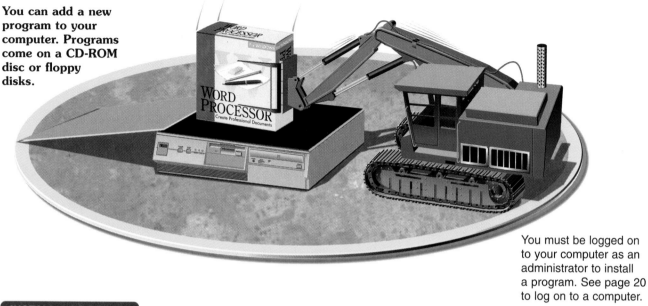

You must be logged on to your computer as an administrator to install a program. See page 20 to log on to a computer.

INSTALL A PROGRAM

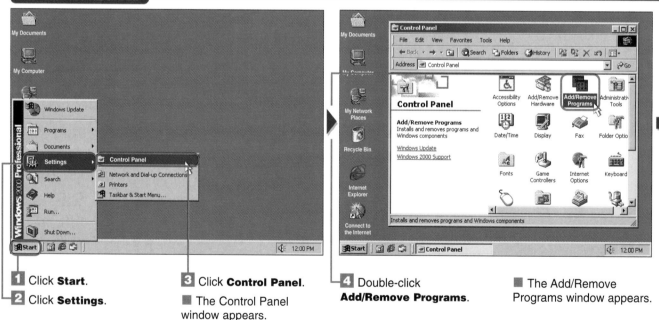

1 Click **Start**.

2 Click **Settings**.

3 Click **Control Panel**.

■ The Control Panel window appears.

4 Double-click **Add/Remove Programs**.

■ The Add/Remove Programs window appears.

? **Why did an installation
program automatically start?**

Most Windows programs
available on a CD-ROM disc
will automatically start an
installation program when
you insert the CD-ROM disc
into the drive. Follow the
instructions on your screen
to install the program.

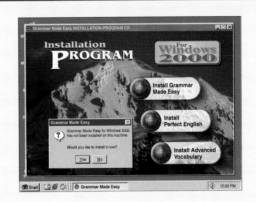

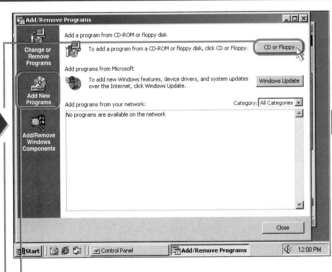

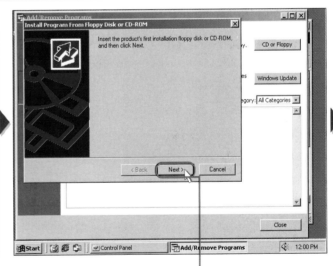

5 Click **Add New Programs**
to install a new program.

6 To install a program from
a CD-ROM disc or floppy
disk, click **CD or Floppy**.

■ The Install Program
From Floppy Disk or
CD-ROM dialog box
appears.

7 Insert the program's
first installation floppy
disk or CD-ROM disc
into a drive.

8 Click **Next** to continue.

CONTINUED

INSTALL A PROGRAM

There are three
common ways to
install a program.

Typical
Sets up the program
with the most common
components.

Custom
Lets you customize
the program to suit
your specific needs.

Minimum
Sets up the program with a
minimum number of components.
This is ideal for computers with
limited disk space.

INSTALL A PROGRAM (CONTINUED)

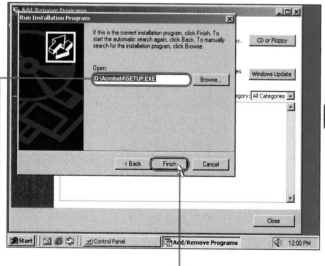

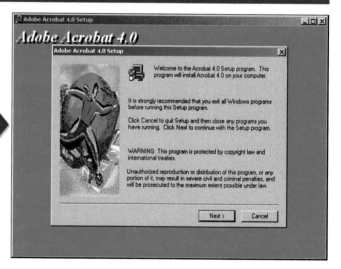

■ Windows locates the
file needed to install the
program.

9 Click **Finish** to install
the program.

10 Follow the instructions
on your screen. Every
program will ask you a
different set of questions.

■ After you install a
program, make sure you
keep the program's CD-ROM
disc or floppy disks in a safe
place. If your computer fails
or you accidentally erase the
program files, you may need
to install the program again.

You can remove a program that you no longer use on your computer. Removing a program will free up space on your hard drive.

REMOVE A PROGRAM

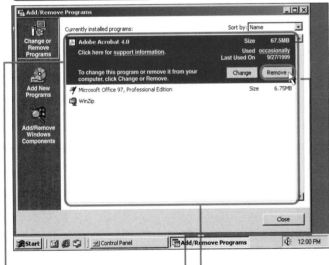
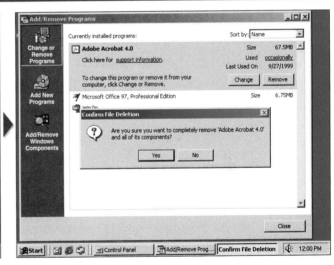

1 To display the Add/Remove Programs window, perform steps 1 to 4 on page 198.

■ This area lists the programs Windows can automatically remove.

2 Click the program you want to remove.

3 Click **Change/Remove** or **Remove**.

Note: The name of the button depends on the program you are removing.

4 Follow the instructions on your screen. Every program will take you through different steps to remove the program.

INSTALL A PRINTER

Before you can use a new printer, you need to install the printer on your computer.

You must be logged on to your computer or network as an administrator to install a printer. See page 20 to log on to a computer or network.

INSTALL A PRINTER

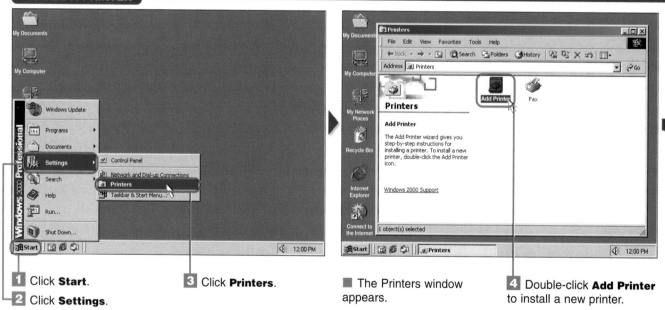

1 Click **Start**.

2 Click **Settings**.

3 Click **Printers**.

■ The Printers window appears.

4 Double-click **Add Printer** to install a new printer.

What is a Plug and Play printer?

A Plug and Play printer is a printer that Windows can automatically set up to work properly with your computer, which makes the printer easy to install. If your printer is Plug and Play, Windows may automatically install the printer for you the first time you turn on your computer after connecting the printer to the computer.

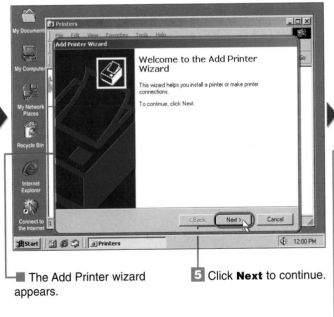

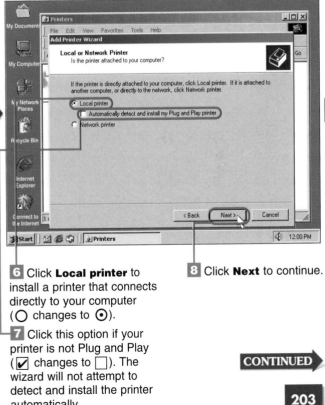

■ The Add Printer wizard appears.

5 Click **Next** to continue.

6 Click **Local printer** to install a printer that connects directly to your computer (○ changes to ⊙).

7 Click this option if your printer is not Plug and Play (☑ changes to ☐). The wizard will not attempt to detect and install the printer automatically.

8 Click **Next** to continue.

CONTINUED

INSTALL A PRINTER

When installing a printer, you must specify which port the printer is connected to. A port is a socket at the back of a computer where you plug in a device.

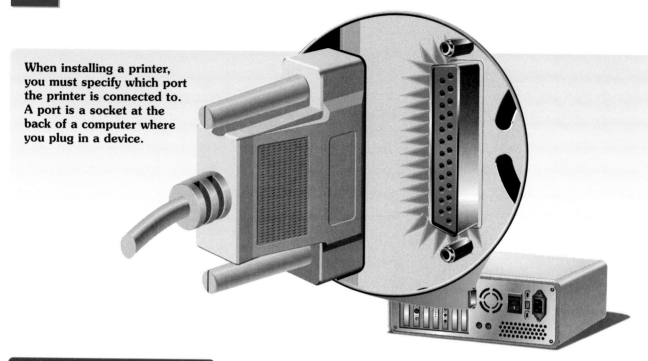

INSTALL A PRINTER (CONTINUED)

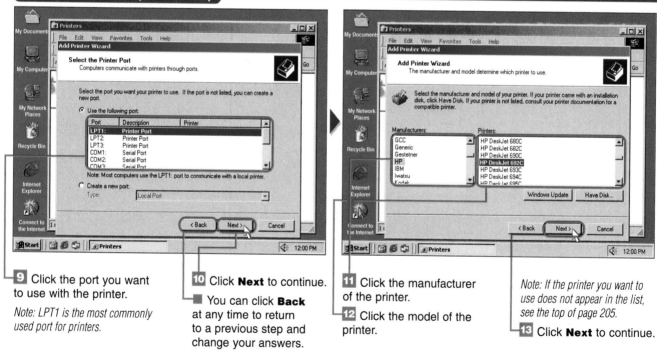

9 Click the port you want to use with the printer.

Note: LPT1 is the most commonly used port for printers.

10 Click **Next** to continue.

■ You can click **Back** at any time to return to a previous step and change your answers.

11 Click the manufacturer of the printer.

12 Click the model of the printer.

Note: If the printer you want to use does not appear in the list, see the top of page 205.

13 Click **Next** to continue.

What if the printer I want to install does not appear in the list?

If the printer you want to install does not appear in the list, you can use the installation disk(s) that came with the printer.

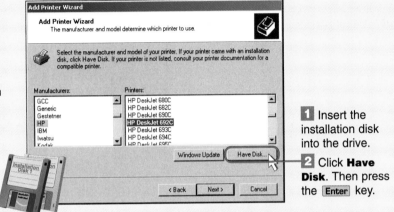

1 Insert the installation disk into the drive.

2 Click **Have Disk**. Then press the **Enter** key.

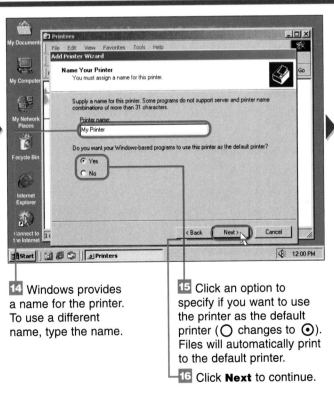

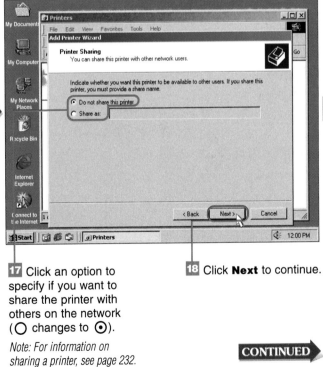

14 Windows provides a name for the printer. To use a different name, type the name.

15 Click an option to specify if you want to use the printer as the default printer (○ changes to ●). Files will automatically print to the default printer.

16 Click **Next** to continue.

17 Click an option to specify if you want to share the printer with others on the network (○ changes to ●).

Note: For information on sharing a printer, see page 232.

18 Click **Next** to continue.

CONTINUED

INSTALL A PRINTER

Windows allows you to print a test page to confirm that your printer is installed properly.

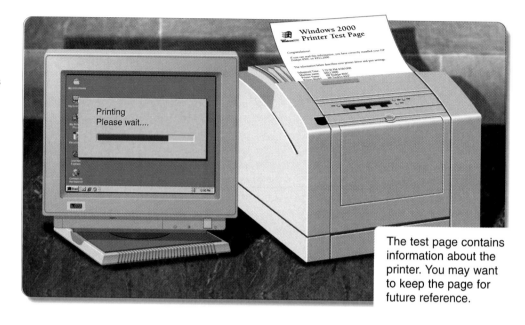

The test page contains information about the printer. You may want to keep the page for future reference.

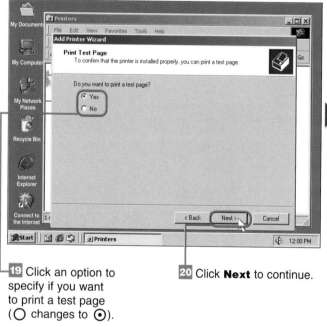

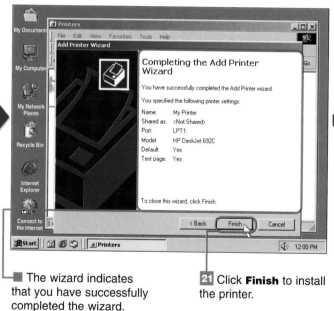

19 Click an option to specify if you want to print a test page (○ changes to ⊙).

20 Click **Next** to continue.

■ The wizard indicates that you have successfully completed the wizard.

21 Click **Finish** to install the printer.

206

? Can I delete a printer?

If you no longer use a printer, you can delete the printer and disconnect the printer from your computer. You can delete a printer from the Printers window as you would delete a file on your computer. For information on deleting a file, see page 94.

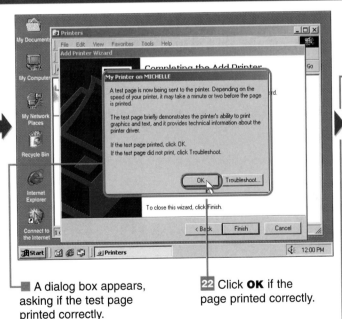

■ A dialog box appears, asking if the test page printed correctly.

*Note: This dialog box does not appear if you selected **No** in step 19.*

22 Click **OK** if the page printed correctly.

■ An icon for the printer appears in the Printers window.

■ The printer displays a check mark (●) if you chose to make the printer the default printer in step **15**.

23 Click ☒ to close the Printers window.

INSTALL NEW HARDWARE

You can have Windows detect and install new hardware for you. You can add hardware such as a modem, mouse or keyboard.

Installing Modem

You must be logged on to your computer or network as an administrator to install new hardware. See page 20 to log on to a computer or network.

INSTALL NEW HARDWARE

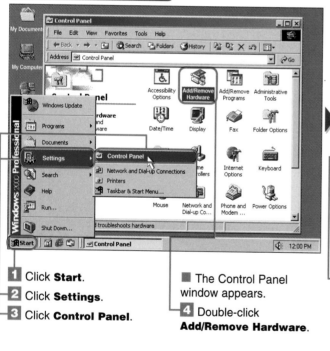

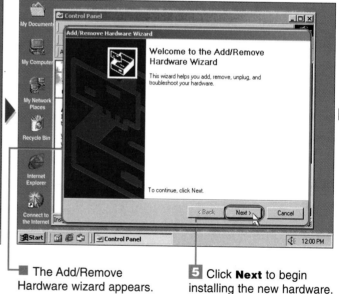

■ Click **Start**.

■ Click **Settings**.

■ Click **Control Panel**.

■ The Control Panel window appears.

■ Double-click **Add/Remove Hardware**.

■ The Add/Remove Hardware wizard appears.

■ Click **Next** to begin installing the new hardware.

Note: The steps you follow in the wizard may depend on the type of hardware device you are installing.

What are Plug and Play devices?

Plug and Play devices are devices that Windows can automatically set up to work properly with your computer, which makes them easy to install. Windows may automatically install a Plug and Play device for you the first time you turn on your computer after connecting the device to the computer.

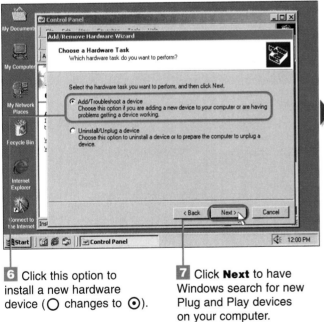

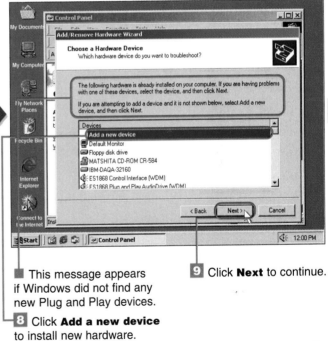

6 Click this option to install a new hardware device (○ changes to ⊙).

7 Click **Next** to have Windows search for new Plug and Play devices on your computer.

■ This message appears if Windows did not find any new Plug and Play devices.

8 Click **Add a new device** to install new hardware.

9 Click **Next** to continue.

CONTINUED

INSTALL NEW HARDWARE

The wizard guides you
step by step through
the installation, first
detecting the hardware
and then installing the
software needed by
the hardware.

INSTALL NEW HARDWARE (CONTINUED)

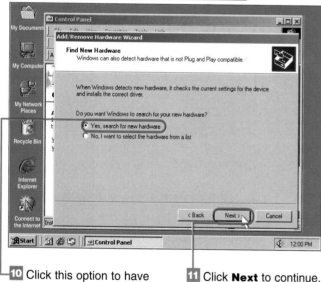

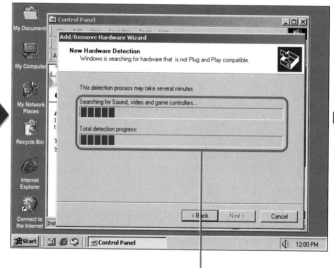

10 Click this option to have
Windows search for new
devices on your computer
that are not Plug and Play
(○ changes to ⊙).

11 Click **Next** to continue.

■ Windows searches for
devices that are not Plug
and Play.

■ This area displays the
progress of the search.
The search may take
several minutes.

*Note: You can click **Cancel** to
stop the search at any time.*

Why didn't my hardware device install properly?

The device you installed may not work properly with Windows 2000. To ensure your new hardware device will work with Windows 2000, check the documentation that came with the device or check Microsoft's Hardware Compatibility List. You can find the Hardware Compatibility List on the World Wide Web at:

www.microsoft.com/hcl

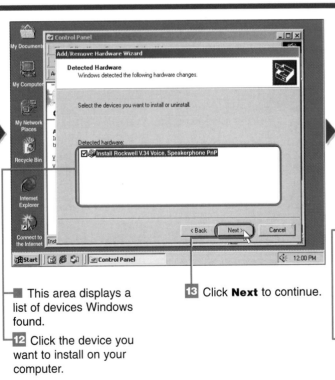

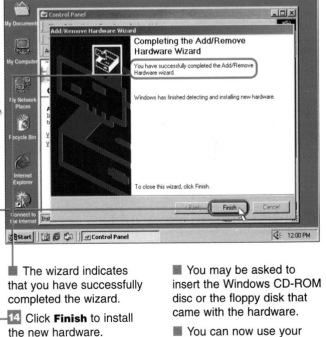

■ This area displays a list of devices Windows found.

12 Click the device you want to install on your computer.

13 Click **Next** to continue.

■ The wizard indicates that you have successfully completed the wizard.

14 Click **Finish** to install the new hardware.

■ You may be asked to insert the Windows CD-ROM disc or the floppy disk that came with the hardware.

■ You can now use your new hardware.

CHAPTER 9

Work With Faxes

Windows allows you to send faxes to family, friends and colleagues. Read this chapter to find out how to send, receive and view faxes using your computer.

USER INFORMAT

Your full name:

Fax number:

E-mail address:

Title:

Office location:

Home phone:

Address:

Company:

Departm

SEND A FAX

You can easily send a fax to a colleague across the city or around the world.

You can use the Send Fax wizard to fax a message on a cover page.

You must have a fax modem installed on your computer to send and receive faxes.

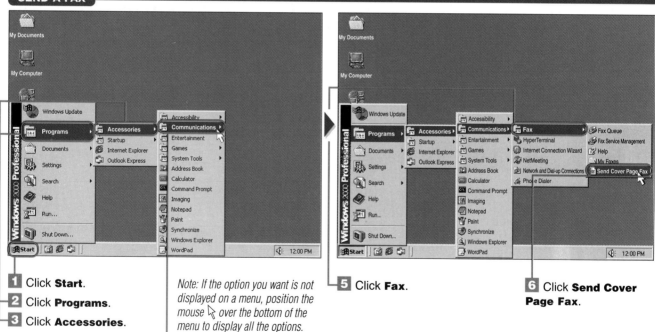

1 Click **Start**.

2 Click **Programs**.

3 Click **Accessories**.

Note: If the option you want is not displayed on a menu, position the mouse ⍊ over the bottom of the menu to display all the options.

4 Click **Communications**.

5 Click **Fax**.

6 Click **Send Cover Page Fax**.

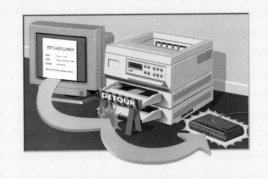

How can I fax a document I created on my computer?

Most programs allow you to use the program's Print feature to fax a document. For example, if you create a document in Microsoft Word, you can use Word's Print feature to fax the document.

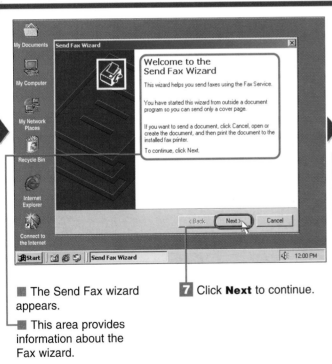

■ The Send Fax wizard appears.

■ This area provides information about the Fax wizard.

7 Click **Next** to continue.

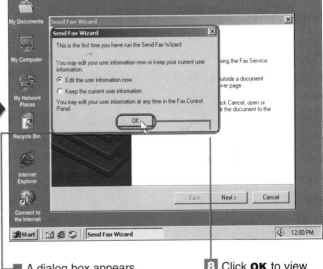

■ A dialog box appears the first time you use the Send Fax wizard, asking if you want to change your user information.

8 Click **OK** to view and change your user information.

CONTINUED

SEND A FAX

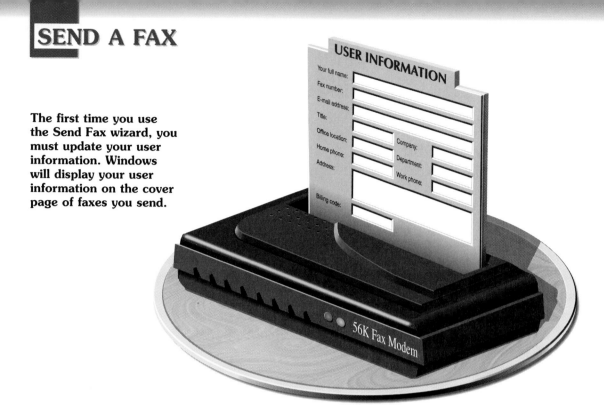

The first time you use the Send Fax wizard, you must update your user information. Windows will display your user information on the cover page of faxes you send.

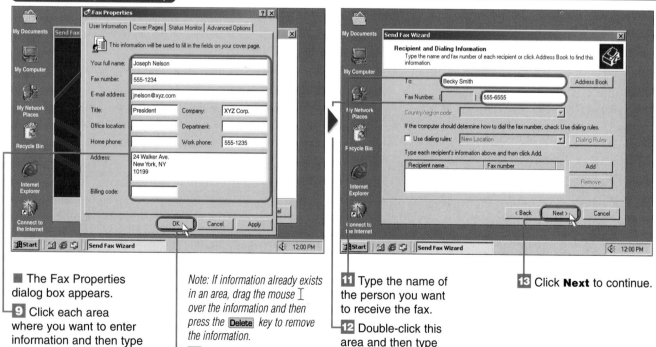

■ The Fax Properties dialog box appears.

9 Click each area where you want to enter information and then type the appropriate information.

Note: If information already exists in an area, drag the mouse I over the information and then press the Delete key to remove the information.

10 Click **OK** to confirm your changes.

11 Type the name of the person you want to receive the fax.

12 Double-click this area and then type the fax number.

13 Click **Next** to continue.

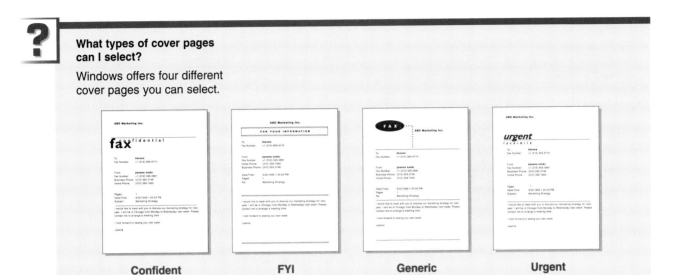

What types of cover pages can I select?

Windows offers four different cover pages you can select.

Confident   FYI   Generic   Urgent

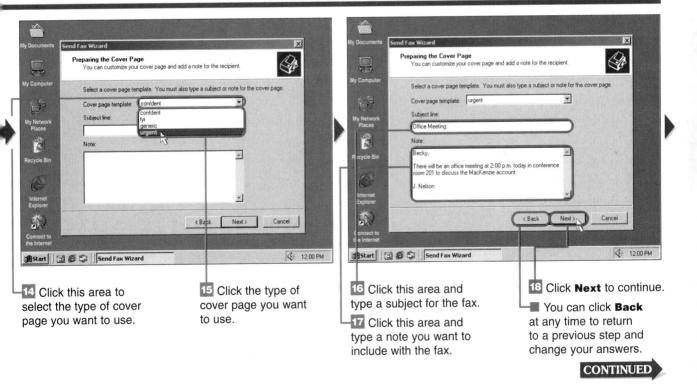

14 Click this area to select the type of cover page you want to use.

15 Click the type of cover page you want to use.

16 Click this area and type a subject for the fax.

17 Click this area and type a note you want to include with the fax.

18 Click **Next** to continue.

■ You can click **Back** at any time to return to a previous step and change your answers.

CONTINUED

SEND A FAX

You can choose when you want to send your fax. You can send the fax immediately, when long-distance rates are lower or at a time you specify.

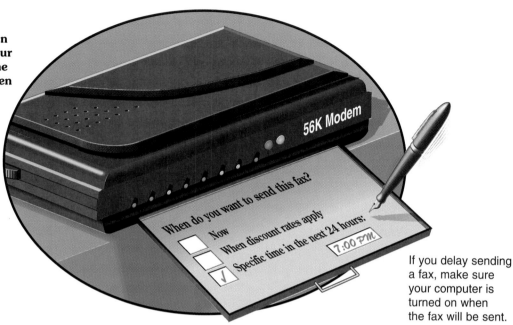

If you delay sending a fax, make sure your computer is turned on when the fax will be sent.

SEND A FAX (CONTINUED)

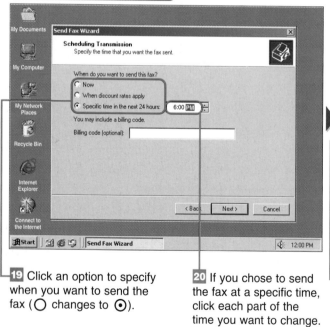

19 Click an option to specify when you want to send the fax (○ changes to ⊙).

20 If you chose to send the fax at a specific time, click each part of the time you want to change. Then type the correct information.

21 To include a billing code, click this area and type the code.

22 Click **Next** to continue.

Why would I include a billing code with a fax I send?

A billing code helps you keep track of the faxes you send and allows you to assign the costs to a specific account. This is useful if you frequently send faxes.

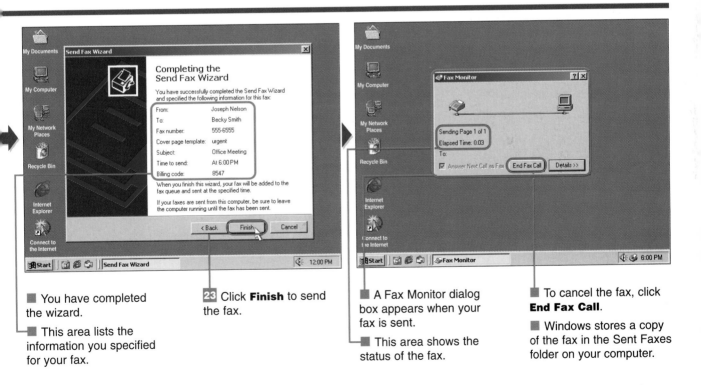

■ You have completed the wizard.

■ This area lists the information you specified for your fax.

23 Click **Finish** to send the fax.

■ A Fax Monitor dialog box appears when your fax is sent.

■ This area shows the status of the fax.

■ To cancel the fax, click **End Fax Call**.

■ Windows stores a copy of the fax in the Sent Faxes folder on your computer.

SET FAX MODEM TO RECEIVE FAXES

Before you can receive faxes on your computer, you must set up your fax modem.

Receive Faxes

You must be logged on to your computer or network as an administrator to set a fax modem to receive faxes. See page 20 to log on to a computer or network.

SET FAX MODEM TO RECEIVE FAXES

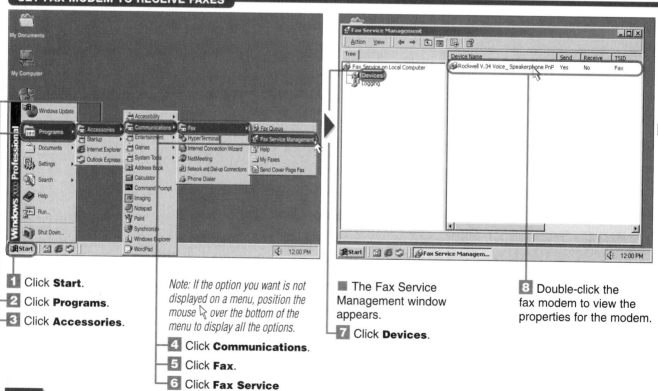

1 Click **Start**.

2 Click **Programs**.

3 Click **Accessories**.

Note: If the option you want is not displayed on a menu, position the mouse ⸻ over the bottom of the menu to display all the options.

4 Click **Communications**.

5 Click **Fax**.

6 Click **Fax Service Management**.

■ The Fax Service Management window appears.

7 Click **Devices**.

8 Double-click the fax modem to view the properties for the modem.

220

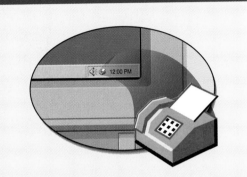

How will I know when I receive a fax?

Your fax modem will automatically answer the fax and the fax will transfer to your computer. The Fax Monitor icon (🖨) will appear at the bottom right corner of your screen to indicate that you received a fax. To view a fax, see page 222.

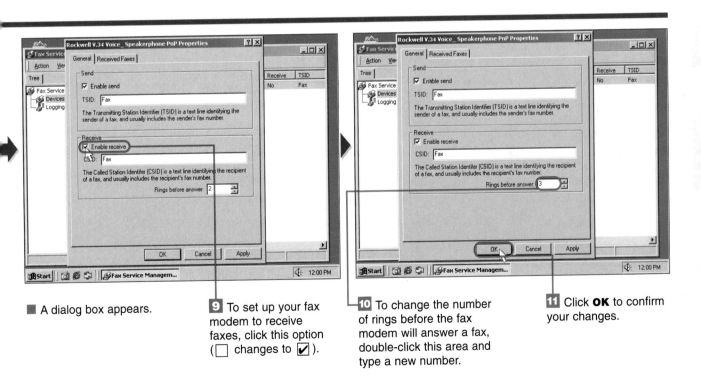

■ A dialog box appears.

9 To set up your fax modem to receive faxes, click this option (☐ changes to ☑).

10 To change the number of rings before the fax modem will answer a fax, double-click this area and type a new number.

11 Click **OK** to confirm your changes.

VIEW FAXES

You can display faxes you have sent and faxes you have received.

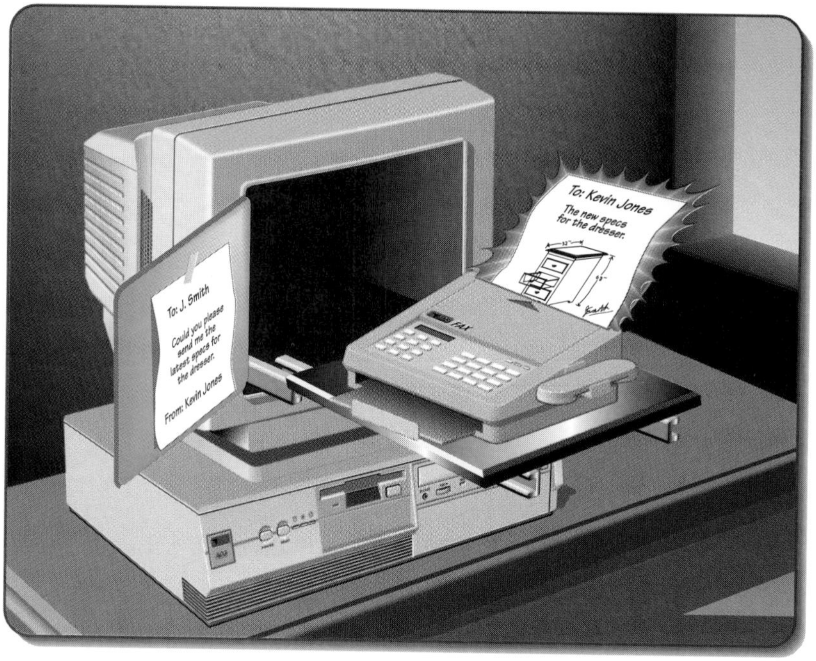

VIEW FAXES

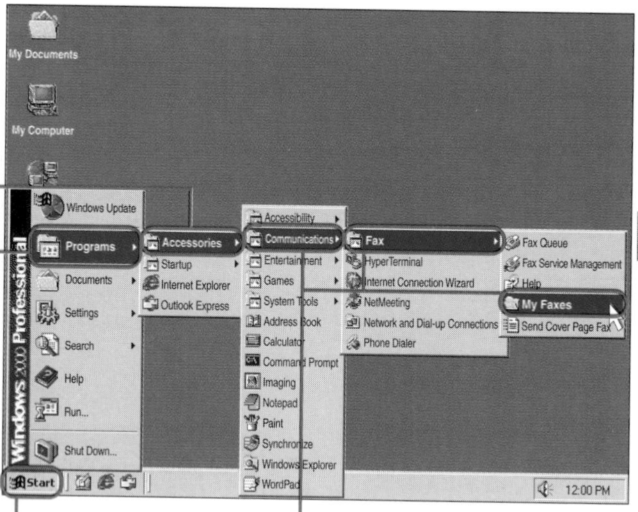

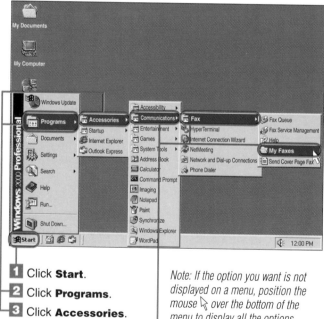

1 Click **Start**.

2 Click **Programs**.

3 Click **Accessories**.

Note: If the option you want is not displayed on a menu, position the mouse over the bottom of the menu to display all the options.

4 Click **Communications**.

5 Click **Fax**.

6 Click **My Faxes**.

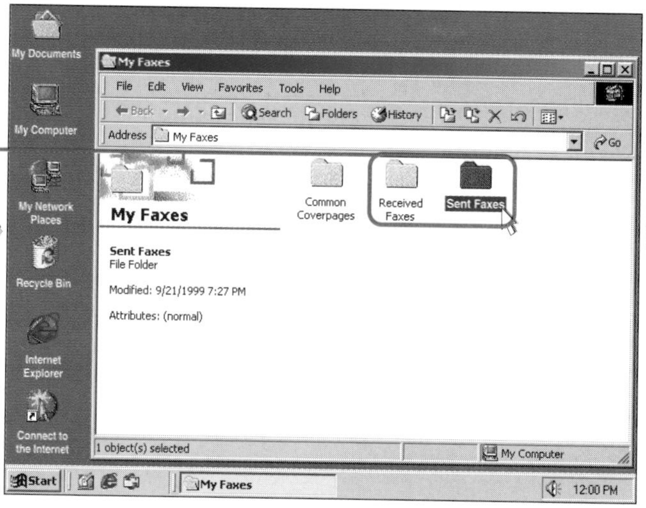

■ The My Faxes window appears.

7 Double-click the folder that contains the faxes you want to view.

Note: The Received Faxes folder stores faxes you have received. The Sent Faxes folder stores faxes you have sent.

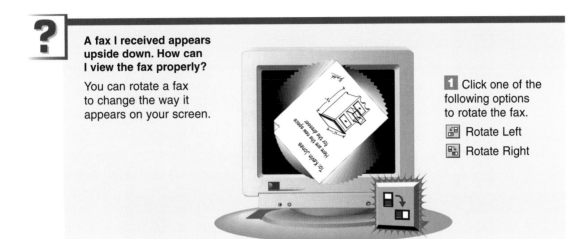

A fax I received appears upside down. How can I view the fax properly?

You can rotate a fax to change the way it appears on your screen.

1 Click one of the following options to rotate the fax.

▢ Rotate Left

▢ Rotate Right

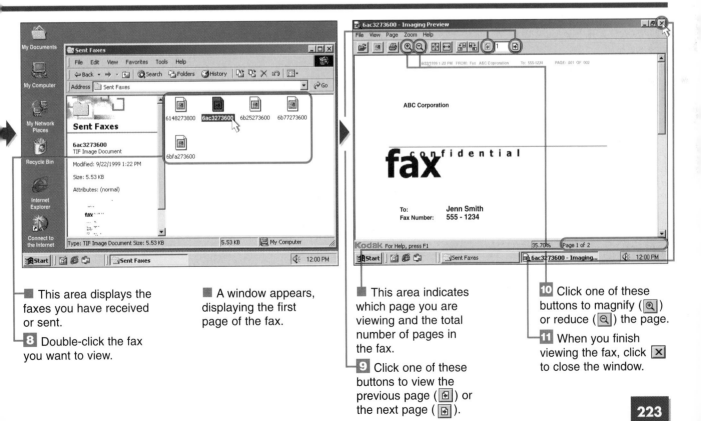

■ This area displays the faxes you have received or sent.

8 Double-click the fax you want to view.

■ A window appears, displaying the first page of the fax.

■ This area indicates which page you are viewing and the total number of pages in the fax.

9 Click one of these buttons to view the previous page (▢) or the next page (▢).

10 Click one of these buttons to magnify (▢) or reduce (▢) the page.

11 When you finish viewing the fax, click ▢ to close the window.

CHAPTER 10

Work on a Network

A network is a group of connected computers that share equipment and information. This chapter teaches you how to browse through a network, share printers and folders and more.

SHARE A FOLDER

You can specify what information on your computer you want to share with individuals on a network.

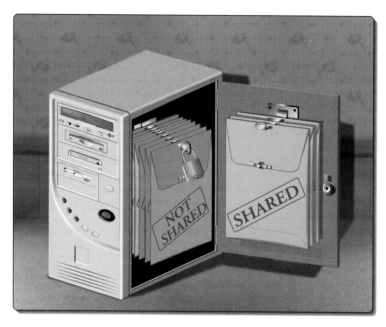

Sharing information is useful if you and your colleagues are working together on a project and need to access the same files.

You must be logged on to your computer or network as an administrator to share a folder. See page 20 to log on to a computer or network.

SHARE A FOLDER

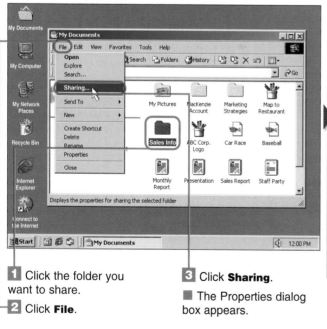

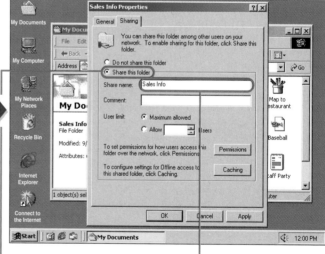

1 Click the folder you want to share.

2 Click **File**.

3 Click **Sharing**.

■ The Properties dialog box appears.

4 Click **Share this folder** to share the folder with others on the network (○ changes to ⊙).

5 This area displays the name of the folder individuals will see on the network. To change the name, drag the mouse I over the text until the text is highlighted. Then type a new name.

? How can I access folders shared by other people on the network?

You can use My Network Places to see a list of the folders shared by your computer and other computers on the network. See page 240 to use My Network Places.

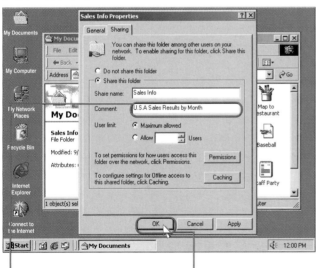

6 To enter a comment about the folder that individuals can see on the network, click this area and then type a comment.

7 Click **OK** to confirm your changes.

■ A hand (👉) appears under the icon for the shared folder. Individuals on the network will have access to all the folders and files within the shared folder.

Note: To specify how people on the network can access the folder, see page 228.

■ To stop sharing a folder, repeat steps **1** to **4**, selecting **Do not share this folder** in step **4**. Then perform step **7**.

CHANGE PERMISSIONS FOR A SHARED FOLDER

You can grant people, computers and groups on the network different types of access to a shared folder on your computer.

By default, everyone on the network has Full Control access to a shared folder on your computer.

You must be logged on to your computer or network as an administrator to change permissions for a shared folder. See page 20 to log on to a computer or network.

CHANGE PERMISSIONS FOR A SHARED FOLDER

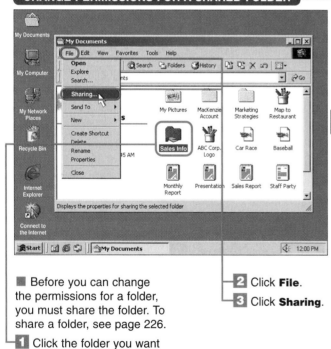

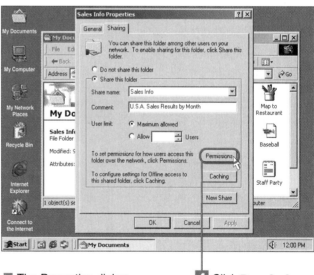

■ Before you can change the permissions for a folder, you must share the folder. To share a folder, see page 226.

1 Click the folder you want to change the permissions for.

2 Click **File**.

3 Click **Sharing**.

■ The Properties dialog box appears.

4 Click **Permissions** to specify how people can access the folder over the network.

What types of access can I allow or deny for a shared folder on my computer?

Full Control

Users can open, change, create, move and delete files in the folder. Users may also be able to administer files.

Change

Users can open, change, create, move and delete files in the folder.

Read

Users can open but not change files in the folder.

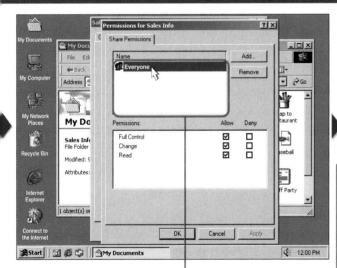

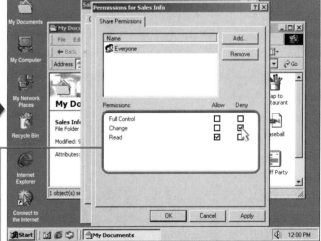

■ The Permissions dialog box appears.

■ This area lists each person, computer and group that can access the folder.

5 Click a person, computer or group to view their permissions.

■ This area displays the permissions granted to the person, computer or group. You can allow or deny permissions for Full Control, Change and Read access.

6 Click an option to allow or deny the permission.

Note: If more than one person, computer or group appears in the list, repeat steps 5 and 6 for each person, computer or group.

CONTINUED

CHANGE PERMISSIONS FOR A SHARED FOLDER

You can limit access to a shared folder on your computer by selecting which people, computers and groups on the network you want to have access to the folder.

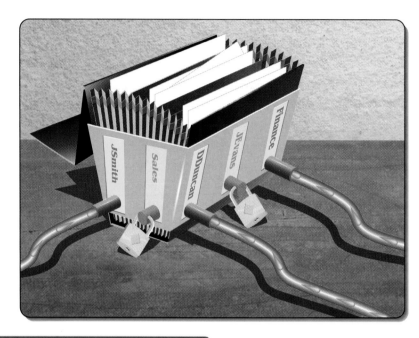

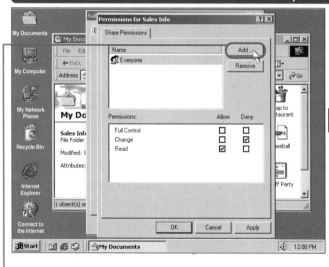

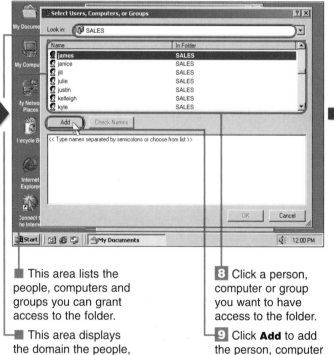

ADD A PERSON, COMPUTER OR GROUP

◾7 To add a person, computer or group to the list, click **Add**.

◾ The Select Users, Computers, or Groups dialog box appears.

◾ This area lists the people, computers and groups you can grant access to the folder.

◾ This area displays the domain the people, computers and groups in the list belong to.

◾8 Click a person, computer or group you want to have access to the folder.

◾9 Click **Add** to add the person, computer or group.

? **How can I remove a person, computer or group from the Permissions dialog box?**

If you no longer want a person, computer or group listed in the Permissions dialog box, click the person, computer or group you want to remove. Then press the Delete key.

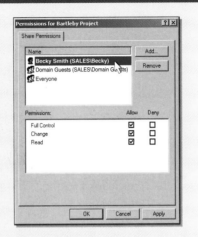

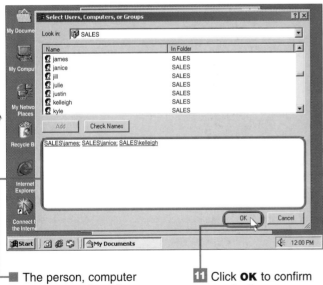

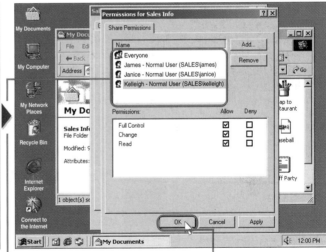

■ The person, computer or group you selected appears in this area.

10 Repeat steps **8** and **9** for each person, computer or group you want to have access to the folder.

11 Click **OK** to confirm your selections.

■ The people, computers and groups you selected appear in this area.

■ To assign permissions to a person, computer or group, perform steps **5** and **6** on page 229.

12 Click **OK** to confirm your changes.

Note: If you chose to deny permission in step **6**, a confirmation dialog box may appear. Click **Yes** to close the dialog box.

SHARE A PRINTER

You can share your printer with other individuals on a network. This allows others to use your printer to print documents.

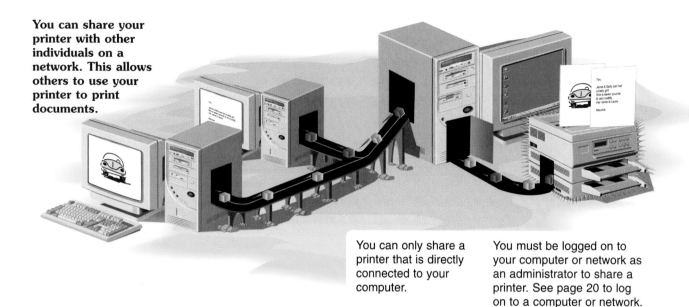

You can only share a printer that is directly connected to your computer.

You must be logged on to your computer or network as an administrator to share a printer. See page 20 to log on to a computer or network.

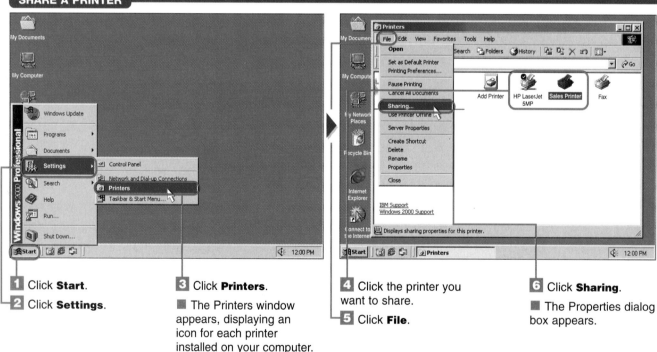

1 Click **Start**.

2 Click **Settings**.

3 Click **Printers**.

■ The Printers window appears, displaying an icon for each printer installed on your computer.

4 Click the printer you want to share.

5 Click **File**.

6 Click **Sharing**.

■ The Properties dialog box appears.

Will sharing a printer affect my computer's performance?

When individuals on the network send files to your printer, your computer temporarily stores the files before sending them to the printer. As a result, your computer will operate more slowly while other people use your printer.

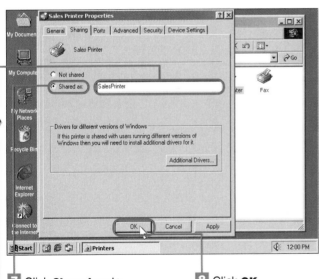

7 Click **Shared as** to share the printer with other people on the network (○ changes to ⊙).

■ This area displays the name of the printer people will see on the network. To change the name, type a new name.

8 Click **OK**.

*Note: A dialog box appears if you typed a printer name that contains spaces or more than 12 characters. Click **Yes** to use the printer name.*

■ A hand (☜) appears under the icon for the printer you have shared, indicating that the printer is available to others on the network.

Note: To specify the type of access people have to the printer, see page 234.

■ To stop sharing a printer, repeat steps **1** to **8**, selecting **Not shared** in step **7**.

CHANGE PERMISSIONS FOR A SHARED PRINTER

You can grant people, computers and groups on the network different types of access to a printer you have shared.

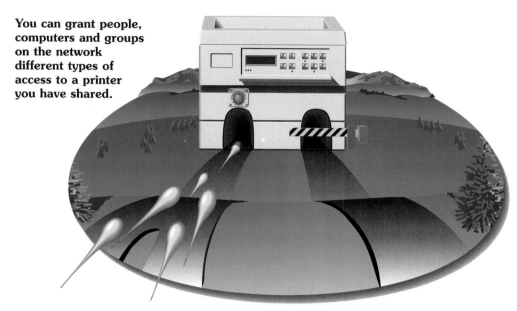

By default, everyone on the network has permission to print documents on the shared printer.

You must be logged on to your computer or network as an administrator to change permissions for a shared printer. See page 20 to log on to a computer or network.

CHANGE PERMISSIONS FOR A SHARED PRINTER

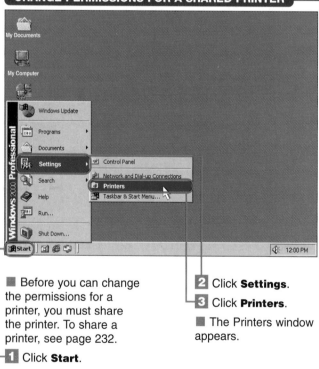

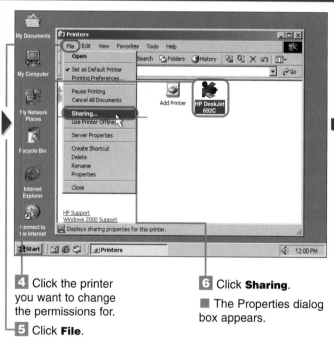

■ Before you can change the permissions for a printer, you must share the printer. To share a printer, see page 232.

1 Click **Start**.

2 Click **Settings**.

3 Click **Printers**.

■ The Printers window appears.

4 Click the printer you want to change the permissions for.

5 Click **File**.

6 Click **Sharing**.

■ The Properties dialog box appears.

What types of permissions can I allow or deny for a shared printer?

Print

Users can print and manage their own documents.

Manage Printers

Users have full control over the printer.

Manage Documents

Users can manage all documents waiting to print.

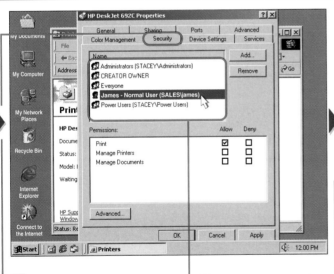

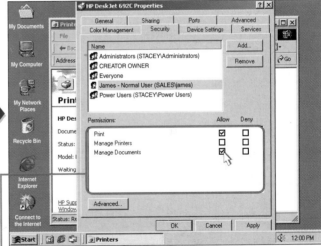

■ 7 Click the **Security** tab.

■ This area lists each person, computer and group that can access the printer.

■ 8 Click a person, computer or group to view their permissions.

■ This area displays the permissions granted to the person, computer or group. You can allow or deny permissions for Print, Manage Printers or Manage Documents.

■ 9 Click an option to allow or deny the permission.

Note: If more than one person, computer or group appears in the list, repeat steps 8 and 9 for each person, computer or group.

CONTINUED

CHANGE PERMISSIONS FOR A SHARED PRINTER

You can select which people, computers and groups on the network you want to have access to your shared printer.

CHANGE PERMISSIONS FOR A SHARED PRINTER (CONTINUED)

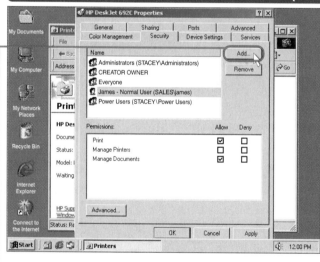

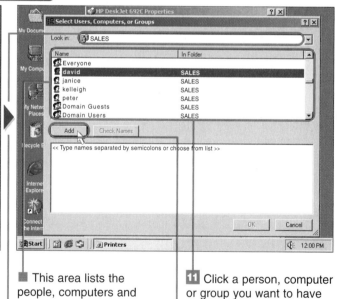

ADD A PERSON, COMPUTER OR GROUP

■10 To add a person, computer or group to the list, click **Add**.

■ The Select Users, Computers, or Groups dialog box appears.

■ This area lists the people, computers and groups you can grant access to the printer.

■ This area displays the domain the people, computers and groups in the list belong to.

■11 Click a person, computer or group you want to have access to the printer.

■12 Click **Add** to add the person, computer or group.

What groups can I allow or deny access to a shared printer?

Windows allows you to grant access to many groups on your computer or network.

Everyone

Every user is a member of this group.

Domain Guests

Users who can perform common tasks but do not have their own user name and password.

Domain Users

Users who can perform common tasks.

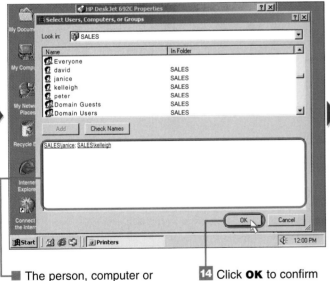

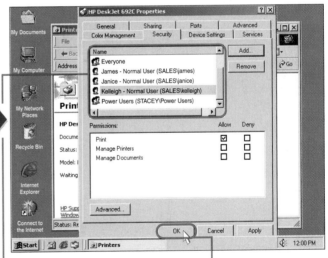

■ The person, computer or group you selected appears in this area.

13 Repeat steps **11** and **12** for each person, computer or group you want to have access to the printer.

14 Click **OK** to confirm your selections.

■ The people, computers and groups you selected appear in this area.

■ To assign permissions to a person, computer or group, perform steps **8** and **9** on page 235.

15 Click **OK** to confirm your changes.

Note: If you chose to deny permission in step **9**, a confirmation dialog box may appear. Click **Yes** to close the dialog box.

CHANGE THE DEFAULT PRINTER

If you have access to more than one printer, you can choose which printer you want to automatically print your documents.

CHANGE THE DEFAULT PRINTER

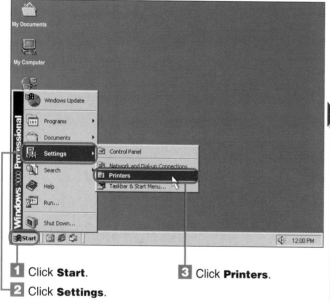

1 Click **Start**.

2 Click **Settings**.

3 Click **Printers**.

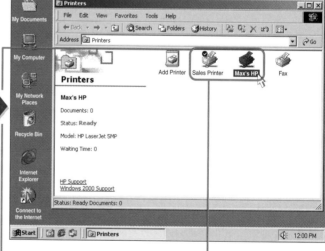

■ The Printers window appears. The window displays the printers you can use to print your documents.

■ The default printer displays a check mark (✓).

4 Click the printer you want to set as your new default printer.

Which printer should I select as my default printer?

When selecting a default printer, you should choose the printer you use most often. The printer you select should also be close to your desk and offer the capabilities you need.

5 Click **File**.

6 Click **Set as Default Printer**.

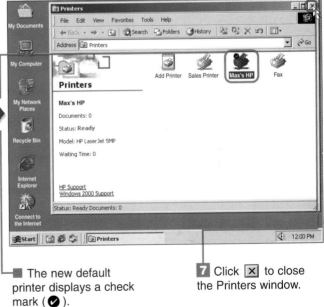

■ The new default printer displays a check mark (✓).

■ Your documents will automatically print to the new default printer.

7 Click ✕ to close the Printers window.

BROWSE THROUGH A NETWORK

You can easily browse through the resources, such as files and printers, available on your network.

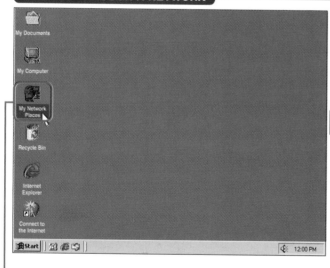

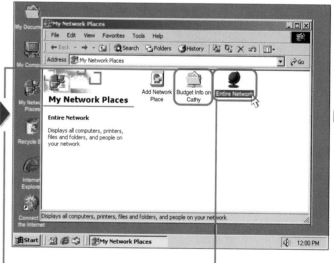

1 Double-click **My Network Places**.

■ The My Network Places window appears.

■ If you have previously worked with files in a shared folder on the network, the shared folder appears in the window. You can double-click the folder to quickly access the contents of the folder.

2 Double-click **Entire Network** to view all the computers and printers on your network.

What do the symbols in the My Network Places window represent?

Each item in the My Network Places window displays a symbol, or icon, to help you distinguish between the different types of items.

Network operating system	Domain	Computer	Folder	Printer

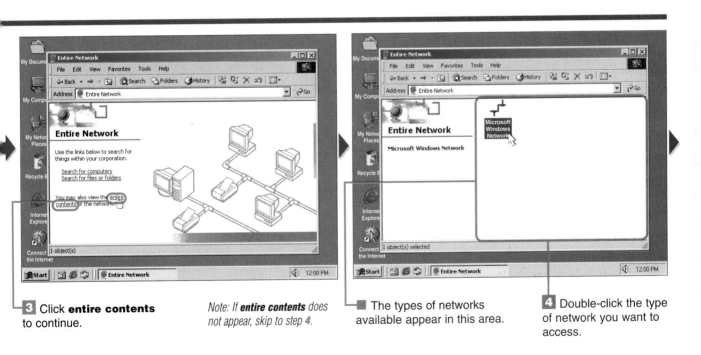

3 Click **entire contents** to continue.

*Note: If **entire contents** does not appear, skip to step 4.*

■ The types of networks available appear in this area.

4 Double-click the type of network you want to access.

CONTINUED

BROWSE THROUGH A NETWORK

You can choose the domain that contains the resources you want to access.

A domain is a collection of computers that are administered together.

BROWSE THROUGH A NETWORK (CONTINUED)

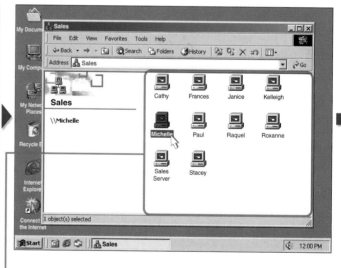

■ This area displays the domains on your network.

5 Double-click the domain containing the computers you want to access.

■ This area displays all the computers in the domain.

6 Double-click the computer containing the files you want to work with.

Note: A dialog box may appear, asking you to enter a user name and password. Contact your system administrator for more information.

? **Why does my My Network Places window look different than the window shown below?**

The items in your My Network Places window depend on the type of network you use and how the network is set up. There are two main types of networks. A client/server network allows people to store their files on a central computer, called a server. A peer-to-peer network allows people to store and share their files on their own computers.

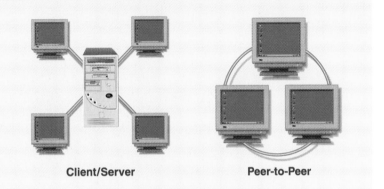

Client/Server   **Peer-to-Peer**

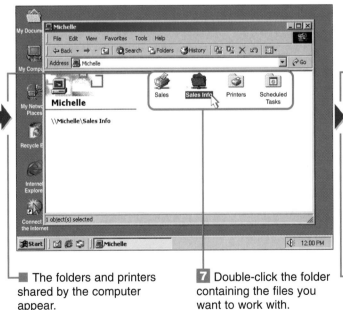

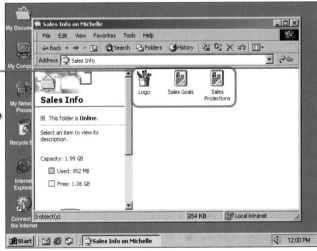

■ The folders and printers shared by the computer appear.

7 Double-click the folder containing the files you want to work with.

■ The contents of the folder appear.

■ You can work with the files and folders as if they were stored on your own computer.

Note: If Windows denies you access to the folder, you do not have permission to access the folder. See page 228 for information on changing permissions for shared folders.

WORK WITH FILES OFFLINE

You can work with files on the network while you are disconnected from the network. This is called working offline.

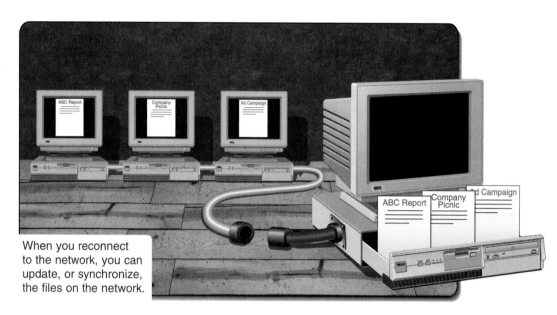

When you reconnect to the network, you can update, or synchronize, the files on the network.

MAKE A FILE AVAILABLE OFFLINE

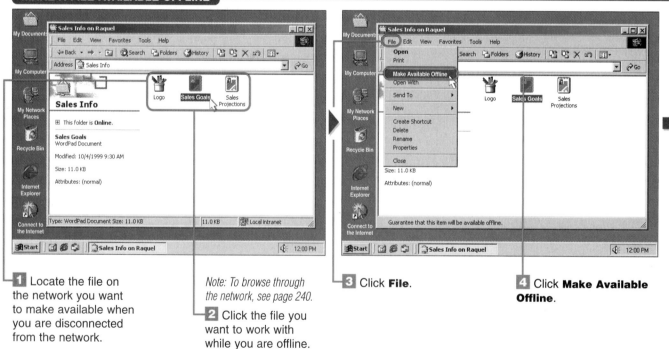

1 Locate the file on the network you want to make available when you are disconnected from the network.

Note: To browse through the network, see page 240.

2 Click the file you want to work with while you are offline.

3 Click **File**.

4 Click **Make Available Offline**.

? **Can I make a folder available offline?**

Yes. To make a folder available offline, perform the steps below, except click the folder in step **2**. When you make a folder available offline, Windows makes all the files in the folder available offline.

■ The first time you make a file available offline, the Offline Files Wizard appears. The wizard helps you set up the way you want to work with offline files.

5 Click **Next** to continue.

6 To have Windows automatically synchronize the files you make available offline when you log on and off your computer or network, click this option (□ changes to ☑).

7 Click **Next** to continue.

CONTINUED ▶

WORK WITH FILES OFFLINE

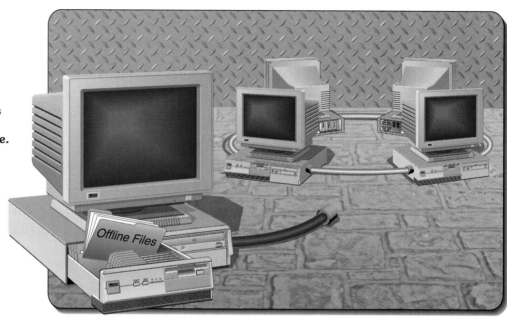

Windows stores files you make available offline in a folder on your computer. You can open the folder at any time to access the files you have made available offline.

Offline Files

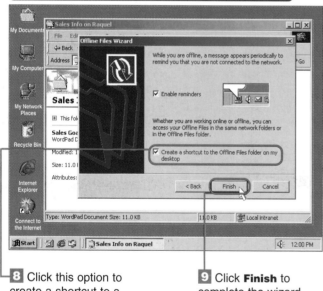

8 Click this option to create a shortcut to a folder that will store all the files you make available offline (☐ changes to ☑).

9 Click **Finish** to complete the wizard.

■ Windows copies the latest version of the file from the network to the folder on your computer.

■ A shortcut to the Offline Files folder appears on your desktop. Windows will store each file you make available offline in this folder.

■ You can repeat steps **1** to **4** on page 244 at any time to make another file available offline.

246

How can I ensure that I have the latest version of each file before I disconnect from the network?

You can synchronize the files you have made available offline at any time to have Windows copy the latest version of the file to your computer. To synchronize the files, see page 248.

WORK WITH FILES OFFLINE

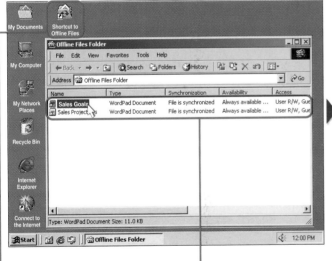

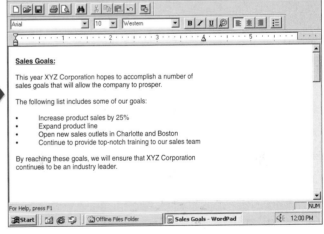

1 When you are disconnected from the network, double-click **Shortcut to Offline Files**.

■ The Offline Files Folder window appears, displaying a list of files you made available offline.

2 Double-click a file you want to work with.

■ Windows opens the file and displays it on your screen. You can now review and make changes to the file.

CONTINUED

WORK WITH FILES OFFLINE

When you reconnect
to the network,
you can update, or
synchronize, the files
you have changed.

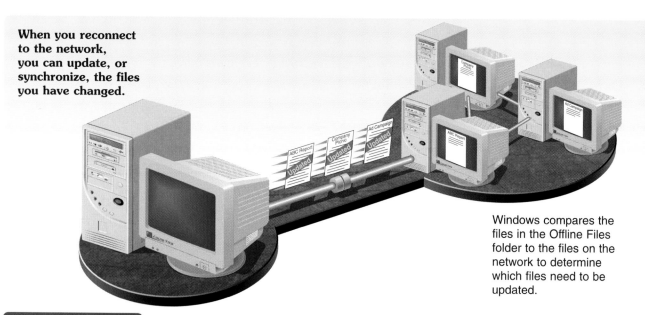

Windows compares the
files in the Offline Files
folder to the files on the
network to determine
which files need to be
updated.

SYNCHRONIZE ITEMS

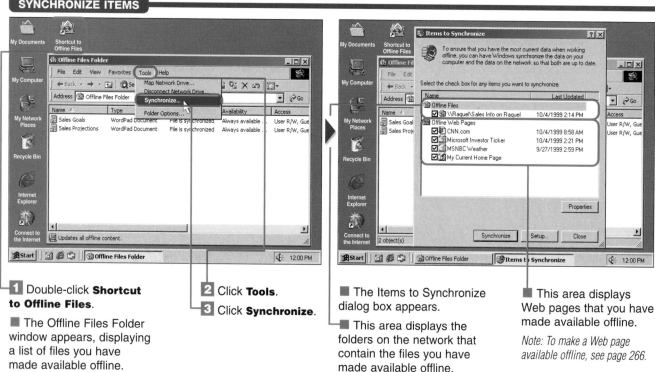

1 Double-click **Shortcut
to Offline Files**.

■ The Offline Files Folder
window appears, displaying
a list of files you have
made offline.

2 Click **Tools**.

3 Click **Synchronize**.

■ The Items to Synchronize
dialog box appears.

■ This area displays the
folders on the network that
contain the files you have
made available offline.

■ This area displays
Web pages that you have
made available offline.

*Note: To make a Web page
available offline, see page 266.*

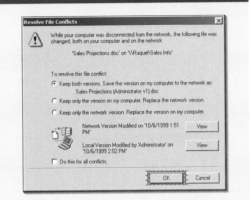

Why did this dialog box appear when I synchronized my files?

This dialog box appears if a file you changed offline was also changed by another person on the network. To save both versions of the file, click **OK**.

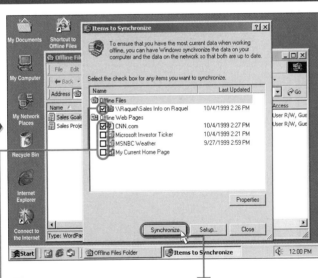

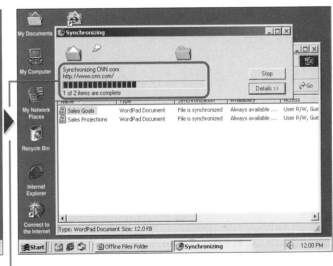

■ **4** Windows will synchronize each item that displays a check mark (☑). You can click the box (☐) beside an item to add or remove the check mark.

■ **5** Click **Synchronize** to update the items you selected.

■ The Synchronizing window appears.

■ This area displays the progress of the synchronization.

Note: If you are synchronizing a Web page and you are not connected to the Internet, a dialog box appears that allows you to connect.

■ The Synchronizing window disappears when the synchronization is complete.

CHAPTER 11

Browse the Web

You can use Windows to browse through information on the World Wide Web. Find out how to set up an Internet connection, display and move through Web pages and more.

INTRODUCTION TO THE WEB

The World Wide Web is part of the Internet, which is the largest computer system in the world. The Web consists of a huge collection of documents stored on hundreds of thousands of computers.

WEB PAGES

A Web page is a document on the Web. You can find Web pages on every subject imaginable. There are Web pages that offer information such as newspaper and magazine articles, movie clips, recipes, Shakespearean plays, airline schedules and more. You can also purchase items, do your banking and get programs and games on the Web.

WEB SITES

A Web site is a collection of Web pages maintained by a college, university, government agency, company or individual.

URLS

Each Web page has a unique address, called a Uniform Resource Locator (URL). You can display any Web page if you know its URL.

Most Web page URLs start with http (HyperText Transfer Protocol).

LINKS

Web pages contain highlighted text or images, called links, that connect to other pages on the Web. You can select a link on a Web page to display another page located on the same computer or a computer across the city, country or world.

Links allow you to easily move through a vast amount of information by jumping from one Web page to another. This is known as "browsing the Web."

CONNECTING TO THE INTERNET

Most people use an Internet Service Provider (ISP) to connect to the Internet. Once you pay your service provider to connect to the Internet, you can exchange information on the Internet free of charge.

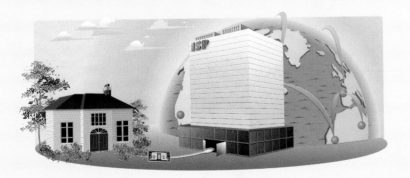

SET UP A CONNECTION TO THE INTERNET

You can use the Internet Connection wizard to set up your computer to use a connection to the Internet.

Internet Connection Wizard

Welcome to the Internet

You must be logged on to your computer or network as an administrator to use the Internet Connection wizard. See page 20 to log on to a computer or network.

SET UP A CONNECTION TO THE INTERNET

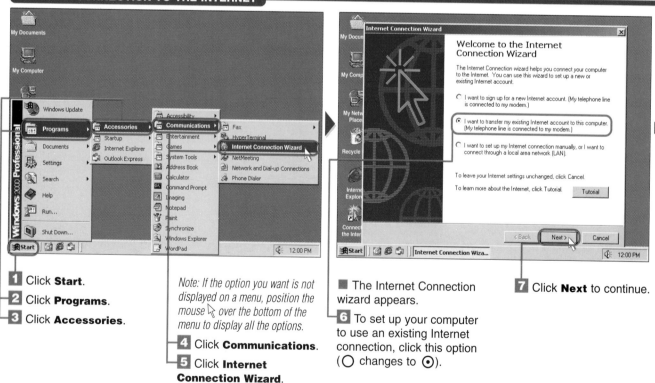

1 Click **Start**.

2 Click **Programs**.

3 Click **Accessories**.

Note: If the option you want is not displayed on a menu, position the mouse ⃗ over the bottom of the menu to display all the options.

4 Click **Communications**.

5 Click **Internet Connection Wizard**.

■ The Internet Connection wizard appears.

6 To set up your computer to use an existing Internet connection, click this option (○ changes to ⊙).

7 Click **Next** to continue.

Can I set up a connection to the Internet if I do not already have an account with an Internet service provider?

The Internet Connection wizard can help you find an Internet service provider in your area. Perform steps **1** to **6** below, except select **I want to sign up for a new Internet account** in step **6**. Then perform steps **7** to **10**, selecting an Internet service provider you want to use in step **8**.

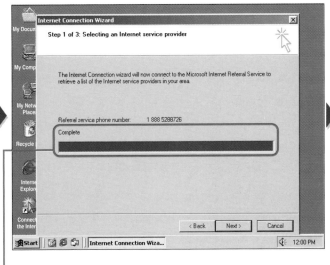

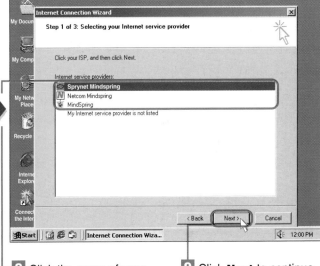

■ The wizard connects to the Microsoft Internet Referral Service to get a list of the Internet service providers available in your area.

■ This area displays the progress of the transfer of information to your computer.

■ When the transfer is complete, a list of Internet service providers in your area appears.

8 Click the name of your Internet service provider.

Note: If your service provider does not appear in the list, click **My Internet service provider is not listed**.

9 Click **Next** to continue.

10 Follow the instructions on your screen to finish setting up the computer to use the Internet connection.

START INTERNET EXPLORER

You can start
Internet Explorer
to browse through
the information
on the Web.

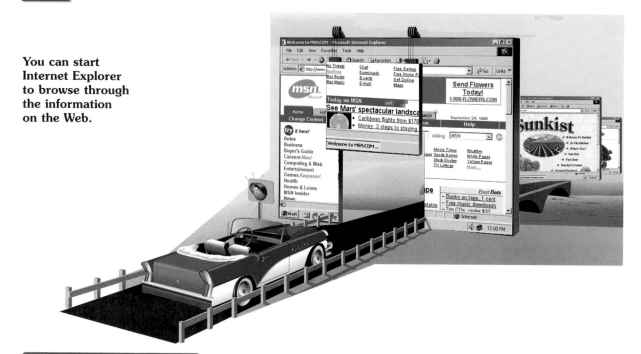

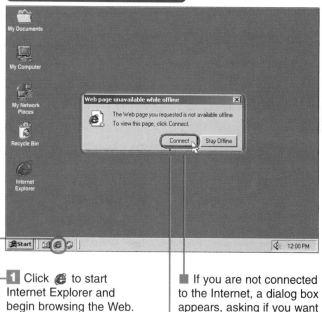

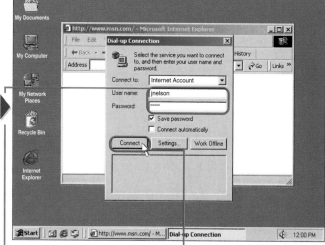

1 Click 🔵 to start
Internet Explorer and
begin browsing the Web.

*Note: If the Internet Connection
wizard appears, see page 254.*

■ If you are not connected
to the Internet, a dialog box
appears, asking if you want
to connect to the Internet.

2 To connect to the
Internet, click **Connect**.

■ The Dial-up Connection
dialog box appears.

■ This area displays your
user name and password.

*Note: A symbol (∗) appears for
each character in your password
to prevent others from viewing
the password.*

3 Click **Connect** to
connect to your Internet
service provider.

Why do the Web pages in this book look different from the Web pages displayed on my screen?

Companies frequently change their Web pages to make the pages more attractive or to add additional information. A Web page displayed on your screen may be a more recent version of the Web page shown in this book.

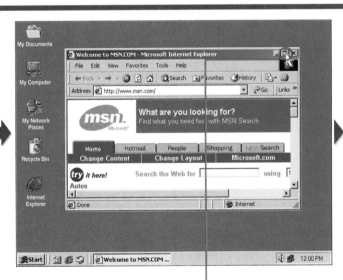

■ The Microsoft Internet Explorer window appears, displaying your home page.

4 Click ▢ to maximize the window to fill your screen.

■ The window maximizes to fill your screen.

DISPLAY A SPECIFIC WEB PAGE

You can easily display a page on the Web that you have heard or read about.

You need to know the address of the Web page you want to view. Each page on the Web has a unique address, called a Uniform Resource Locator (URL).

DISPLAY A SPECIFIC WEB PAGE

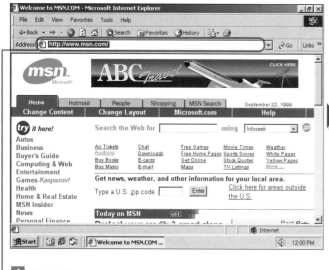

1 Click this area to highlight the current Web page address.

2 Type the address of the Web page you want to view and then press the Enter key.

*Note: You do not have to type **http://** when typing the Web page address.*

■ The Web page appears on your screen.

258

What are some popular Web pages that I can display?

Blue Mountain Arts	www.bluemountain.com
CBS SportsLine	www.sportsline.com
CNN	www.cnn.com
eBay	www.ebay.com
maranGraphics	www.maran.com
MSNBC	www.msnbc.com
MTV	www.mtv.com
NASA	www.nasa.gov
Sony	www.sony.com
Time.com	www.pathfinder.com

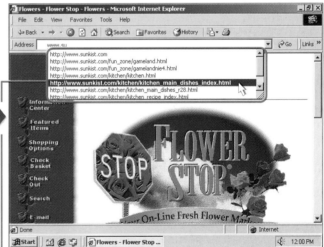

Internet Explorer remembers the addresses of Web pages you recently visited. You can select one of these addresses to quickly redisplay a Web page.

■ When you begin typing the address of a Web page you previously visited, a list of matching addresses appears.

■ You can also click ▼ to display the list of addresses at any time.

1 Click the address of the Web page you want to display.

■ The Web page appears on your screen.

SELECT A LINK

You can select a link on a Web page to display another page on the Web.

A link is highlighted text or an image on a Web page that will take you to another Web page.

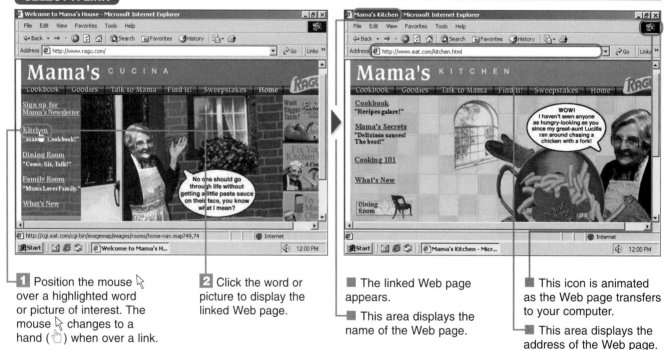

1 Position the mouse over a highlighted word or picture of interest. The mouse changes to a hand ( ) when over a link.

2 Click the word or picture to display the linked Web page.

■ The linked Web page appears.

■ This area displays the name of the Web page.

■ This icon is animated as the Web page transfers to your computer.

■ This area displays the address of the Web page.

You can refresh a Web page to update the displayed information, such as the current news. Internet Explorer will transfer a fresh copy of the Web page to your computer.

REFRESH A WEB PAGE

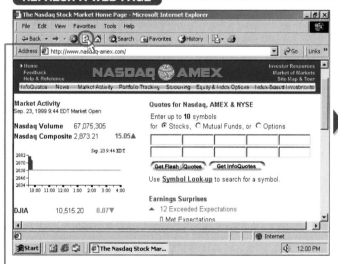

1 Click 🔄 to transfer a fresh copy of the displayed Web page to your computer.

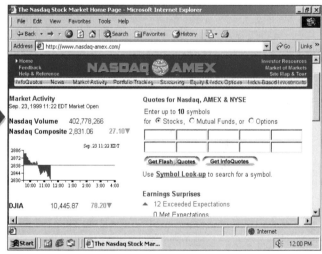

■ A fresh copy of the Web page appears on your screen.

STOP TRANSFER OF INFORMATION

If a Web page is taking a long time to appear on your screen, you can stop transferring the page and try connecting again later.

The best time to try connecting to a Web site is during off-peak hours, such as nights and weekends, when fewer people are using the Internet.

STOP TRANSFER OF INFORMATION

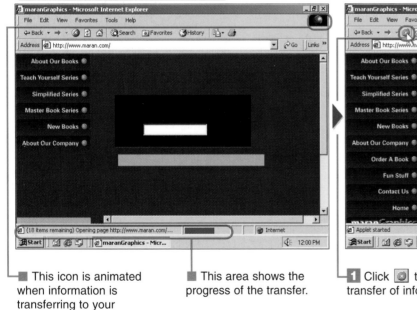

■ This icon is animated when information is transferring to your computer.

■ This area shows the progress of the transfer.

1 Click 🔘 to stop the transfer of information.

■ You may also want to stop the transfer of information if you realize a Web page is of no interest to you.

You can easily move back and forth through Web pages you have viewed since you last started Internet Explorer.

MOVE THROUGH WEB PAGES

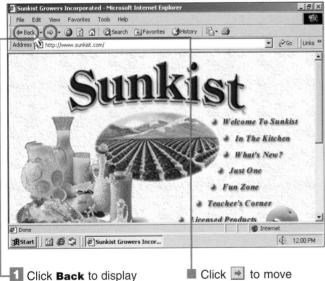

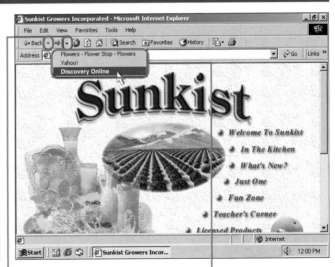

1 Click **Back** to display the last Web page you viewed.

■ Click → to move forward through the Web pages you have viewed.

You can display a list of the Web pages you have viewed.

1 Click ⬝ beside **Back** or → to display a list of Web pages you have viewed.

2 Click the Web page you want to view.

DISPLAY AND CHANGE YOUR HOME PAGE

You can specify which Web page you want to appear each time you start Internet Explorer. This page is called your home page.

DISPLAY AND CHANGE YOUR HOME PAGE

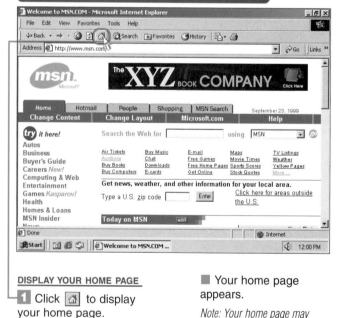

DISPLAY YOUR HOME PAGE

1 Click 🏠 to display your home page.

■ Your home page appears.

Note: Your home page may be different than the home page shown above.

CHANGE YOUR HOME PAGE

1 Display the Web page you want to set as your home page.

2 Click **Tools**.

3 Click **Internet Options**.

**Which Web page should
I use as my home page?**

You can choose any page
on the Web as your home
page. Your home page
can be a Web page you
frequently visit or a Web
page that provides a good
starting point for exploring
the Web.

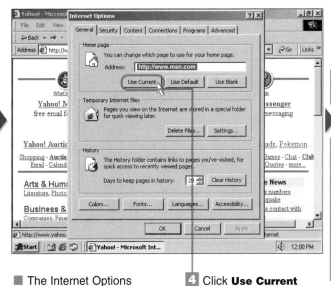

■ The Internet Options
dialog box appears.

4 Click **Use Current**
to set the Web page
displayed on your screen
as your new home page.

■ This area displays
the address of the new
home page.

5 Click **OK** to confirm
your change.

ADD A WEB PAGE TO FAVORITES

You can use the Favorites feature to create a list of Web pages you frequently visit. You can quickly return to any Web page in the list.

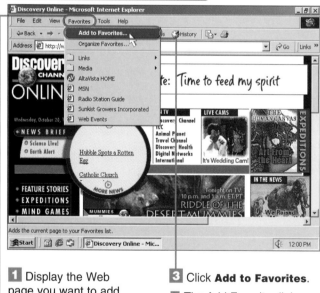

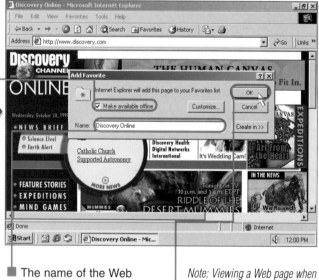

1 Display the Web page you want to add to your collection of favorite Web pages.

2 Click **Favorites**.

3 Click **Add to Favorites**.

■ The Add Favorite dialog box appears.

■ The name of the Web page appears in this area.

4 To be able to view the Web page when you are not connected to the Internet, click this option (☐ changes to ☑).

Note: Viewing a Web page when you are not connected to the Internet is called working offline. For information on working offline, see pages 244 to 249.

5 Click **OK** to add the Web page to your list of favorites.

?

What are the benefits of adding a Web page to my list of favorites?

Web page addresses can be long and complex. Selecting Web pages from your list of favorites saves you from having to remember and constantly retype the same addresses over and over.

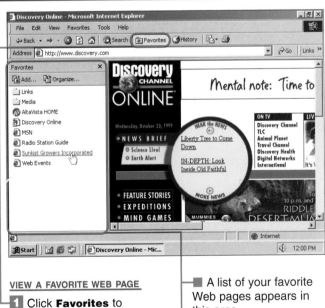

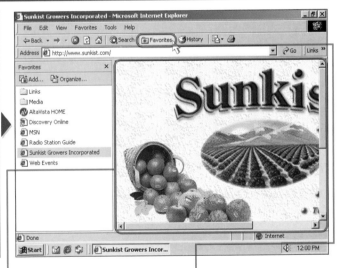

VIEW A FAVORITE WEB PAGE

1 Click **Favorites** to display a list of your favorite Web pages.

■ A list of your favorite Web pages appears in this area.

2 Click the favorite Web page you want to view.

Note: To display the favorite Web pages in a folder, click the folder ( ).

■ The favorite Web page you selected appears in this area.

■ You can repeat step **2** to view another favorite Web page.

3 When you finish viewing your list of favorite Web pages, click **Favorites** to hide the list.

DISPLAY HISTORY OF VIEWED WEB PAGES

Internet Explorer keeps track of the Web pages you have recently viewed. You can easily return to any of these pages.

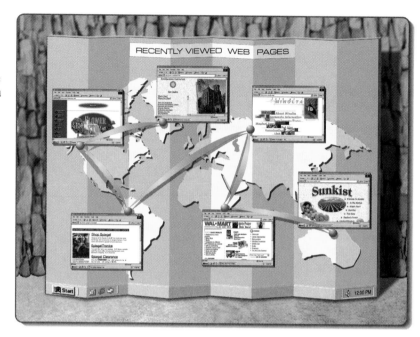

Internet Explorer keeps track of the Web pages you have viewed during the last 20 days.

DISPLAY HISTORY OF VIEWED WEB PAGES

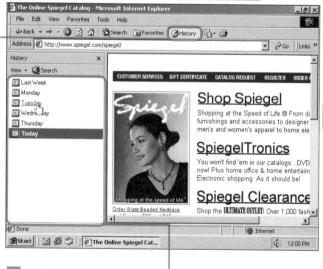

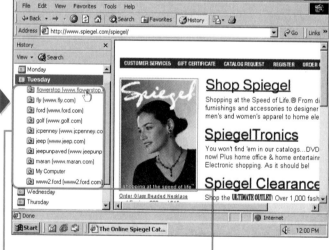

1 Click **History** to display a list of the Web pages you have recently viewed.

■ A history of Web pages you have recently viewed appears in this area.

2 Click the week or day you viewed the Web page you want to view again. The ▦ symbol appears beside each week and day.

■ The Web sites you viewed during the week or day appear. The 🔲 symbol appears beside each Web site.

3 Click the Web site of interest.

Why do folders on my computer and network appear in the History list?

The History list also keeps track of files you have viewed and worked with on your computer and the network. You can click a folder in the History list to view a list of files you have worked with. You can then click a file to display the file on your screen.

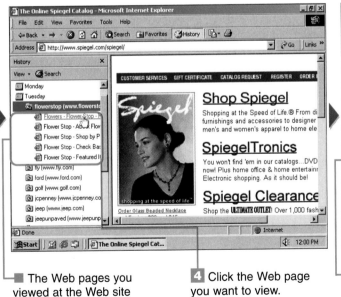

■ The Web pages you viewed at the Web site appear. The ⎙ symbol appears beside each Web page.

4 Click the Web page you want to view.

■ The Web page appears in this area.

■ You can repeat step **4** to view another Web page.

5 When you finish displaying recently viewed Web pages, click **History** to hide the list.

SEARCH THE WEB

You can find pages on the Web that discuss topics of interest to you.

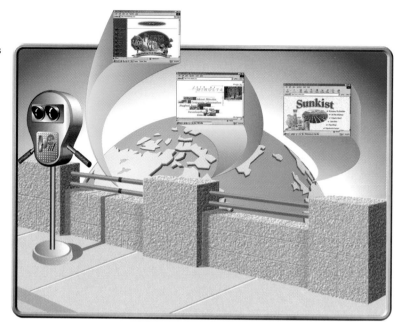

There are search tools available on the Web that catalog information about millions of Web pages. Popular search tools include Excite, Yahoo! and Lycos.

SEARCH THE WEB

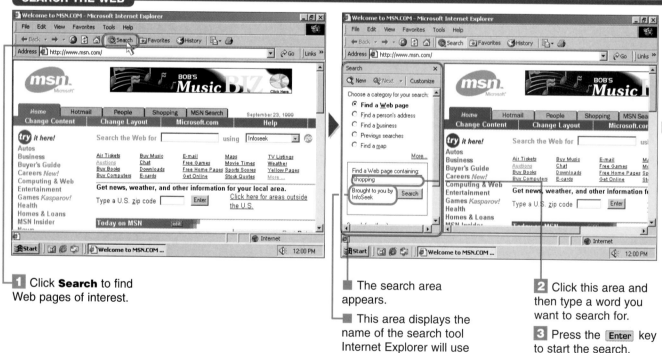

1 Click **Search** to find Web pages of interest.

■ The search area appears.

■ This area displays the name of the search tool Internet Explorer will use to search the Web.

2 Click this area and then type a word you want to search for.

3 Press the Enter key to start the search.

How do search tools find Web pages?

Some search tools use a program, called a robot, to scan the Web for new and updated pages. Thousands of new Web pages are located and cataloged by robots every day. New pages are also cataloged when people submit information about the pages they have created.

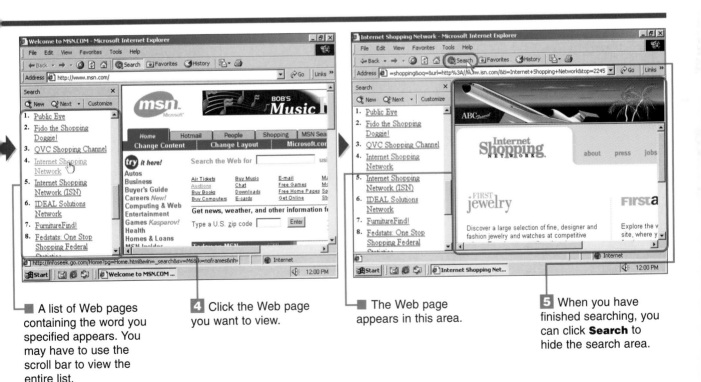

■ A list of Web pages containing the word you specified appears. You may have to use the scroll bar to view the entire list.

4 Click the Web page you want to view.

■ The Web page appears in this area.

5 When you have finished searching, you can click **Search** to hide the search area.

CHAPTER 12

Exchange Electronic Mail

You can exchange electronic mail with people around the world. In this chapter you will learn how to send and work with e-mail messages.

START OUTLOOK EXPRESS

You can start Outlook
Express to exchange
electronic mail (e-mail)
messages with people
around the world.

E-mail provides a
fast, economical and
convenient way to
send messages to
family, friends and
colleagues.

START OUTLOOK EXPRESS

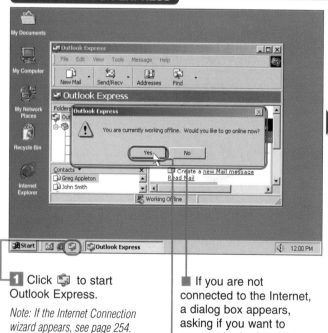

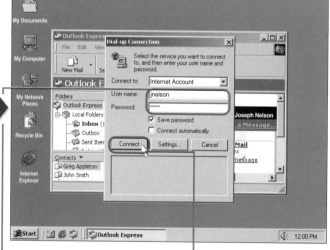

1 Click 🖼 to start
Outlook Express.

*Note: If the Internet Connection
wizard appears, see page 254.*

■ If you are not
connected to the Internet,
a dialog box appears,
asking if you want to
connect to the Internet.

2 To connect to the
Internet, click **Yes**.

■ The Dial-up Connection
dialog box appears.

■ This area displays your
user name and password.

*Note: A symbol (ˣ) appears
for each character in your
password to prevent others
from viewing the password.*

3 Click **Connect** to
connect to your Internet
service provider.

Can I use Outlook Express to e-mail famous people?

You can send a message to anyone around the world if you know the person's e-mail address. Here are the e-mail addresses of some famous people.

NAME	ADDRESS
Bill Gates	askbill@microsoft.com
Brad Pitt	CIAOBOX@MSN.com
James Woods	jameswoods@aol.com
President	president@whitehouse.gov
Tom Brokaw	nightly@nbc.com

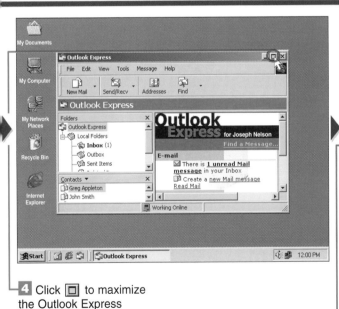

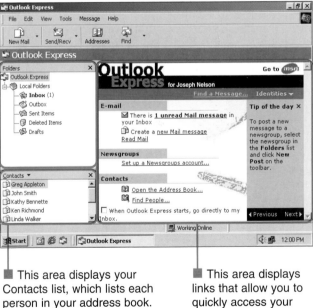

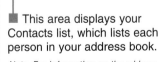

4 Click ⬜ to maximize the Outlook Express window to fill your screen.

■ This area displays your Contacts list, which lists each person in your address book.

Note: For information on the address book, see page 280.

■ This area displays the folders that contain your messages.

■ This area displays links that allow you to quickly access your messages and contacts.

READ MESSAGES

You can easily open
your messages to
read their contents.

Chris,

The drafts for the advertising
campaign are ready. Will you
be free at 2:00 p.m. tomorrow
to discuss them?

Henry

READ MESSAGES

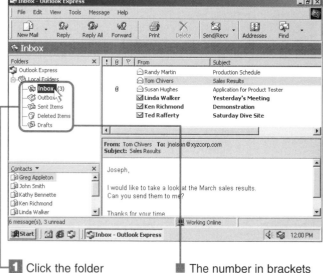

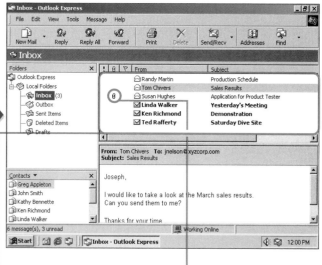

1 Click the folder
containing the messages
you want to read. The
folder is highlighted.

■ The number in brackets
beside the folder indicates
how many unread messages
the folder contains. The
number disappears when
you have read all the
messages in the folder.

■ This area displays the
messages in the highlighted
folder. Messages you have
not read display a closed
envelope (✉) and appear
in **bold** type.

■ A paper clip icon (📎)
appears beside a message
with an attached file.

*Note: To open an attached file,
see page 286.*

276

What folders does Outlook Express use to store my messages?

Inbox

Stores messages sent to you.

Outbox

Temporarily stores messages that have not yet been sent.

Sent Items

Stores copies of messages you have sent.

Deleted Items

Stores messages you have deleted.

Drafts

Stores messages you have not yet completed.

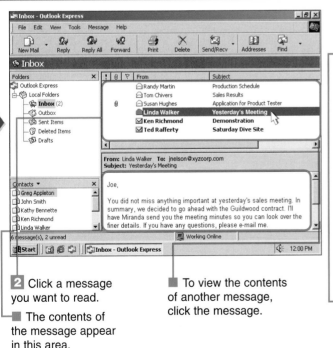

2 Click a message you want to read.

■ The contents of the message appear in this area.

■ To view the contents of another message, click the message.

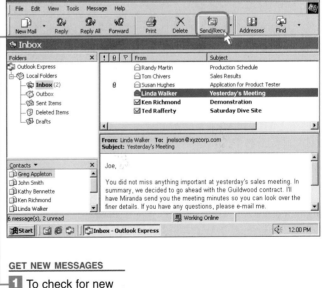

GET NEW MESSAGES

1 To check for new messages at any time, click **Send/Recv**.

SEND A MESSAGE

You can send a message to express an idea or request information.

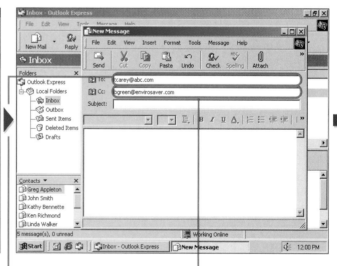

SEND A MESSAGE

1 Click **New Mail**.

■ The New Message window appears.

2 Type the e-mail address of the person you want to receive the message.

Note: To select a name from the address book, see page 282. Then skip to step 4.

3 To send a copy of the message to a person who is not directly involved but would be interested in the message, click this area and then type the e-mail address.

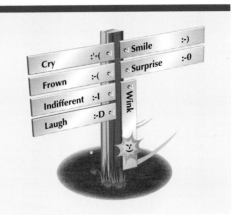

How can I express emotions in my e-mail messages?

You can use special characters, called smileys or emoticons, to express emotions in e-mail messages. These characters resemble human faces if you turn them sideways.

Smile	:-)
Surprise	:-0
Wink	
Cry	:'-(
Frown	:-(
Indifferent	:-I
Laugh	:-D

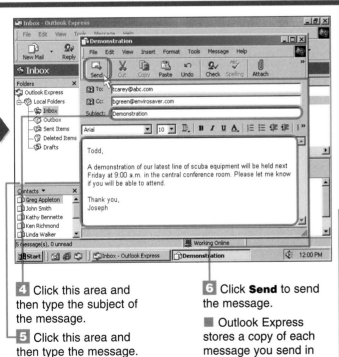

4 Click this area and then type the subject of the message.

5 Click this area and then type the message.

6 Click **Send** to send the message.

■ Outlook Express stores a copy of each message you send in the Sent Items folder.

QUICKLY SEND A MESSAGE

■ The Contacts list displays the name of each person in your address book. For information on the address book, see page 280.

1 To quickly send a message to a person in the Contacts list, double-click the name of the person.

■ The New Message window appears. Outlook Express addresses the message for you.

2 To complete the message, perform steps **3** to **6** starting on page 278.

ADD A NAME TO THE ADDRESS BOOK

You can use the address book to store the e-mail addresses of people you frequently send messages to.

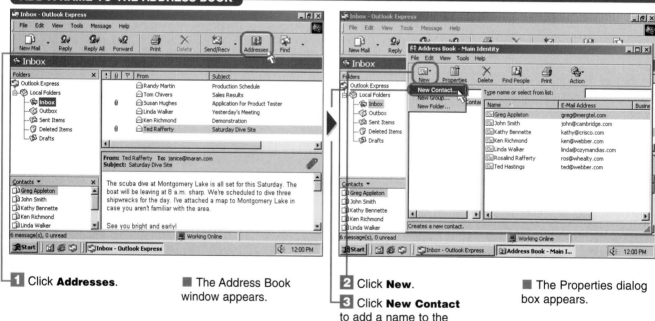

1 Click **Addresses**.

■ The Address Book window appears.

2 Click **New**.

3 Click **New Contact** to add a name to the address book.

■ The Properties dialog box appears.

Can Outlook Express automatically add names to my address book?

Each time you reply to a message, the author's name and e-mail address are automatically added to your address book.

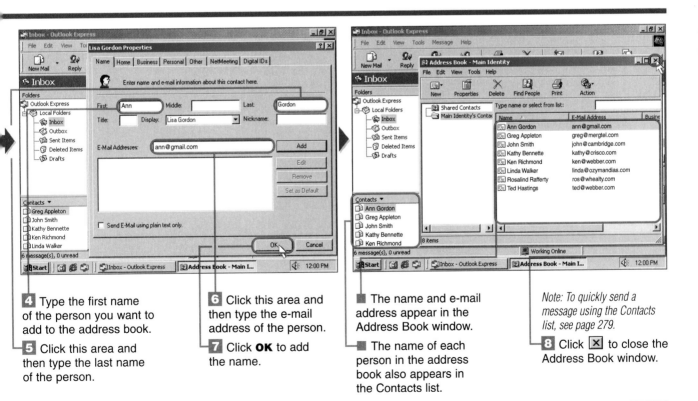

4 Type the first name of the person you want to add to the address book.

5 Click this area and then type the last name of the person.

6 Click this area and then type the e-mail address of the person.

7 Click **OK** to add the name.

■ The name and e-mail address appear in the Address Book window.

■ The name of each person in the address book also appears in the Contacts list.

Note: To quickly send a message using the Contacts list, see page 279.

8 Click ⊠ to close the Address Book window.

SELECT A NAME FROM THE ADDRESS BOOK

When sending a
message, you can
select the name
of the person you
want to receive the
message from the
address book.

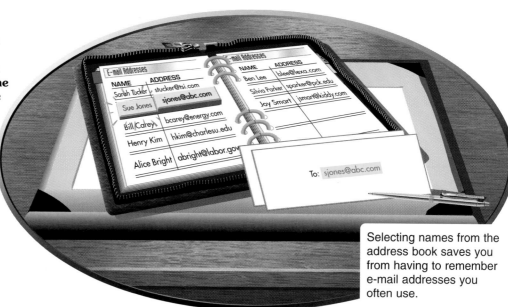

Selecting names from the
address book saves you
from having to remember
e-mail addresses you
often use.

SELECT A NAME FROM THE ADDRESS BOOK

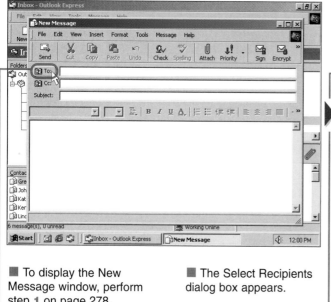

■ To display the New
Message window, perform
step 1 on page 278.

1 To select a name from
the address book, click **To**.

■ The Select Recipients
dialog box appears.

2 Click the name of
the person you want to
receive the message.

3 Click **To**.

■ This area displays the
name of the person you
selected.

■ You can repeat steps **2**
and **3** for each person you
want to receive the message.

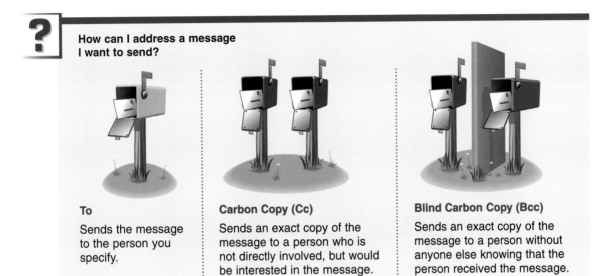

How can I address a message I want to send?

To

Sends the message to the person you specify.

Carbon Copy (Cc)

Sends an exact copy of the message to a person who is not directly involved, but would be interested in the message.

Blind Carbon Copy (Bcc)

Sends an exact copy of the message to a person without anyone else knowing that the person received the message.

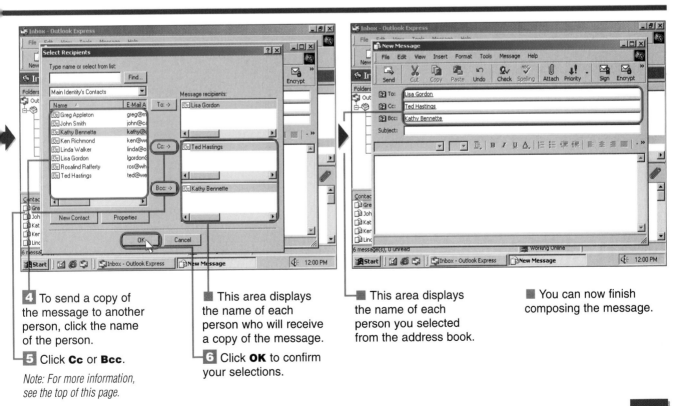

4 To send a copy of the message to another person, click the name of the person.

5 Click **Cc** or **Bcc**.

Note: For more information, see the top of this page.

■ This area displays the name of each person who will receive a copy of the message.

6 Click **OK** to confirm your selections.

■ This area displays the name of each person you selected from the address book.

■ You can now finish composing the message.

ATTACH A FILE TO A MESSAGE

You can attach a file
to a message you are
sending. Attaching a file
is useful when you want
to include additional
information with a
message.

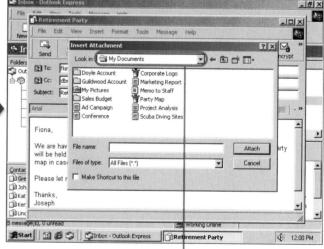

Fishing Derby Winner

From:
To:
Subject:
Cc:

Congratulations on your achievement! I'm looking forward to seeing you at the awards ceremony! I've also included photos from the event in an attached file.

ATTACH A FILE TO A MESSAGE

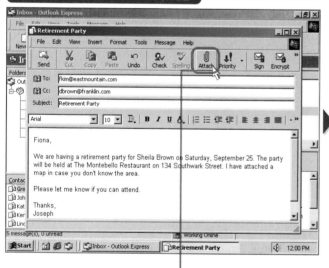

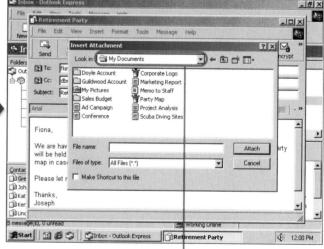

1 To compose a
message, perform
steps **1** to **5** starting
on page 278.

2 Click **Attach** to
attach a file to the
message.

■ The Insert Attachment
dialog box appears.

■ This area shows
the location of the
displayed files. You
can click this area to
change the location.

What types of files can I attach to a message?

You can attach files such as documents, pictures, programs, sounds and videos to a message. The computer receiving the message must have the necessary hardware and software to display or play the file.

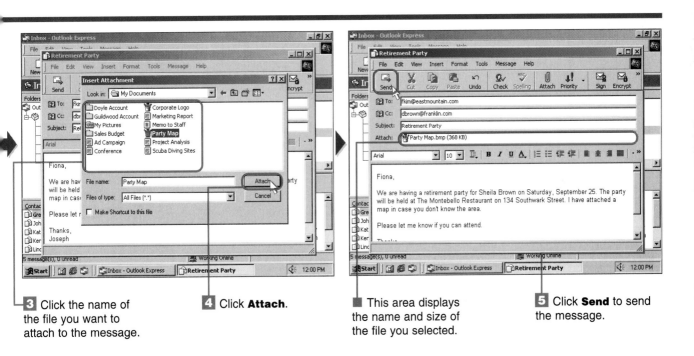

3 Click the name of the file you want to attach to the message.

4 Click **Attach**.

■ This area displays the name and size of the file you selected.

5 Click **Send** to send the message.

VIEW AN ATTACHED FILE

You can view a
file attached to
a message you
receive.

VIEW AN ATTACHED FILE

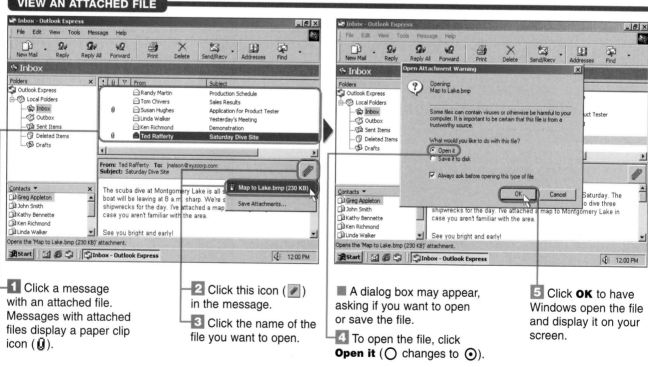

1 Click a message
with an attached file.
Messages with attached
files display a paper clip
icon (📎).

2 Click this icon (📎)
in the message.

3 Click the name of the
file you want to open.

■ A dialog box may appear,
asking if you want to open
or save the file.

4 To open the file, click
Open it (○ changes to ⊙).

5 Click **OK** to have
Windows open the file
and display it on your
screen.

After reading a message, you can add comments and then forward the message to a friend or colleague.

Forward to: Jim Berry

FORWARD A MESSAGE

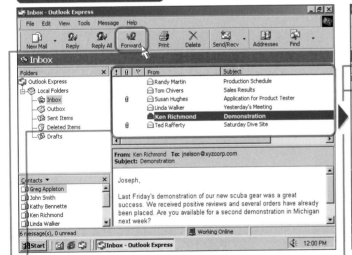

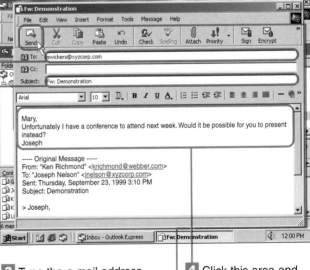

1 Click the message you want to forward.

2 Click **Forward**.

■ A window appears, displaying the message you are forwarding.

3 Type the e-mail address of the person you want to receive the message.

Note: To select a name from the address book, see page 282.

■ Outlook Express fills in the subject for you, starting the subject with **Fw:**.

4 Click this area and then type any comments about the message you are forwarding.

5 Click **Send** to forward the message.

REPLY TO A MESSAGE

You can reply to a message to answer a question or comment on the message.

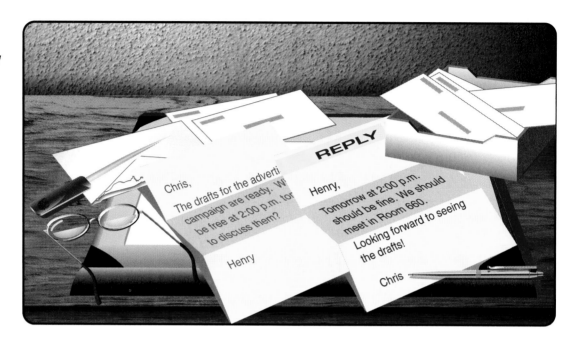

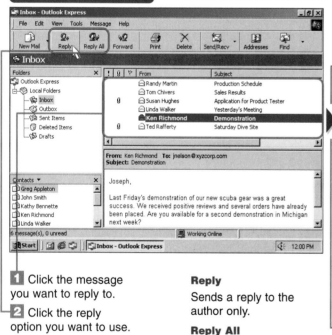

1 Click the message you want to reply to.

2 Click the reply option you want to use.

Reply

Sends a reply to the author only.

Reply All

Sends a reply to the author and everyone who received the original message.

■ A window appears for you to compose the message.

■ Outlook Express fills in the e-mail address(es) for you.

■ Outlook Express also fills in the subject, starting the subject with **Re:**.

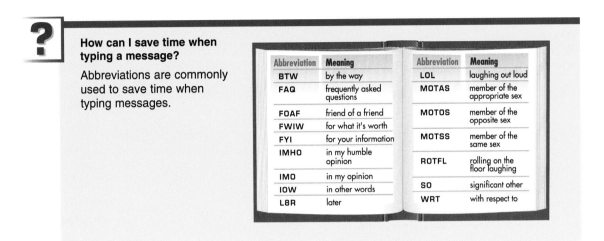

How can I save time when typing a message?

Abbreviations are commonly used to save time when typing messages.

Abbreviation	Meaning	Abbreviation	Meaning
BTW	by the way	LOL	laughing out loud
FAQ	frequently asked questions	MOTAS	member of the appropriate sex
FOAF	friend of a friend	MOTOS	member of the opposite sex
FWIW	for what it's worth		
FYI	for your information	MOTSS	member of the same sex
IMHO	in my humble opinion	ROTFL	rolling on the floor laughing
IMO	in my opinion		
IOW	in other words	SO	significant other
L8R	later	WRT	with respect to

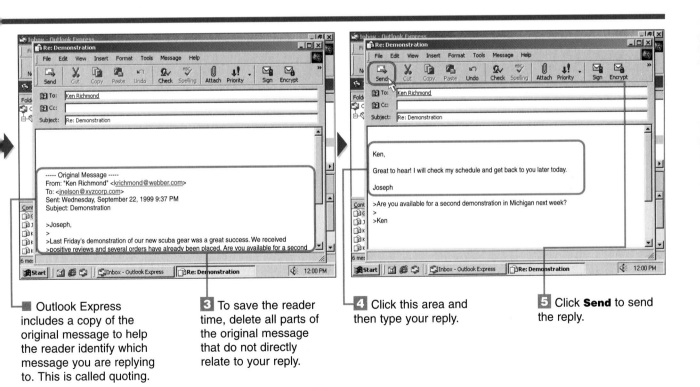

■ Outlook Express includes a copy of the original message to help the reader identify which message you are replying to. This is called quoting.

3 To save the reader time, delete all parts of the original message that do not directly relate to your reply.

4 Click this area and then type your reply.

5 Click **Send** to send the reply.

DELETE A MESSAGE

You can delete a
message you no
longer need. Deleting
messages prevents
your folders from
becoming cluttered
with messages.

DELETE A MESSAGE

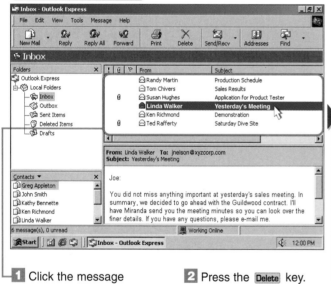

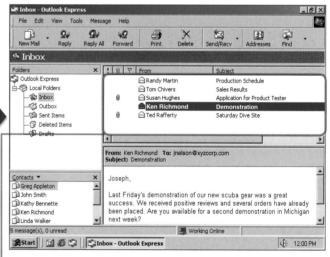

1 Click the message
you want to delete.

2 Press the Delete key.

■ Outlook Express
removes the message
from the current folder
and places the message
in the Deleted Items folder.

*Note: Deleting a message
from the Deleted Items folder
will permanently remove the
message from your computer.*

You can produce
a paper copy of
a message you
received.

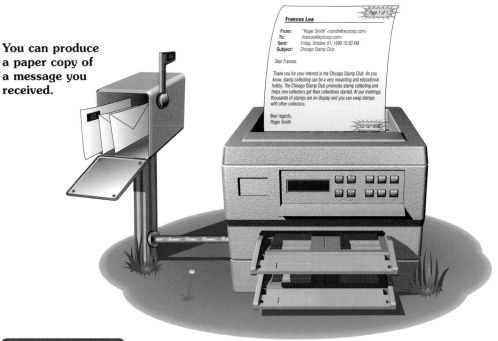

Outlook Express prints
the page number and
total number of pages
at the top of each page.
The current date prints
at the bottom of each
page.

PRINT A MESSAGE

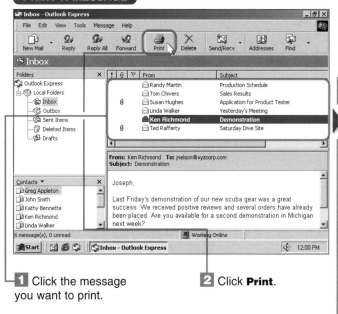

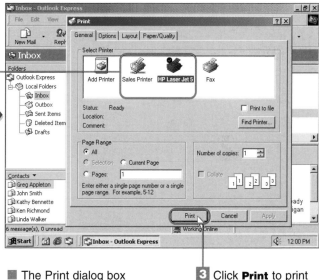

1 Click the message
you want to print.

2 Click **Print**.

■ The Print dialog box
appears.

■ This area displays
the available printers.
The printer that will print
the message displays
a check mark (✓).

3 Click **Print** to print
the message.

ADD A SIGNATURE TO MESSAGES

You can have Outlook Express add information about yourself to the end of every message you send. A signature saves you from having to type the same information every time you send a message.

ADD A SIGNATURE TO MESSAGES

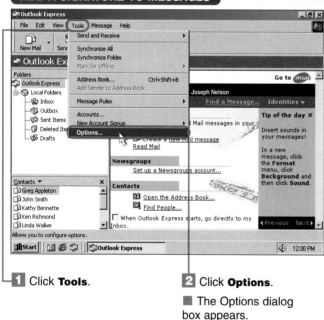

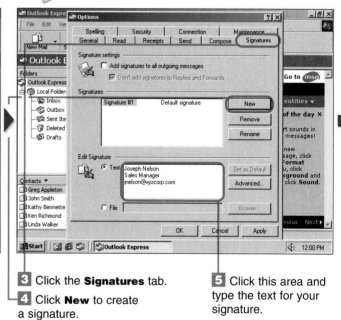

1 Click **Tools**.

2 Click **Options**.

■ The Options dialog box appears.

3 Click the **Signatures** tab.

4 Click **New** to create a signature.

5 Click this area and type the text for your signature.

? What can I include in a signature?

A signature can include information such as your name, e-mail address, occupation, favorite quotation or Web page address. You can also use plain characters to display simple pictures.

As a courtesy to people who will read your messages, do not create a signature that is more than four lines long.

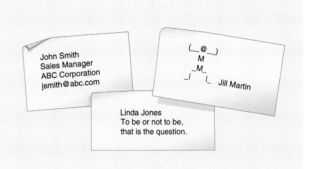

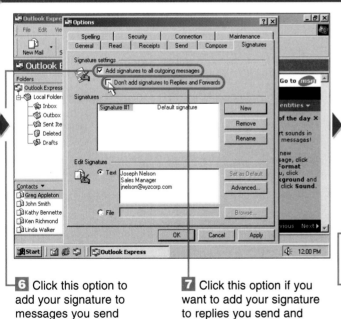

6 Click this option to add your signature to messages you send (☐ changes to ☑).

7 Click this option if you want to add your signature to replies you send and messages you forward (☑ changes to ☐).

8 Click **OK** to confirm your changes.

■ If you no longer want to add a signature to messages you send, repeat steps 1 to 3. Perform step 6 (☑ changes to ☐) and then press the Enter key.

INDEX

INDEX

INDEX

INDEX

INDEX

stretch wallpaper on desktop, 125
switch
    between
        songs on CDs, 164
        windows, 16
    mouse button functions, 134
symbols in My Network Places window, 241
synchronize files, 248-249
system fonts, 197

T

Task Scheduler, use, 190-193
taskbar
    move, 120
    overview, 4
    size, 121
tasks
    remove from Task Scheduler, 193
    schedule, 190-193
temporary Internet files, 189
temporary offline files, 189
text
    in Notepad
        enter, 28
        wrap, 28-29
    in Paint
        add to pictures, 56-57
        size, 57
    in WordPad
        align, 47
        bold, 46
        copy, 39
        delete, 37
        edit, 36-37
        fonts,
            size, change, 45
            type, change, 44
        insert, 36
        italicize, 46
        move, 38-39
        underline, 46
Text Toolbar, display, 57
Thumbnails view, 69
tile
    pictures on desktop, 63
    wallpaper on desktop, 125
time
    change in computer, 122-123
    enter current, in Notepad, 29

title bar, 4
to, in e-mail messages, 283
toolbars, Text, display, 57
tools, in Paint, display description, 51
transfer
    files, to Briefcase, 110-111
    of Web pages, stop, 262
TrueType fonts, 197
turn off
    Auto Arrange feature, 72-73
    screen saver, 127
    volume, 165
turn on
    Auto Arrange feature, 72-73
    Num Lock, 27
    volume, 165
type
    search for files using, 104-107
    sort items in windows by, 70-71
types
    of files, 89
    of fonts, 197
    of printers, 101
typical, installation option, 200

U

underline text, 46
Undo feature, 37
unlock computers, 23
update files
    in Briefcase, 114-116
    changed offline, 248-249
URL (Uniform Resource Locator), 253, 258
user names, log on using, 6-7, 21
users
    create on computers, 152-154
    delete from computers, 155

V

VGA color schemes, 129
videos, play, 166-167
view
    Active Desktop items, 144
    amount of disk space, 182-183
    computers, on networks, 240-242
    contents
        of computers, 66-67
        of folders, 75
    date set in computer, 122
    description of tools, in Paint, 51

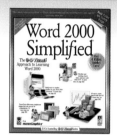

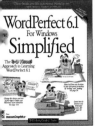

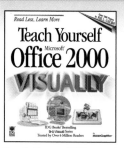

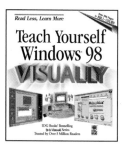
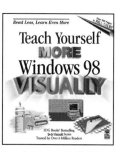

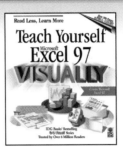

IDG BOOKS

TRADE & INDIVIDUAL ORDERS

Phone: **(800) 762-2974**
or **(317) 596-5200**
(8 a.m. – 6 p.m., CST, weekdays)
FAX : **(800) 550-2747**
or **(317) 596-5692**

EDUCATIONAL ORDERS & DISCOUNTS

Phone: **(800) 434-2086**
(8:30 a.m.–5:00 p.m., CST, weekdays)
FAX : **(317) 596-5499**

CORPORATE ORDERS FOR 3-D VISUAL™ SERIES

Phone: **(800) 469-6616**
(8 a.m.–5 p.m., EST, weekdays)
FAX : **(905) 890-9434**

Qty	ISBN	Title	Price	Total

Shipping & Handling Charges

	Description	First book	Each add'l. book	Total
Domestic	Normal	$4.50	$1.50	$
	Two Day Air	$8.50	$2.50	$
	Overnight	$18.00	$3.00	$
International	Surface	$8.00	$8.00	$
	Airmail	$16.00	$16.00	$
	DHL Air	$17.00	$17.00	$

Subtotal _____

CA residents add
applicable sales tax _____

IN, MA and MD
residents add
5% sales tax _____

IL residents add
6.25% sales tax _____

RI residents add
7% sales tax _____

TX residents add
8.25% sales tax _____

Shipping _____

Total _____

Ship to:

Name _____

Address _____

Company _____

City/State/Zip _____

Daytime Phone _____

Payment: ☐ Check to IDG Books (US Funds Only)
            ☐ Visa   ☐ Mastercard   ☐ American Express

Card # _____ Exp. _____ Signature _____

*maran*Graphics™